The Paradox of Generosity

The Paradox of Generosity

Giving We Receive, Grasping We Lose

CHRISTIAN SMITH

HILARY DAVIDSON

OXFORD
UNIVERSITY PRESS

OXFORD
UNIVERSITY PRESS

Oxford University Press is a department of the University of Oxford.
It furthers the University's objective of excellence in research, scholarship,
and education by publishing worldwide.

Oxford   New York
Auckland   Cape Town   Dar es Salaam   Hong Kong   Karachi
Kuala Lumpur   Madrid   Melbourne   Mexico City   Nairobi
New Delhi   Shanghai   Taipei   Toronto

With offices in
Argentina   Austria   Brazil   Chile   Czech Republic   France   Greece
Guatemala   Hungary   Italy   Japan   Poland   Portugal   Singapore
South Korea   Switzerland   Thailand   Turkey   Ukraine   Vietnam

Oxford is a registered trademark of Oxford University Press
in the UK and certain other countries.

Published in the United States of America by
Oxford University Press
198 Madison Avenue, New York, NY 10016

Library of Congress Cataloging-in-Publication Data
Smith, Christian, 1960–
The paradox of generosity : giving we receive, grasping we lose / by Christian Smith and Hilary
Davidson.
pages cm
Includes index.
ISBN 978–0–19–939490–6 (hardcover : alk. paper)—ISBN 978–0–19–939491–3
(ebook)—ISBN 978–0–19–939492–0 (ebook)—ISBN 978–0–19–939493–7 (online
content)   1. Generosity.   I. Title.
BJ1533.G4S53 2014
179'.9—dc23
2014007240

9 8 7 6 5 4 3 2
Printed in the United States of America
on acid-free paper

For Helen Q. Smith, R.I.P., generous to the end—C.S.S.

For my grandparents, Carl and Anise Swartz,
whose lifelong practices of generosity are an inspiration—H.D.

CONTENTS

ACKNOWLEDGMENTS

Thanks to Trish Snell Herzog for her fantastic administrative work on the first half of the Science of Generosity Initiative; without her contribution this book would not exist. Thanks also to Emmie Mediate and Catherine Braunlich for data coding. Matt, Tammy, Mallory, and Natalie Davidson, Alison Miller, Katherine Sorrell, and Paul Ullrich helped to sharpen some of our ideas. Thanks finally to the John Templeton Foundation, particularly to Kimon Sargeant, our program officer, for generously funding the research and collection of data on which this book is based.

The Paradox of Generosity

Introduction

GENEROSITY IS PARADOXICAL. THOSE who give, receive back in turn. By spending ourselves for others' well-being, we enhance our own standing. In letting go of some of what we own, we better secure our own lives. By giving ourselves away, we ourselves move toward flourishing. This is not only a philosophical or religious teaching; it is a sociological fact.

The generosity paradox can also be stated in the negative. By grasping onto what we currently have, we lose out on better goods that we might have gained. In holding onto what we possess, we diminish its long-term value to us. By always protecting ourselves against future uncertainties and misfortunes, we are affected in ways that make us more anxious about uncertainties and vulnerable to future misfortunes. In short, by failing to care for others, we do not properly take care of ourselves. It is no coincidence that the word "miser" is etymologically related to the word "miserable."[1]

This paradox of generosity should not be surprising. Very many wise observers of human life across all of recorded history have taught different versions of the generosity paradox. An ancient Hebrew proverb, for example, teaches that, "One man gives freely, yet gains even more; another withholds unduly, but ends up impoverished." The Buddha teaches, "Giving brings happiness at every stage of its expression." A Hindu proverb holds that, "They who give have all things, they who withhold have nothing." And Jesus of Nazareth teaches, "Whoever tries to keep his life will lose it, and whoever loses his life will preserve it."

But many people today seem not much shaped by the sayings of wise teachers from thousands of years ago. So, if we want to understand the power of generosity in a way that might influence our lives today, it may help to add to this traditional wisdom some empirical findings from social-scientific research. The addition of that knowledge is what this book is about. In recent years, I (Smith) have been leading a study called the "Science of Generosity Initiative" at the University of Notre Dame, in which I (Davidson) have been deeply involved. In that study, we have been conducting a nationally representative survey of Americans' practices and beliefs about generosity, hundreds of interviews with Americans around the country on generosity, and participant-observation studies of local religious congregations. This book presents some key findings of that Science of Generosity Initiative which illuminate the paradox of generosity.

What we have learned is the following. First, the more generous Americans are, the more happiness, health, and purpose in life they enjoy. This association between generous practices and personal well-being is strong and highly consistent across a variety of types of generous practices and measures of well-being. Second, we have excellent reason to believe that generous practices actually create enhanced personal well-being. The association between generosity and well-being is not accidental, spurious, or simply an artifact of reverse causal influence. Certain well-known, explicable causal mechanisms explain to us the specific ways that generous practices shape positive well-being outcomes. Third, the way Americans talk about generosity confirms and illustrates the first two points. The paradox of generosity is evident in the lives of Americans. Fourth, despite all of this, it turns out that many Americans fail to live generous lives. A lot of Americans are indeed very generous—but even more are not. And so the latter are deprived, by their lack of generosity, of the greater well-being that generous practices would likely afford them. This is the second paradox of generosity. Finally, as we mentioned above, many wise writers, philosophers, religious teachers, sages, and mystics have been teaching us about the paradox of generosity for thousands of years. What today's empirical social-science research tells us only confirms what we might have known all along, had we trusted traditional teachers.

That, in brief, is the story of this book. By the time we are done with that story, the inescapable existential questions will have also grown clearer and sharper: Will *we* live generous lives or won't we—both as persons and as a society? Why or why not? And what will that mean for the quality of our own lives, for the lives of those around us, and for our entire society? In the end, all responsible science comes back to basic human questions about what is finally good and valuable in life. That is certainly true about the science of generosity, and will remain one reference point of this book.

What Is "Generosity"?

The modern English word "generosity" derives from the Latin word *generōsus*, which means "of noble birth." That Latin word was passed down to English through the Old French word *genereus*, later *généreux* ("noble, magnanimous"). The Latin stem *gener-* is the declensional stem of *genus*, meaning "kin," "clan," "race," or "stock," with the root Indo-European meaning of *gen* being "to beget." The same root gives us the words "genesis," "gentry," "gender," "genital," "gentile," "genealogy," and "genius," among others.[2]

Most recorded English uses of the word "generous" up to and during the sixteenth century reflect an aristocratic sense of being of noble lineage or high birth. To describe someone as generous was literally a way of saying "to belong to nobility." During the seventeenth century, however, the meaning and use of the word began to change. Generosity came increasingly to identify not literal family heritage, but rather a nobility of *spirit* thought to be associated with high birth—that is, with various admirable qualities that could vary from person to person, depending not on family history but on whether a person actually possessed the qualities. In this way, "generosity," in seventeenth-century English, increasingly signified a *variety* of traits of character and action historically associated (whether accurately or not) with the ideals of actual nobility: gallantry, courage, strength, richness, gentleness, and fairness. In addition to describing these diverse human qualities, "generous" also became a word during this period used to describe fertile land, the strength of animal breeds, abundant provisions of food, vibrancy of colors, the strength of liquor, and the potency of medicine.

During the eighteenth century, the meaning of "generosity" continued to evolve in directions denoting the more specific, contemporary meaning of munificence, open-handedness, and liberality in the giving of money and possessions to others. This more specific meaning came to dominate English usage by the nineteenth century. Over the last five centuries in the English-speaking world, then, "generosity" developed from primarily the description of an ascribed status pertaining to the elite nobility, to an achieved mark of admirable personal quality and action capable of being exercised in theory by any person who had learned virtue and noble character.

This etymological genealogy tells us that the word "generosity" that we have inherited and use today entails certain historical associations which may still inform, however faintly, our contemporary cultural sensibilities on the matter. Generosity has not long been viewed as a normal trait of ordinary or of all people, but rather one expected to be practiced by those of higher quality or greater goodness. Generosity—unlike, say, truth telling or not stealing—is often considered an ideal which the best may aspire to achieve, rather than a "democratic" obligation that is the duty of all to practice. "Generosity" may thus, on the positive side, properly call any given person to a higher standard. Yet simultaneously, and morally more problematically, this two-tier understanding may have the effect of "excusing" the majority from practicing generosity because of their more ordinary perceived status. Thus, practicing generosity broadly today may run up against the contemporary analogue of an old cultural mindset of, "Let the nobility take care of people in need, we ordinary folk don't need to."

At the same time, we learn from this historical review that the meanings of words can and do evolve. They often do so in response to changing macro social conditions, such as long-term transitions from aristocratic to more democratic societies and cultures. Humans are self-reflexive creatures who learn and sometimes change their lives in response to what they learn. That means that human outlooks and actions are not absolutely fixed by nature, but can grow and adjust to new understandings. And that means that books—such as this one—possess the potential power to change people and social institutions. That is one reason we have conducted this research and written this book.

But, still, what does "generosity" mean for us? For our purposes, by generosity we mean *the virtue of giving good things to others freely and abundantly*. Generosity thus conceived is a learned character trait that involves both attitudes and actions—entailing as a virtue both a disposition to give liberally and an actual practice of giving liberally. Generosity is not a random idea or a haphazard behavior, but rather, in its mature form at least, a basic, personal, moral orientation to life. Generosity also involves giving to others not simply anything in abundance but rather giving those things that are beneficial to others. Generosity always intends to enhance the true well-being of those to whom something is being given. For this reason, we think, generosity is ultimately an expression of love, even if in specific instances it takes on an appearance of responsibility, justice, duty, or citizenship exercised.

What, exactly, generous people give can vary: money, possessions, time, attention, aid, encouragement, emotional availability, and more. Furthermore, in a world of moral contrasts, generosity involves not only the good of love expressed, but also many vices and counterproductive emotions rejected, such as selfishness, greed, fear, and meanness.

Generosity, to be clear, is not identical to pure altruism, since people can be authentically generous in part for reasons that serve their own interests as well as those of others. Indeed, insofar as generosity is a virtue, to practice it for the good of others also necessarily means that doing so achieves benefits for oneself as well. The evidence, as we will see below, bears this lesson out. And so generosity, like all of the virtues, is in people's genuine and true interest to learn and practice. All of this helps to make clear why research on generosity is warranted to increase our understanding of it.

In this book, survey measures of generosity, which attempt to capture a diversity of its expressions, include voluntary financial giving, volunteering for work without pay, relational expressions of generosity to family, "neighborly" expressions of generosity to residential neighbors and friends, giving blood, becoming an organ donor, loaning possessions, and estate giving in the form of including nonprofit organizations outside of one's family in one's will.

The Science of Generosity

The findings of this book are based on a national study of American adults which collected different kinds of empirical evidence about their generosity and their lives more broadly. First, we examine data from an extensive, nationally representative survey on generosity that was completed by nearly two thousand Americans in 2010. That survey asked a host of carefully designed questions informed by many previous studies about people's beliefs, attitudes, feelings, backgrounds, and practices about different kinds of generosity. The survey also asked about many other aspects of people's lives, including their happiness, health, mental well-being, sense of purpose in life, and much more.[3] The chapters that follow present statistical findings from that survey in clear, easily understandable ways.

Second, we analyze rich qualitative data collected through in-depth interviews with adult Americans around the country. These interviews were also conducted in 2010, with the members of forty carefully selected American households. Each of these households contained one adult who had completed our survey. Because we had extensive data on these households from their survey answers, we were able to select those we interviewed with great precision, based mostly on how generous or ungenerous they reported themselves to be in their surveys. Our confidential interviews with these respondents went into great depth about their lives generally and their experiences of generosity specifically. Each interview lasted about four hours on average. We conducted a total of sixty-two of these in-depth interviews, representing altogether twelve states around the country.[4] All of the interviews were digitally recorded and then carefully transcribed. The interview transcripts were systematically and carefully analyzed by a small team of project investigators for their common themes and varying meanings. The results of those analyses are also presented in some of the chapters that follow.

In addition to conducting interviews, we also collected visual data on the forty households that we studied, by taking more than one thousand digital photographs of their families, homes, and neighborhoods. We also recorded hundreds of pages of fieldnotes to supplement the photographs.[5] People's lives consist of more than simply what they say in interviews, so to try to capture a richer sense of Americans' lives, we recorded and studied this visual photographic data and written fieldnotes. Oftentimes they helped to put flesh on the bones of what people said in their interviews. Sometimes the photographs revealed tensions or even contradictions between what people said and what seemed to be the reality of their lives.[6] In short, the research and data behind the analysis of this book are carefully gathered, extensive, varied, and in-depth. Altogether, they help give us a clear picture of the nature, extent, and causes of Americans' generosity or lack thereof, and their consequences in people's lives.

Last Thoughts

A few miscellaneous thoughts before proceeding. First, we have written this book to be of interest to both general readers and academic scholars. Those are not always easy audiences to bridge, but the argument of this book is relevant to both. We rely on detailed endnotes to provide the kind of scholarly particulars expected by researchers; and by relegating the details of the scholarship to the notes, the main body of the text remains accessible to the general reader. We try to keep the main text as simple and clear as possible. For many readers, we expect the primary text of the chapters will suffice. Readers who want more details—including elaborated methodological and theoretical discussions—should also study the endnotes.

Second, this book operates on two levels at the same time. At an analytical level, the exploration that follows tells us about some basic social processes and outcomes that interest social scientists. In that sense, this book contributes to scholarly social science literatures on altruism, "prosocial" behavior, charitable giving, volunteering, morality, positive psychology, and other topics. But at a more personal level, as we noted above, this book presents a human challenge and promise to readers. Inescapable in this book's analysis is a profound existential question: How generously or ungenerously will each of us live our own lives, why will we choose to do so, and with what effects on ourselves and those around us? So, the issue here is not only "academic," but also deeply personal, often powerfully emotional, and profoundly consequential. We can also extend the question to the social level. How generous or not will our families, friendship networks, neighborhood associations, schools and colleges, religious congregations, voluntary organizations, for-profit companies, and other institutions in our lives be? How generous will American society be? And what outcomes, good and bad, will that produce? Again, these are big and consequential questions. We hope the evidence and argument of this book helps readers answer them well.

Third, we assume in what follows that humans have natural capacities that operate in different ways when it comes to being both generous and ungenerous with their resources. Some theories posit that humans are naturally selfish and acquisitive, and must be trained, with difficulty, to behave generously, if that is even possible. Other theories suppose that humans are naturally social and charitable toward others, only curtailing their generosity when social conditions damage their normal munificent tendencies. Neither of these one-sided starting points will do. Rather, we should suppose that humans have a variety of interests, desires, and tendencies, which sometimes reinforce each other and sometimes conflict, and which produce a range of actions that can be relatively generous or ungenerous.[7] The potential for generosity, that is, can shift strongly in different directions, depending upon a variety of factors.[8] One of those factors is human conviction and decision.

While we hope that many will read this book in order to become more generous people—and thereby likely enhance over time their own happiness, health, and purpose in life—the paradox of generosity also seems to entail this relevant truth: generosity cannot be faked in order to achieve some other, more valued, self-serving end. Generosity *itself* needs to be desired. The good of *other* people must be what we want. Nobody can reap the personal rewards that generous practices tend to produce by going through the motions of generosity simply in order to reap those desired rewards. Such practices are not really generous, but rather self-serving—and self-serving actions do not enhance anyone's well-being. Generosity cannot be counterfeited, and fake generosity does not make us happier, healthier, and more purposeful in life. To live generously, one must in due time *really become* a generous person. Generosity must be authentic. It must actually be believed and practiced as a real part of one's life. Only then might its well-being-enhancing powers kick in.[9]

Generosity is like love in this way. People often say that we increase the love we have by giving it away. When we love other people more, we often then find that the love we feel and enjoy only grows more. But that dynamic requires *really* loving the others, really giving them our love. Faking it will not do. Love must be genuine, and then when it is, the normal, bigger consequences of loving tend to follow. It is the same with generosity. For generosity to enhance well-being, it must be the generosity, not the well-being, that we are after. The enhanced well-being comes then indirectly and secondarily.

However, that fact does not mean that people must first somehow fully internalize and totally, authentically personalize generosity before they can practice being generous at all. One of the best ways of starting to become a truly generous person, if one really *wants* to, is simply to first start *behaving* like a generous person. Right attitudes often do follow right actions. New beliefs and insights are frequently provoked by new behaviors and instigations of habits. Like many things in life, we usually learn best by doing; we perfect activities and attitudes by practicing them. So, while generosity cannot ultimately be faked, people certainly can *learn* generosity, and can come to personally believe in and practice real generosity, by first setting into motion new behaviors that are generous, and then reflecting upon and soaking in their meaning and consequences.

Even so, we must realize throughout what follows that even genuinely generous practices do not increase people's well-being in any automatic, mechanical, or guaranteed way. It is not like putting coins in a machine, pressing a button, and having candy drop out the bottom. Life is rarely that straightforward about anything. The scientific evidence, as we will see, does indeed show that generosity significantly increases well-being among Americans as a whole—but the processes by which that happens often vary from person to person, and are influenced by other factors often operating varyingly in different people's lives. So, the strong causal tendency for generosity to enhance well-being is there. But, again, nothing about it is necessarily simple or surefire in any given case. Helping to understand some of those complexities is also one of the purposes of this book.

What Follows

Here, briefly, is what comes in the chapters that follow. Chapter 1 demonstrates, with empirical evidence, that Americans' generous practices are strongly associated with greater well-being of the generous givers. The evidence examined involves a variety of forms of generous practice and a diversity of kinds of measures of well-being. In this first chapter, the relationship between generosity and well-being, the significant correlation between the two, is clearly established.

Chapter 2 then turns to the crucial issue of cause and effect. Many readers will ask this question about the findings of the first chapter: Does generosity actually increase well-being or, rather, is it prior well-being that produces more generosity? Which causes which? It may be, some skeptics will suspect, that generosity does not itself enhance well-being; rather, they might believe, happier, healthier, and more purposeful people simply tend to behave more generously, because those kinds of people have more energy, vision, and physical capacity to be generous than unhappy, unhealthy, purposeless people. Our answer in Chapter 2 is that the causal arrows run in both directions. Greater well-being indeed often facilitates generosity. But, at the same time, generosity also enhances well-being. It does so through specific causal mechanisms that we can understand, explain, and test. So we are not, with this causal question, dealing with a simple either/or choice, but rather with a more complicated, both/and dynamic.

Chapter 3 examines the extent of Americans' generous practices. Having seen the relationship between generous practices and positive life well-being, we might then ask: Just how generous or not are Americans as a people? The answer, it turns out, is mixed. Many Americans are indeed quite generous in various ways—and they are more likely to enjoy the happiness, health, and sense of purpose that their generosity tends to produce. But many other Americans, by their own admission, live fairly ungenerous lives. They do not, for example, engage in much or any voluntary financial giving to valued organizations and good causes. They do not volunteer their time and labor to help others in need. They do not extend themselves much in relationships with family, friends, and neighbors. Consequently, these less generous people are also less likely to be happy, healthy, and leading purposeful lives. That, again, is the second paradox of generosity: that many people fail to live in ways that would actually give them more of what they want in life.

Chapters 4 and 5 introduces stories about the role of generosity in the lives of some of the people we interviewed. Here we step aside from survey data to examine qualitative-interview case studies and themes to illustrate and develop many of the findings of the survey analysis. This chapter examines the lives of Americans we have studied whose experiences help us to more clearly understand the generosity paradox, its dynamics and consequences, as they affect real people's lives. This chapter fleshes out some of the principles developed in the previous chapters and demonstrates some of the complexities and variants at work in the generosity paradox.

Finally, the Conclusion briefly reflects theoretically on the findings of this book. What does what we have learned here tell us more generally about human action and social life? What are the implications of our story for personal and social change? And where does future research on this topic need to go? The Conclusion of this book steps back, summarizes our major findings, and returns to the existential question lurking in the background of this study: namely, what implications do these social-science conclusions present to readers? What does this all mean for how we actually live our lives?

Throughout the book, the words of wise teachers from various time periods and backgrounds on human generosity and its consequences will be offered in sidebars. While most of this book uses nationally representative empirical survey and interview data as evidence to make its case, we will occasionally glance toward literature, proverbs, essays, religious scriptures, and other forms of traditional writings for "data" of the sort that sociologists do not normally analyze. The consistency of these observations about the paradox of generosity across so many thousands of years of history, we believe, tells us something important that is entirely consistent with the systematic empirical evidence.

Before getting to all of that, however, we need to start at the beginning. In the next chapter, we address the question: What is the relationship, if any, between generous practices and well-being in life?

CHAPTER 1 | The Paradox of Giving and Getting

IT MIGHT SEEM OBVIOUS that generously giving money away involves a loss—of the money itself, of course, and of the goods, experiences, or savings that the money might have provided the giver had it not been given away. It also seems evident that donating one's own limited time, energy, and attention to someone else's concerns similarly represents a loss. Other people benefit—the recipients, but not the person who gives something away. Again, spending one's own resources to take care of the physical and emotional needs of other people—whether family, friends, or neighbors—would also seem to imply a loss, in the form of fewer resources left over with which to take care of oneself. In these and other ways, being a generous giver would appear to exact a net cost to the giving person. Generosity should *seem* to balance out to a relative deficit. The giver loses not only the forfeited resources directly transferred, but also the "opportunity costs" of other goods to which the money, time, energy, attention, and emotions might have been devoted for themselves.

Not so. Not at all. The reality of generosity is instead actually *paradoxical*. Generosity does not usually work in simple, zero-sum, win-lose ways. The results of generosity are often instead unexpected, counterintuitive, win-win. Rather than generosity producing net losses, in general the more generously people give of themselves, the more of many goods they receive in turn. Sometimes they receive more of the same kind of thing that they gave—money, time, attention, and so forth. But, more often and importantly, generous people tend to receive back goods that are even more valuable than those they gave: happiness, health, a sense of purpose in life, and personal growth.

People rightly say that money cannot buy happiness. But money and happiness are still related in a curious way. Happiness can be the result, not of spending more money on oneself, but rather of giving money away to others. Generous financial givers are happier people, as we will see. So, while money cannot buy happiness, giving it away actually associates with greater happiness. The same holds true for other forms of generous giving, such as volunteering and taking care of family and neighbors. This win-win outcome of generosity also holds true for other kinds of well-being, such as health, avoidance of depression, purpose in life, and personal growth. This paradox of generosity has very significant implications. It points to an important general principle that people ought to be aware of, which is that—contrary to the "common sense" suggested by strict economic cost-benefit analysis—generous givers actually tend to enhance themselves personally by reducing what they spend on themselves. People actually grow by giving themselves away. By caring for other people, those who give generously end up increasing the quality of their own lives.

For people who want to be happy, to enjoy health, to lead purposeful lives—which we assume includes nearly everyone—this paradox of generosity is important to understand. It tells us that we ought not simply work to acquire, to accumulate, to save, to grasp and keep and spend for ourselves. We need instead to live *into* the paradox of generosity. We need to learn to share our resources generously with others. Then, in turn, we will likely find ourselves happier, healthier, and more purposeful in life. The data examined here show this to be not simply a nice idea, but a social-scientific fact. The evidence presented in this chapter follows a certain method that is helpful to understand from the start. Here we examine the relationship between a variety of specific forms of generosity and five particular measures of human well-being. We will explain the specific forms of generosity examined as the chapter develops. The five measures of well-being are:

1. Happiness
2. Bodily health
3. Purpose in living
4. Avoidance of depression
5. Interest in personal growth

Again, we assume that nearly everyone wants to be happy and healthy, and to live with purpose. We further assume that most people would prefer to not be depressed rather than to suffer depression, and would generally wish to be able to grow as persons rather than to stagnate. Thus, if people report being unhappy, unhealthy, purposeless, depressed, and uninterested in personal growth, something is wrong. They are not flourishing. Something is getting in the way of their realizing their own personal good.

This chapter proceeds by exploring the relationship between these five measures of basic human well-being and a variety of generous practices. The key question is this: *Is greater generosity, measured in various ways, positively associated with greater well-being?* The clear and consistent answer is *yes*. Generous practices of different sorts are positively related to greater well-being of different kinds. That positive relationship is not absolute nor overwhelming. But it is clear, consistent, and statistically significant—strong enough to make a real difference in people's lives.

Our emphasis here, to begin to give away part of our story, is on *practices* of generosity, not on single generous acts. What matters about practices, compared to one-time acts, is that they are *repeated behaviors that involve recurrent intention and attention*. Those are the kinds of expressions of generosity that actually enhance people's well-being. That is because *practices* of generosity—such as financial giving, volunteering, and relational and neighborly generosity—have the capacity to *shape* people in processes of human formation over time. By contrast, one-time (or infrequent) acts of generosity seem not to be associated with greater well-being. These include being an organ donor, estate giving through wills, lending possessions, and donating blood infrequently.[1] How all of this works, and what it means, will be explained as the chapter unfolds: but first, the empirical evidence.

Happiness

Most people (arguably all normal people) want to be happy. Happiness appears to be a human good that is not useful for achieving some other end. Rather, it seems to be a final end in life itself. Human happiness needs little justification; it is a self-evident good. To be able to live a truly happy life, in fact, appears to be an ultimate good that people nearly everywhere hope and strive for. People do many things to try to be happy. Some of them work, many do not. Our question here is, how, if at all, does generosity relate to happiness among Americans?

The answer is that the practice of generosity toward others in a variety of ways is positively associated with greater happiness. That relationship is clear and statistically significant. For clarity of presentation and ease of comprehension, we show this positive association between generosity and happiness in a series of bar graphs. Each graph in this section compares the percent of Americans who are "very happy" versus "very or somewhat *un*happy," by how generous they are on a variety of measures of generosity. In every case, we see that more generous Americans are clearly more likely to be very happy and less likely to be unhappy than their less generous counterparts. Happiness here is measured by a standard survey question asking, "Taking all things together, how happy or unhappy are you with your life these days?"[2] The bar graphs presented below show the relationship between two variables: happiness and the generous practice in question—in what social scientists call their "bivariate" relationship.

To test whether the observed differences in happiness are not spurious, that is, are not explained away by some other more important factor, we also ran more complicated, "multivariate" statistical analyses. These more complicated analyses "control for," by removing the influence of, thirteen other variables that might affect both generosity and happiness.[3] That test produces the "net" or "independent" association of the generosity variable with happiness, isolating generosity's independent relationship with happiness as if there were no influence from the other variables. Those more complicated tests show that, even after statistically controlling for many other potentially related factors, the differences examined in the simpler bivariate relationships presented below remain statistically significant in almost all cases.[4] This means that the odds of finding these generosity-related differences in happiness as a result of random error in our original sampling of survey respondents are extremely low.

Thus, for example, the positive association between financial giving and happiness that we are about to see is not explained by differences in, say, household income—that is, by higher income producing both more generous financial giving and greater happiness. We statistically control for any effects of household income, as well as many other factors, and the positive association between financial giving and happiness remains. In short, the data allow us to argue that the observed differences in happiness between more and less generous Americans are real and related to generosity. Having explained that method, we can now proceed to the findings.

Voluntary Financial Giving

One of the main ways that people act generously is by giving away money to people in need or to worthy organizations or causes. Different Americans give away different amounts of money; some give no money at all (as we will see in Chapter 3). One standard that has traditionally set a fairly high bar for generous voluntary financial giving is the giving away of 10 percent of one's income. Some, especially religious people, call this "tithing." But people do not have to be religious to give away 10 percent of their income. We begin here by taking this fairly strong measure of generous financial giving and examining whether those who give at least 10 percent of their income are happier than those who do not.[5] Figure 1.1 suggests that they indeed are.

Nearly four out of ten (38 percent) Americans who say that they give away 10 percent of their income report that they are very happy, according to the findings presented in Figure 1.1. And only 10 percent of them are somewhat or very unhappy. Compare that to those who do not give away 10 percent of their income. The percentage of those less generous financial givers who are very happy drops by 10 percent, to 28 percent. And the number of those who report being somewhat or very unhappy increases by half again as much (from 10 to 15 percent).

What should we make of these differences? They are not enormous, but they are sizeable, and they are statistically significant, even after

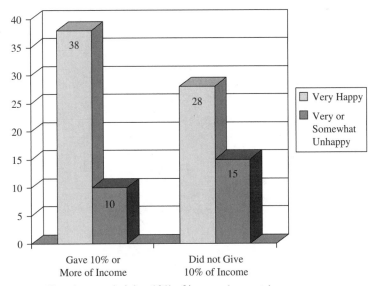

FIGURE 1.1 Happiness and giving 10% of income (percents)

controlling for the possible effects of other variables that we have reason to believe might matter here. At the very least, we can conclude that the practice of giving away 10 percent of one's income is associated with the greater probability of being happy in life. Stated in the reverse, Americans who do not give away 10 percent of their income run the significant risk of ending up less happy than they might have otherwise been. In fact, as a group they *are* less happy. So, whatever Americans lose monetarily by giving away 10 percent of their income is offset by the greater likelihood of being happier in life. And we have good reason to think that increased happiness is more valuable than the last dollar given away. Again, too, while these differences in happiness are not absolute, and greater happiness cannot be guaranteed to a more generous person in any particular case, this generosity-happiness pattern holds across all Americans, and the differences are large enough to be taken quite seriously. Considering the *value* of happiness, anything associated with a 10 percent increase in being very happy and a one-third proportion decrease (from 15 to 10 percent) of being very or somewhat unhappy should be taken seriously.

Volunteering

Americans also believe that one can act generously by volunteering time and skills to help other people. Just as with giving a portion of one's income, volunteering is empirically associated with greater happiness in life. In our survey we asked respondents whether they had volunteered in

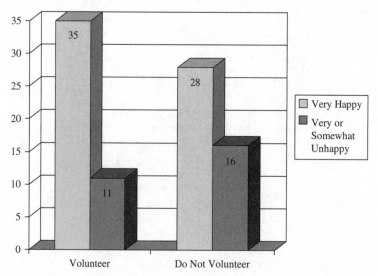

FIGURE I.2 Happiness and volunteering (percents)

the previous year. The answer was a simple yes or no. The differences in happiness between those who volunteered and those who did not are presented in Figure 1.2.

The trends are similar to those observed in Figure 1.1. Those Americans who volunteered are more likely to be very happy than those who did not (35 percent compared to 28 percent). And those who did not volunteer are more likely to be very or somewhat *un*happy than those who did (16 percent compared to 11 percent). Note that this measure is based upon a pretty blunt instrument. Someone might have only volunteered once in the previous year to be counted here as a volunteer. Yet the difference between the volunteers and non-volunteers is evident and statistically significant. At least when it comes to life happiness, then, the simple act of volunteering does not function as a loss, but as a gain.

What about how much time volunteers invest in their volunteer work? Is time spent associated with greater or lesser happiness? Yes, according to the data compiled in Figure 1.3. The bar graph below shows that Americans who are very happy volunteer an average of 5.8 hours per month. Those who are somewhat happy volunteer 4.9 hours. And as people become less happy, the average number of hours they volunteer per month drops. Those who are very unhappy, for instance, volunteer on average only about 36 minutes per month. Comparing the extremes, very happy Americans volunteer nearly ten times the amount of hours that very unhappy Americans do.[6] Again, greater happiness is significantly associated with higher levels of generosity in the form of volunteering one's time for other people and causes.

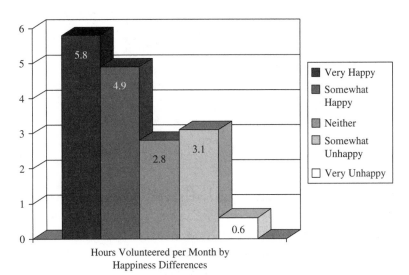

Hours Volunteered per Month by
Happiness Differences

FIGURE 1.3 Happiness and volunteering hours per month (hours)

Relational Generosity

There are more ways to be generous, however, than simply giving away money and time. Some people, after all, do not have a lot of money or time to spare. Another available type of generosity is one we call "relational generosity." By this we mean being generous with one's attention and emotions in relationships with other people. People vary in their relational generosity with others: some are extremely generous in their relationships, while others are concerned mostly with themselves. The Science of Generosity Survey asked respondents ten pretested questions designed to measure relational generosity. All focus on differences in people's attention to, effort for, and emotional investment in friends and family. The ten questions asked respondents to report the extent to which they agreed or disagreed with these statements:

1. When one of my loved ones needs my attention, I really try to slow down and give them the time and help they need.
2. I am known by family and friends as someone who makes time to pay attention to others' problems.
3. I'm the kind of person who is willing to go the "extra mile" to help take care of my friends, relatives, and acquaintances.
4. When friends or family members experience something upsetting or discouraging I make a special point of being kind to them.
5. When it comes to my personal relationships with others, I am a very generous person.
6. It makes me very happy to give to other people in ways that meet their needs.
7. It is just as important to me that other people around me are happy and thriving as it is that I am happy and thriving.
8. My decisions are often based on concern for the welfare of others.
9. I am usually willing to risk my own feelings being hurt in the process if I stand a chance of helping someone else in need.
10. I make it a point to let my friends and family know how much I love and appreciate them.[7]

Despite being the kinds of questions that might lead people to provide unrealistically positive answers, in an attempt to "look good," and so thus involving what survey researchers call a possible "social desirability bias," our respondents actually provided a reasonable range of answers. More than a few reported that they in fact did not practice

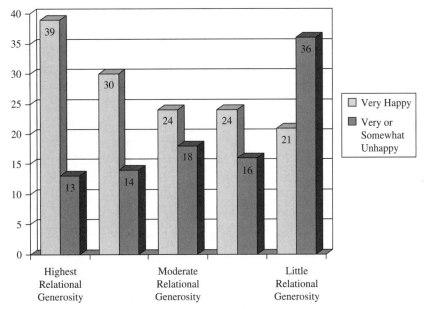

FIGURE 1.4 Happiness and relational generosity (percents)

much relational generosity.[8] That reassured us that our data about relational generosity are valid. We then took the answers to these ten questions and combined them into a single scale of relational generosity, to make our analysis and presentation simpler.[9] So how does practicing generosity in interpersonal relationships in these ten ways relate to happiness?

The general pattern we have seen with financial giving, volunteering, and happiness also holds with relational generosity. Americans who practice the highest levels of relational generosity are also those who report being more happy, according to Figure 1.4. Thirty-nine percent of those most relationally generous are very happy. Only 21 percent of those who practice little relational generosity are very happy. The latter percentage is nearly cut in half, in other words, compared to the most relationally generous people (21 percent compared to 39 percent). Scanning across the bars from left to right, we see that, as a pattern, the less relationally generous people are, the less likely they are to be very happy. Conversely, the less generous Americans are relationally with friends and family, the more likely they are to be very or somewhat *un*happy. Only 13 percent of the most relationally generous people are very or somewhat unhappy. But of those who are the least relationally generous, fully 36 percent—*three times the proportion* of the most generous—are very or somewhat unhappy. Later in this book we will explore how and why this is likely the case. But for now, this simple association is what concerns us: relational generosity and life happiness are strongly, significantly, and positively related to each other. The more generous people are, the happier they are.

Neighborly Generosity

Our survey also asked a different set of questions attempting to measure a kind of generosity we call "neighborly." This type of generosity is still centered on relationships, but it is less concerned with personal attention and emotions, and more focused instead on hospitality, friendliness, assistance with chores, and such neighborly expressions of care. Six survey questions together measured this form of neighborly generosity, asking, "How often, if ever, would you say you have done these things during the last year (12 months)?":

1. Visited family relatives in person or had them visit you?
2. Had friends over to your home?
3. Taken care of other people's children?
4. Watched over the house or property of friends who were away?
5. Helped a friend or neighbor with a job at their house or property?

Respondents were asked to report the frequency with which they practiced these acts in the previous year, with answers ranging on an eight-point scale from "more than once a week" to "never."[10] As we did above, we combined respondents' five answers into a single scale for analysis and presentation.

Figure 1.5 continues to show the pattern we have consistently observed so far: personal happiness is significantly associated with the practice of neighborly generosity. More than half (52 percent) of Americans who practice neighborly generosity most frequently are very happy. Only 20 percent of those who practice neighborly generosity the least are very happy. That is well less than half the proportion of happiness of the most generous Americans. At the same time, the unhappier people are, the less neighborly generosity they practice. Only 10 percent of the most generous are very or somewhat unhappy, while that number more than doubles to 22 percent for the least generous. In short, Americans who are more generous in neighborly ways are happier, while those who are less generous are less happy.

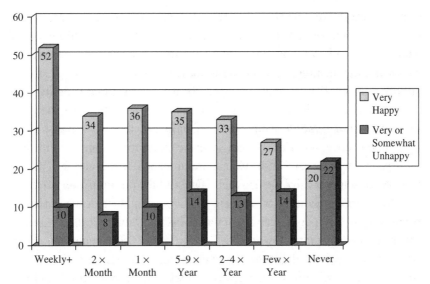

FIGURE 1.5 Happiness and neighborly generosity (percents)

Self-Evaluated Financial Generosity

The kinds of generosity considered thus far concern objective behaviors, such as donating money, volunteering, giving attention to needy friends, and visiting with friends and relatives. While surveys always rely on respondents' reports, so far the questions themselves have mostly asked about the existence or frequency of objective actions. In every case, we have found that the greater the generosity practiced, the more happy those who practice generosity are. But there are other ways to measure generosity. A different approach, one that proves another helpful angle on the matter, is to simply ask people to rate themselves on how generous they consider themselves to be when it comes to different, specific forms of giving. This renders a more subjective, self-evaluative approach to generosity, rather than an objective report or count. With this approach, we ask survey respondents to step back and consider their own overall character on matters of generosity in different areas.

This subjective self-assessment of course potentially enables people to flatter themselves and provide inaccurate answers. But it also provides a way to measure overall self-understandings and images concerning generosity, which can have the advantage of accounting for situational complexities that more objective counts might fail to capture. And, in fact, our respondents as a whole self-reported a wide variance in their own evaluations of their generosity, increasing our confidence that everyone was not simply deceiving themselves and us.[11] Furthermore, the objective measures and self-evaluative measures of generosity correlate as one would expect. In any case, this self-evaluation approach does not displace or compete against more objective measures of generous behavior. It only provides a complement to them, which is at least worth considering. So, when we examine these self-evaluative measures of generosity, what do we find when it comes to happiness?

This subjective, self-evaluative gauge of generosity agrees with and reinforces our findings so far. Consider people's self-evaluations of their own financial generosity, for example. Our survey question was, "Overall, when it comes to giving away money, what kind of person do you consider yourself to be?" Answers ranged on a seven-point scale from "extremely generous" to "extremely ungenerous" (with "very," "somewhat," and "neither" being the points between the two extremes). Figure 1.6 shows that, similarly to the figures above, Americans who consider themselves to be the most financially generous are also the most happy—and happiness declines as self-evaluated financial generosity decreases. Likewise, the people least likely to be very or somewhat *un*happy are the most generous financially, measured by self-evaluation. And the less generous people consider themselves to be, the more likely they are to be very or somewhat unhappy. In this figure, the differences in happiness across generosity categories are not enormous, but they are noticeable and statistically significant. Again, considering the great value of life happiness, even these relatively modest differences are worth noting.

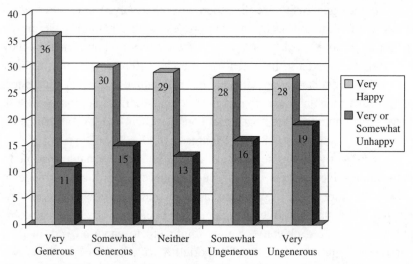

FIGURE 1.6 Happiness and self-evaluations of financial generosity (percents)

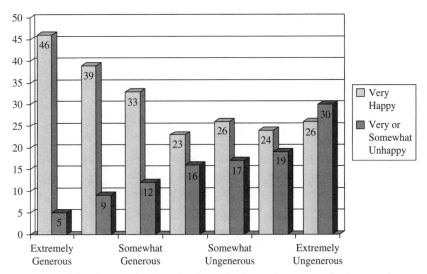

FIGURE 1.7 Happiness and self-evaluations of volunteering generosity (percents)

Self-Evaluated Volunteering Generosity

The same finding, but much more strongly evident, is clear in Figure 1.7, which focuses on self-evaluations of generosity in volunteering. The survey question asked, "Overall, when it comes to volunteering your time for others, do you consider yourself to be. . .?," with answers ranging on a seven-point scale from "extremely generous" to "extremely ungenerous." Figure 1.7 shows, once again, that those who self-evaluate as the most generous when it comes to volunteering are nearly twice as likely to be very happy as those who rate themselves as ungenerous. At the same time, those who are the most generous here are only one-sixth as likely to be very or somewhat unhappy as those who say that they are extremely ungenerous (5 percent compared to 30 percent). Yet again, as we move from the more to the less generous Americans, even by their own self-evaluations, the chances of being very happy significantly decline and the odds of being unhappy significantly increase. The consistency of this pattern of findings across different measures of generosity is becoming impressive.

Self-Evaluated Relational Generosity

The Science of Generosity Survey also asked respondents, "Overall, in relationships, when it comes to making yourself available to other people, being emotionally open, and being hospitable, do you consider yourself to be. . .?" The same seven answer categories were offered. Here the general

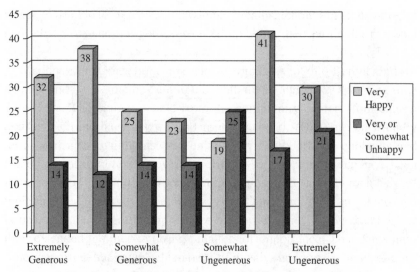

FIGURE 1.8 Happiness and self-evaluations of relational generosity (percents)

pattern of findings is similar, although the distribution of answers is less clear-cut, and the associations are weaker than in the previous figure, although they are still statistically significant. This lack of clarity could be because self-evaluations of relational generosity in particular, which involve fewer concrete referents than financial giving and volunteering, are more subject to social desirability biases and thus produce less reliable data. In any case, the results of this analysis are presented in Figure 1.8. There we observe a slight trend of increasing unhappiness associated with less self-evaluated relational generosity. Differences in "very happy" responses across levels of generosity are much less clear in this case.

Personal Importance of Generosity

Finally, in addition to the eight behavioral and self-evaluative measures of generosity examined above, we also asked survey respondents to report how much they agreed or disagreed with this general statement: "It is very important to me to be a generous person." Answers ranged on a seven-point scale from "strongly agree" to "strongly disagree" (with "mostly," "slightly," and "neither" providing the answer points in the middle of the scale). Because so relatively few answered either "slightly," "mostly," or "strongly" disagree, for the sake of statistical reliability we combined these answers into one "disagree" category. The relationship between overall personal importance of generosity and happiness is shown in Figure 1.9.

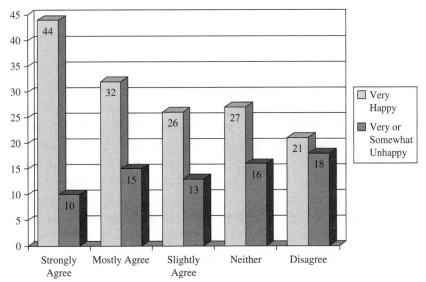

FIGURE 1.9 Happiness and "It is very important to me to be a generous person" (percents)

Here we observe again the strong pattern we have seen repeated (with the exception of Figure 1.8) thus far. Forty-four percent of those who strongly agree that it is important for them to be generous are very happy. As the importance of being generous decreases, so do the percentages of those who are very happy. Americans who outright disagree that it is important to them to be generous turn out to be very happy at less than *half* the rate of those who strongly agree (21 percent compared to 44 percent). Conversely, the percent of Americans who are very or somewhat unhappy gradually increases as the importance of generosity diminishes, from 10 percent on the low end (among those for whom generosity is most important) to 18 percent on the high end (for those who disagree that being generous is important).

To summarize, then, nine different measures of varying types of generosity that take different approaches to asking about the issue all reveal a positive, statistically significant, and oftentimes quite strong relationship between generosity and happiness. In general, the more generous Americans are, the more likely they are to be happy—and the less generous, the less happy. That pattern has been evident with more or less clarity across all nine measures of generosity examined so far. And that association remains statistically significant even after the effects of ten other potentially related variables are controlled for in multivariate analyses.[12] We can therefore safely conclude that happiness in life is definitely related to Americans' practices of financial, volunteering, relational, and neighborly generosity and to the overall personal importance of generosity in their lives.

The Logic of Non-Findings

Curiously, given the pattern of our empirical findings so far, four other measures of generosity prove to have no statistically significant association with reported happiness. They are giving blood at least once in the previous year, being an organ donor, lending personal possessions, and giving money or possessions through estate planning in a legal will to a nonprofit not involving one's own family. None of these are significantly associated with greater happiness after the effects of other relevant variables are statistically controlled for. At first this might seem odd. If some obvious kinds of generosity are so clearly associated with happiness, as we have seen, then why are not all forms of generosity positively correlated with happiness? Why wouldn't people who are organ donors, for instance, be more happy than those who are not, if generosity increases happiness? Is there any more specific logic of explanation for this breakdown of the more general pattern of relationship between generosity and happiness? A few different explanations suggest themselves.

For example, becoming an organ donor is relatively easy and many Americans (about 44 percent according to our survey) are organ donors. Typically, all one has to do is check a box in the paperwork of the Department of Motor Vehicles while getting or renewing one's driver's license, and one has become an organ donor. Since not many people expect to suffer life-ending accidents, few likely take seriously the idea that they will actually donate their body organs anytime soon to other people who need them. For most, being an organ donor is essentially a formal status, the consequences of which are considered extremely remote and, in any case, are mostly irrelevant to the extent that they would only transpire after one's death. Furthermore, relatively few Americans have legal wills governing the transfer of their estates upon death. And only some who do provide for the transfer of resources to nonprofits instead of family members. So we are working with relatively little variance when it comes to estate giving, and that might make statistical analysis more difficult.

But these seem like ad hoc explanations, which is a problem. Had any of these four forms of generosity proved to be significantly associated with happiness, we certainly would have reported them as such and claimed them as further evidence for our larger argument. So it hardly seems fair under the current circumstances to be offering reasons particular to each one of these measures to explain why they are not significantly related to happiness—even if those particular reasons seem to make sense on an ad hoc basis. We need a better account—and in fact, we can offer a better, more systematic account. The explanation for why these four forms of generosity do not associate with greater happiness, while the nine measures examined above do, has to do, we suggest, with the crucial difference between generous *practices* and generous *one-time events*. Generous practices simply have much more capacity to shape people's lives over time. One-time events typically have less capacity, unless they are major, memorable, or traumatic occurrences.

By definition, a practice is an activity or behavior that is *repeated*—it continues over time. A practice by definition is also a *meaningful* activity—it holds some significance or import for the person engaging in it. Practices therefore require some degree of attention and intention. To practice something, people have to devote some interest and awareness to make it happen and keep it going. People have to sufficiently intend to do it, to desire to make the repeated activity part of their lives. Otherwise, entropy and distraction take their toll. Of course, many practices can eventually become routines, and even sometimes mindless habits. But practices of generosity that involve repeated partings with money, time, attention, emotional energy, and other resources rarely become meaningless, mechanical habits. The resources parted with are usually too valuable to allow one to be mindless about them.

Giving away 10 percent of one's income on an ongoing basis, for example, requires a real commitment and continual actions to make it happen. The same is usually true for volunteering and generously attending to family, friends, and neighbors. But compare the nature of those practices with the four forms of generosity that are not associated with greater happiness. Becoming an organ donor, as we have already noted, can be carried out with the check of a bureaucratic box that one can essentially forget about for the rest of one's life (until asked about it on a survey). Likewise, deciding to include a favorite nonprofit organization in one's will is often a one-time decision that takes place decades before that donation is eventually made and the results accomplished. Similar to being an organ donor, the estate distribution to that nonprofit by definition and law also does not happen until one is dead, and so the givers do not have the opportunity to see the results of that generous giving.

What about lending possessions to others? That need not be a one-time event. But neither in most cases does lending possessions have the character of a generous practice, the way liberal financial giving and volunteering do, for example. For one thing, the loaning of possessions is usually instigated not by the loaner, but by requests from borrowers. They are the ones who usually take the initiative to make loaning possessions happen. The activity of loaning thus depends in character and timing on the needs of the borrower, which are often intermittent at best. Furthermore, willingness to loan possessions sometimes, if not often, takes place under some duress, insofar as the refusal to loan a possession to someone who feels entitled to borrow it in the first place communicates negative signals that can be socially uncomfortable. Many prospective lenders would prefer to risk lending out a possession knowing that it may be damaged or lost rather than to flatly tell the asker, "No, sorry." Of course, sometimes financial giving and volunteering also take place under the duress of someone significant asking for money or time. But usually a bit of money or time given in response can satisfy the request and avoid social awkwardness. By comparison, those who *practice* giving money and volunteering generously on a significant and ongoing basis are typically self-motivated, rather than operating primarily under duress from others.

Finally, what about giving blood? Some people give blood on a regular, scheduled basis as a matter of generous practice, don't they? Yes, although half of the blood that is donated in the US is provided by first-time or irregular donors.[13] More relevant for present purposes, however, is the fact that the survey question analyzed here does not distinguish between different kinds of donors of blood. Ideally, the survey question would have asked probes to separate one-time and irregular blood donors from regularly recurring donors. But this question only asked, "In the past year (12 months), have "you" donated blood for which you did not receive pay?" Those who answered yes might be people who generously give blood as a practice as often as they can. Or they might have only given blood once or a few times in their entire lives. Unfortunately, we do not have the data here to say. Consequently, we are not able to test whether donating blood as a practice of generosity is also associated with greater happiness in life. If our theory developed here is correct, it should be.[14] But establishing that one way or the other will require a different analysis than we can accomplish at present.

Summary

Both the theoretical logic and the empirical evidence considered so far suggest the following initial interpretation. Regular practices of generosity that are repeated over time and involve some amount of ongoing intention and attention have the capacity to form people in ways that increase their happiness in life. Exactly how and why they do so we explore in depth in the next chapter. For now it is enough to note the consistent association between generous practices and greater life happiness. By comparison, one-time decisions about or sporadic events involving generosity (organ donation, writing a will, lending some possessions, giving blood on occasion) appear to have less capacity to increase happiness over time. They lack the kind of recurrence, attention, and sustained meaning needed, we suggest, to shape people's lives in ways that stick. Thus, when people give of themselves through *practices* of generosity, they receive back in greater happiness. But when they give through isolated choices or sporadic events, they are less affected in happiness by those generous acts.

Bodily Health

Happiness is not the only positive outcome that people seek in life. Bodily health is another basic good that nearly all people value. Health is of course affected by many disparate factors, including genetics, environment, social-class position, occupation, and lifestyle choices, such as smoking and drinking alcohol heavily. Could it be that, amid these many other influences, practicing generosity is also related to better health? Let us examine the empirical evidence and see. The following exploration studies the same nine measures of generous practices related above to happiness, only here we relate them to bodily health. What do we find? The answer is, the same pattern of positive associations that we observed regarding generosity and happiness.

Voluntary Financial Giving

Americans who give away 10 percent of their income are healthier than those who do not, as evident in Figure 1.10. Forty-seven percent of those who give that much say that they are in excellent or very good health, compared to 39 percent who do not. That is a modest but real difference. Conversely, more Americans who do not give away 10 percent of their income report being in poor or only fair health than those who do (23 percent compared to 18 percent). Again, the difference is not enormous. But, considering the many non-generosity factors that influence health, and the great value of bodily health, even those degrees of difference matter.

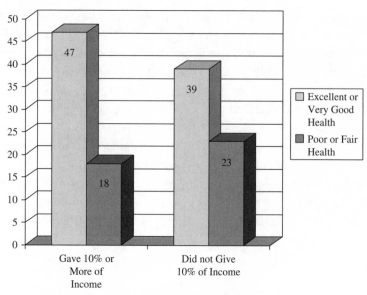

FIGURE 1.10 Health and giving 10% of income (percents)

Volunteering

The results on volunteering and health continue the established pattern, as shown in Figure 1.11. Those who volunteered in the previous year are 13 percent more likely to be in excellent or very good health than those who did not. Comparatively, those who did not volunteer are more likely to be in poor or fair health than those who did (25 percent compared to 14 percent). Again, practicing generosity in the form of volunteering is clearly associated with greater physical health—a finding that is statistically significant even after taking into account our standard set of control variables. In the next chapter we will argue that this is not only because healthy people are more able to volunteer, but also because certain aspects or results of volunteering have the capacity to improve and sustain better physical health.

The same general pattern is also evident when it comes to hours volunteered and health. Figure 1.12 shows that physical health is positively associated with the average number of hours volunteered per month. Those who volunteer the most are in the best health. Those who volunteer the least are in the poorest health. These differences are statistically significant even after taking into account our standard control variables. Once again, some of this effect is no doubt because healthier people are generally able to volunteer more. But, as we argue in the next chapter, we have good reason to believe that this only explains part of this association. In addition, volunteering itself helps to bolster people's physical health.

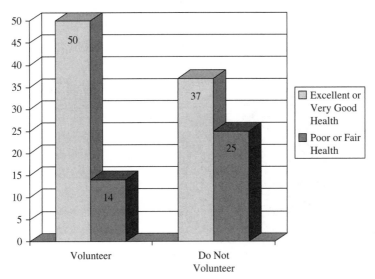

FIGURE I.11 Health and volunteering (percents)

Relational Generosity

Figure 1.13 examines the relationship between relational generosity and physical health. There we see again that the difference between excellent or very good versus poor or only fair health is greatest among those who are most generous relationally, while those differences in health diminish and eventually converge among the least relationally generous. Relationally generous people are clearly healthier than the ungenerous. The proportion of those in poor or only fair health more than doubles for the least generous relationally compared to the most generous (36 percent versus 17 percent). These differences in health are statistically significant net of all control variables. Something about relational generosity itself, and not other likely variables, appears to be associated with greater health.

Neighborly Generosity

We also observe the same trends in Figure 1.14, which focuses on neighborly generosity. Here, 48 percent of those who practice this form of generosity most frequently are in excellent or very good health. Only 30 percent of those who never practice neighborly generosity are that healthy—a drop of 18 percentage points. Meanwhile, the increase in the percent experiencing poor or only fair health grows from 17 percent at the highest end of generosity to 28 percent at the lowest end—an increase of 11 percent. These differences in health by extent of generosity are, again, statistically

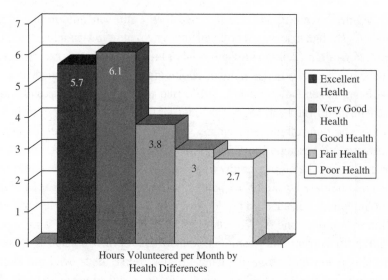

FIGURE I.I2 Health and volunteering hours per month (hours)

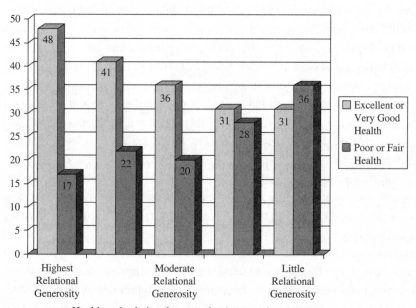

FIGURE I.I3 Health and relational generosity (percents)

significant even after control variables are factored in. So, once again, we see that generosity and physical health are positively associated in noticeable ways.

Self-Evaluated Financial Generosity

The same overall trend is also evident in Figure 1.15, which displays the relationship between physical health and self-evaluations of financial generosity. The percentage of those in excellent or very good health declines as Americans become less financially generous, according to their own self-reports, from 49 percent at the high end to 38 percent at the low end. Meanwhile, the percentage of those in poor or only fair health nearly doubles between the most financially generous compared to the least, increasing from 15 percent to 29 percent. These differences are highly significant in the bivariate relationship (though, after taking all control variables into account, the statistical odds of these differences being found by random error in sampling increases from less than 5 out of 100 to about 10 out of 100).[15] Once again, then, we see that generosity and physical health are positively, observably associated with each other.

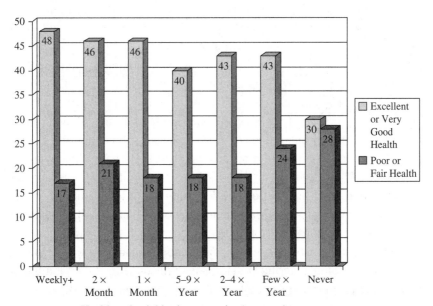

FIGURE 1.14 Health and neighborly generosity (percents)

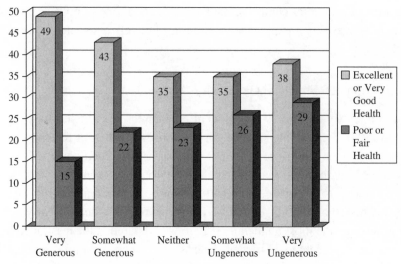

FIGURE 1.15 Health and self-evaluations of financial generosity (percents)

Self-Evaluated Volunteering Generosity

Figure 1.16 shows the same general pattern yet again. The findings are beginning, in other words, to become very repetitive, though in a revealing way. When it comes to self-evaluations of volunteering generosity, the most generous are much more likely to be in excellent or very good health than the least generous (54 percent compared to 32 percent). And the percentage of Americans in poor or only fair health more than doubles from the most to the least generous in volunteering, as measured by overall self-evaluation. Once more, these differences are statistically significant in multivariate analyses that include ten control variables.[16] Thus, the larger patterns of findings reflecting the specific pattern of associations between generosity and positive outcomes—in this case, physical health—are growing clearer and stronger with each analysis.

Self-Evaluated Relational Generosity

Examining the correlation of self-evaluated relational generosity and health, we see again in Figure 1.17 that the most generous are in significantly better health than the least generous. Those in excellent or very good health drop a whopping 30 percent between the most and least generous (from 50 percent to 20 percent). Meanwhile, those in poor or only fair health increase by 20 percent from the most to the least generous (from 19 percent to 39 percent). Those differences are not only statistically

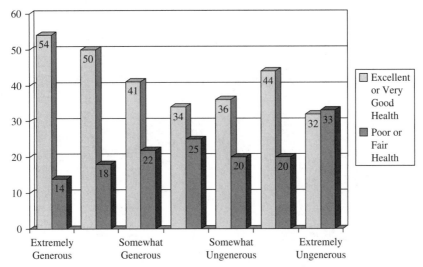

FIGURE 1.16 Health and self-evaluations of volunteering generosity (percents)

significant but also substantively large. Certainly, anyone gambling on ways to achieve better physical health who sees these numbers should be willing to wage a very large bet on the role of relational generosity in influencing the process and outcome.

Personal Importance of Generosity

Finally, physical health is also related, for Americans, to the overall value they place on being a generous person. While the relatively good health of those who most disagree about being generous stands out as an anomaly, the overall trend lines are the same as those above, as we see in Figure 1.18. Americans for whom it is most important to be generous are the healthiest, while those for whom being generous is less important are less healthy. These differences, too, are significant in a multivariate context and comport with the accumulated findings of a positive relationship between generosity and physical health.

Non-Significant Forms of Generosity

Just as with happiness, so with physical health. The above practices of generosity are statistically and substantively significant. But four other forms of generosity that we tested are not: giving blood, being an organ donor, loaning possessions, and estate giving.[17] Our explanation for this contrast is the same for health as it was for happiness. Only generous *practices*

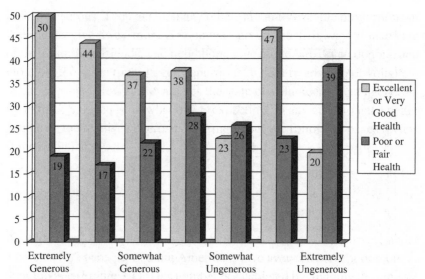

FIGURE 1.17 Health and self-evaluations of relational generosity (percents)

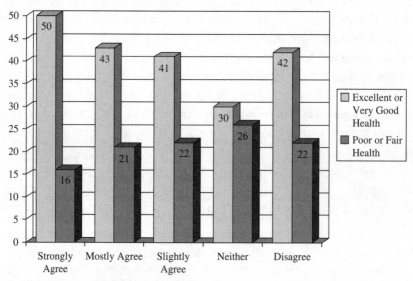

FIGURE 1.18 Health and "It is very important to me to be a generous person" (percents)

have the capacity to inform life outcomes, including physical health, in positive ways. By contrast, one-time decisions or acts of generosity do not do so nearly as much. Once again, the larger patterns that our analyses are revealing are not weak, spotty, and confusing, but rather clear, consistent, and theoretically explicable.

Purpose in Life

A third basic good in human experience is to live with purpose. Few people believe that it is good to live aimlessly, with no direction, having little sense of what one's life is about or what purposes one ought to achieve. Purpose provides clarity and direction in life. It helps supply the meaning of one's existence, the value of one's contribution to the world. To live without purpose is to be lost, merely drifting, uncertain, and confused about the very bearing and significance of one's life experience. Some people may be happy to live without purpose. But by all reasonable accounts they are not thriving as human beings, for to thrive as persons, we humans need purpose.

What relation, then, does purpose have to generosity? The Science of Generosity Survey asked its respondents the extent to which they agreed or disagreed with these three statements about purpose:

1. I don't have a good sense of what it is I'm trying to accomplish in life.
2. Some people wander aimlessly through life, but I am not one of them.
3. My life often seems to lack any clear goals or sense of direction.

The answer categories ranged on a seven-point scale from "strongly agree" to "strongly disagree." Together, these three questions form a single scale measuring life purpose.[18] How, then, does purpose in life measured in this way relate to generosity?

The short answer, in keeping with everything good about generosity that we have seen in this chapter thus far, is that Americans who are more generous in a variety of ways also enjoy greater purpose in life. Figures 1.19–1.27 reveals once again a clear, consistent, and significant pattern of positive associations between various forms of generous practices and Americans' reports of living their lives with greater purpose. Conversely, Americans who are not engaged in different kinds of generous practices report higher levels of a lack of purpose in life.

Readers are by now familiar with the patterns of measurement and presentation concerning generosity and well-being outcomes. So we will not review the findings presented in Figures 1.19–1.27 in as much detail as we have those concerning happiness and health. The overall patterns are the same as those we have already reviewed: greater generosity correlates with the human good of greater life purpose. For present concerns, then,

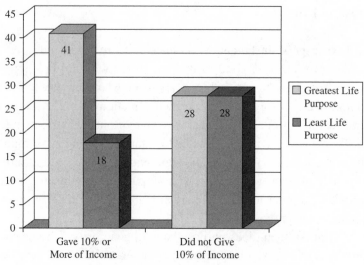

FIGURE 1.19 Life purpose and giving 10% of income (percents)

it is sufficient to simply emphasize some of the high points of the findings concerning purpose in life.

Consider Figure 1.19, for example. Whether or not Americans give away 10 percent of their income makes a difference of thirteen percentage points in the likelihood of living life with strong purpose. Forty-one percent of those who give 10 percent of income report enjoying strong purpose, while only 28 percent of those who do not report the same. Meanwhile, the percent of people reporting weak purpose in their lives increases by nearly half the original number, when comparing those who give ten percent to those who do not (18 percent compared to 28 percent). Figure 1.20 shows a similar pattern: volunteering is associated with greater life purpose.[19] Likewise, Figure 1.21 demonstrates that volunteering more hours per month is clearly correlated with enjoying greater purpose in life; those who volunteer more, also live with the strongest purpose.

The same holds true with relational and neighborly generosity (see Figures 1.22 and 1.23). Those who are most generous in these ways enjoy the greatest life purpose, while those who are least generous report the least purpose. In some cases, the magnitude of difference is major. For example, 52 percent of Americans who practice the least relational generosity also exhibit the weakest life purpose, compared to only 22 percent of those who practice the most relational generosity—a difference of 30 percent (Figure 1.22). Likewise, Americans who practice neighborly generosity most frequently are more than twice as likely to enjoy the strongest life purpose, at 48 percent

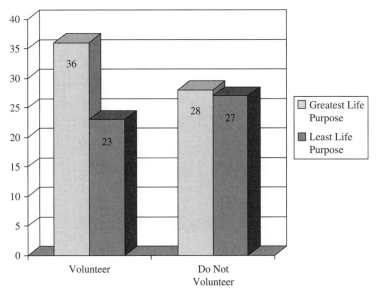

FIGURE I.20 Life purpose and volunteering (percents)

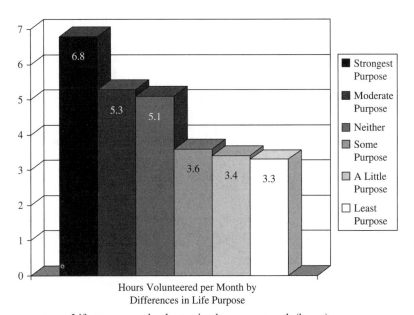

FIGURE I.21 Life purpose and volunteering hours per month (hours)

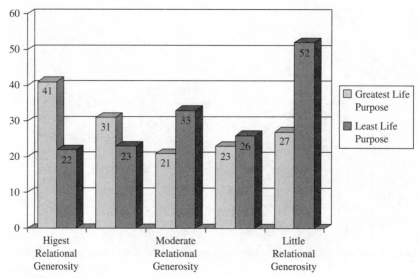

FIGURE I.22 Life purpose and relational generosity (percents)

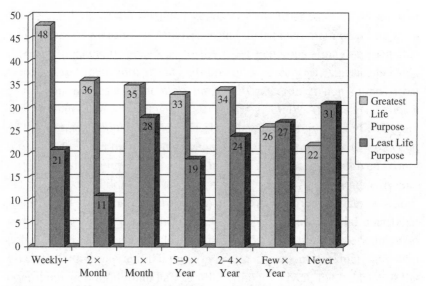

FIGURE I.23 Life purpose and neighborly generosity (percents)

compared to 22 percent (Figure 1.23; also see similar associations in Figures 1.24 and 1.25). Again, all of these differences are statistically significant even after accounting for the possible effects of ten other variables.

The findings concerning Americans' self-evaluations of financial, volunteer, and relational generosity replicate the pattern already well established in this chapter. Overall, the more generously people rate themselves

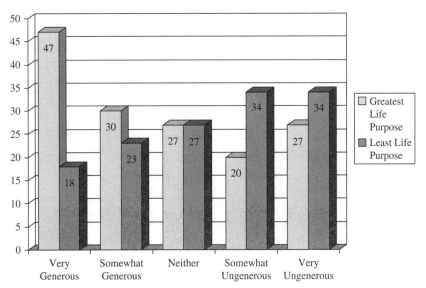

FIGURE 1.24 Life purpose and self-evaluations of financial generosity (percents)

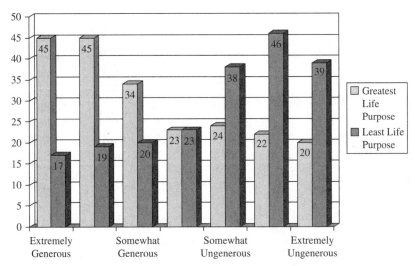

FIGURE 1.25 Life purpose and self-evaluations of volunteering generosity (percents)

in these ways, the more purpose in life they enjoy. The less generous they report themselves to be, the less life purpose they enjoy. If the implications of these findings were not so interesting and important, the consistency with which they are presenting themselves would almost be boringly repetitive. Greater generosity clearly correlates with greater well-being on this matter of life purpose, just as it did with greater happiness and physical health above (Figure 1.26).[20] Finally, the identical configuration of

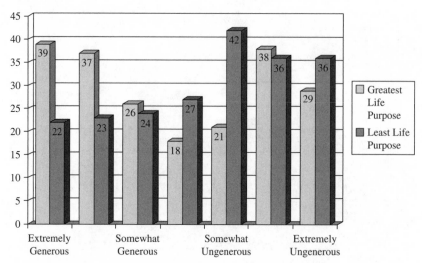

FIGURE 1.26 Life purpose and self-evaluations of relational generosity (percents)

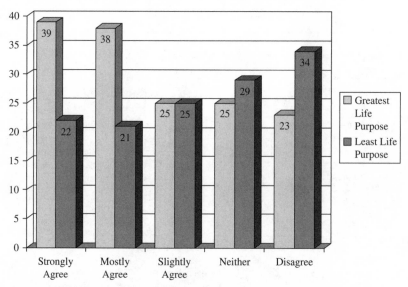

FIGURE 1.27 Life purpose and "It is very important to me to be a generous person" (percents)

relationships replicates itself in Figure 1.27, where we see that Americans for whom being a generous person is most important are also much more likely to enjoy the strongest purpose in life. Compared to them, Americans who most disagree about the importance of being a generous person are 16 percentage points less likely to enjoy the greatest life purpose (23 percent compared to 39 percent).

At the same time, and remaining perfectly consistent with the pattern of findings observed about happiness and health above, the four specific acts of generosity that were not significantly associated with either of those outcomes are also not associated with greater purpose. None of giving blood, being an organ donor, lending possessions, or estate giving significantly correlates with greater life purpose. The reason why, we propose, is the same reason they did not associate significantly with happiness or health. That is, that they are not ongoing *practices* of generosity, but rather only one time or irregular decisions or acts of generosity. They may be very valuable to do in and of themselves. But the evidence indicates that they, taken alone, do not enhance the well-being of the givers.

In sum, once again, the more generous Americans are in their *practices*, the more they enjoy greater well-being in their personal lives—in this case, in the form of living with greater purpose. Every one of the nine different measures of generous practices reflected this clear, positive, and statistically significant relationship between generosity and enhanced personal well-being. The answer to the question running throughout this chapter thus grows ever more clear. Far from being a draining cost that leaves the generous giver at a net loss, practicing generosity for the good of others actually tends to enrich the lives of the givers in ways that are of fundamental human value. Rather than leaving generous people on the short end of an unequal bargain, practices of generosity are actually likely instead to provide generous givers with essential goods in life—happiness, health, and purpose—which money and time themselves simply cannot buy. That is an empirical fact well worth knowing.

Avoiding Depression and Enjoying Personal Growth

In addition to analyzing the relationship between generosity, happiness, health, and purpose in life, we also examined the relationship of generosity to avoiding symptoms of depression and to people's expressed interest in personal growth. Again, we take both to be positive life outcomes. What did we find?

The very same clear, significant, and understandable patterns between generosity and positive life outcomes reviewed above bore themselves out down to the detail when it came to symptoms of depression and interest in personal growth. Namely, the more generous Americans are through different practices, the less likely and frequently do they suffer depressive symptoms. Also, the more generous Americans are, the more likely they are to express an interest in personal growth. Each of the nine tested generosity variables examined above reveals clear patterns of lower depression and greater interest in personal growth. And each of the patterned differences is statistically significant even net of the influence of ten control variables. So, with this, the larger pattern of positive associations between various forms of generosity and different measures of positive well-being is extended to two more major types of well-being outcomes. Both—depression and personal growth—are consequences about which most people care a great deal. The empirical evidence that generosity is definitely related to those basic goods in life that most, if not nearly all, people desire is increasingly convincing.

Readers are already familiar from the discussion above with the style and substance of the presentation of figures that show these positive relationships. And we do not wish to belabor the point by showing a seemingly endless stream of figures and percentages. So we are putting into the Appendix all of the figures presenting the relationships between the nine measures of generosity used in this chapter and the well-being outcomes of avoiding depression and being interested in personal growth. While we wish to move on in this book's larger argument, rather than to spell out every last finding in this first chapter, we still encourage readers to review those findings as they confirm our summary of them here.

Conclusion

This chapter has established that a variety of kinds of practices of generosity are positively and significantly associated with five important good life outcomes. Giving money, volunteering, being relationally generous, being a generous neighbor and friend, and personally valuing the importance of being a generous person are all significantly, positively correlated with greater personal happiness, physical health, a stronger sense of purpose in life, avoidance of symptoms of depression, and a greater interest in personal growth. These findings have not been weak, inconsistent, or requiring convoluted explanations to make sense of. Nearly every test and comparison came out similarly. The more generous Americans are in their practices (though not necessarily one-time decisions and acts), the more likely they are to enjoy positive life goods and well-being outcomes. Not often do social science results come out so clear and consistent in their patterning. And not often do social science findings so closely match theoretically explicable interpretations and expectations, such as the differences between practices and one-time acts, as they did here.

People may rightly wonder whether being a generous person and acting generously is a costly course of life. They might ask whether spending money, time, attention, energy, and emotions on and for the good of others proves to be a net loss in the overall scheme of things. The answer here is clear and compelling. Greater generosity is clearly, positively associated with many of the characteristics that most people consider essential to a good life: happiness, health, purpose, and growth. That is a significant finding with major implications for living.

So far, however, we have only established a statistical association or correlation between generosity and positive life well-being outcomes. But, if the greater generosity is not in part the cause of, but rather is entirely caused by, greater well-being, as some skeptical readers might suspect, then that does not speak well of the power of generosity to shape life for the better. In that case, generosity becomes not a causally important force, but simply a dependent variable that is driven by other factors. Which one of those two options really is true about generosity matters a great deal. So, we turn in the next chapter to address and answer head-on the key question of causal relations: Does generosity cause greater well-being, or vice versa?

CHAPTER 2 | How Generosity Enhances
         | Well-Being

THE PREVIOUS CHAPTER ESTABLISHED a clear association between the practice of generosity and Americans' greater well-being in life. The central question of this chapter concerns how the causal forces that produce that association actually work. Does generosity causally produce greater well-being? Or is it actually greater well-being that causes more generosity?

The need to address these questions stems from the reasonable doubts of some who are skeptical about claims that generous practices could have causal influences on outcomes like happiness, health, and purpose in life. How or why could giving money liberally, for example, cause someone to be happier or healthier? Oftentimes, in social science analyses, it is difficult to know exactly which variables causally influence which other variables and in what ways. That is especially true when studies use cross-sectional survey data, as we do here—that is, data gathered at one point in time, rather than in multiple waves of data collection with the same respondents across time, called panel or longitudinal studies. So it is important that we not presume that generosity causally enhances well-being. Correlation, as everyone knows, does not mean causation. So what is going on there causally?

Thinking Clearly About Causation

The first thing to be clear about is that causal questions cannot be ultimately answered by empirical data alone.[1] Causation is not "in" the data. Causation is not even "in" our theories that try to make sense of our data. Causation, rather, happens in the *real world* itself. Causes *are* real, they really exist and work in reality "out there" and in our own lives. Our job is to use the conceptual and theoretical tools at our disposal to better understand those causes, so that the understandings in our heads match the causal dynamics actually happening in reality. In that process, our data simply and only model more or less well those real causal processes. And our theories merely more or less well make conceptually knowable the actual causal processes that seem to operate in the real world. In short, our minds, which seek knowledge and understanding about how the real world works, have at their disposal both empirical data about the world that we have gathered, and concepts and theories that attempt to make sense of patterns we see in the data.

We can be confident about our understanding of how and why causes work in the real world, then, under two conditions. The first is that we have patterned empirical findings from reliable data that fit our larger understandings about how the world we observe and in which we ourselves participate as causal actors operates. The second is that we can provide conceptual theories that offer the arguably best interpretations of the patterned findings of our data, in terms of how the data seem to fit the reality they model and our best understanding of how the world works causally. This means that developing a good theoretical account of what seems to be going on in our empirical findings—an inference to the best explanation[2]—is crucial for building a credible interpretation and explanation of how the real world works. Providing just such a good theoretical account on the matter of generosity and well-being is the purpose of this chapter.[3]

Our job here is to relieve causal skeptics—those who believe that generosity does or could not possibly cause greater human well-being—of their skepticism. Our strategy will be not to argue that the skeptics are entirely wrong, because they are not completely wrong. Our strategy, rather, will be to argue that the causal skeptics are only *partially* right. Their proposal is fine as far as it goes, but it does not go far enough. We need to add in a second theoretical move. The skeptic's view of how things work, in other words, is one-sided. It can be affirmed. But it also needs to be complemented by another side. Then we will have a fuller picture about the relationship between generous practices and human well-being.

Let us venture two game metaphors to try to explain how we should and should not approach these issues. All too often, social scientists build their explanations on the assumption that the real social world works something like a game of pool (that is, the game played with balls on a billiard table). Explanatory models in this case are set up as if some outside ("exogenous") force (a person's arm) moves a cue stick (some variable), which pushes a white cue ball (an outcome) in a certain linear direction, which in turn exerts impacts on one or more other balls that sit within the trajectory of the moving cue ball. That then has the causal effect of propelling those balls through the transfer of kinetic energy to also move in different directions, thus bouncing off of other balls and side cushions and sometimes dropping into pockets. In this case, the causal forces at play are limited, fairly simple, linear, operating in discrete moves or plays, and in theory are mathematically calculable.

We suggest, however, that this pool-table model is often not an adequate way to think about how social life works. Sometimes it is positively misleading. We think we are often better served to think instead about the way social reality works as something more like a soccer game (what outside the US is called "football"). In this case, the model is complex, action is in continuous flow, and causal relations are nonlinear and highly interactive. A key difference here is that the players in a soccer game continuously monitor each other and the overall flow of the game and adjust their own play accordingly. Each player is doing this at every moment, with consequences of more or less obvious importance depending on their proximity to the ball, so that causal influences are operating in multiple, interactive directions. Focusing our vision on a simple piece of the game, one player may make a move to which another responds, which in turn affects the next move of the first player. Put that together with all of the players interacting at the same time, and we have a better model of how social life normally works. It is complex, interactive, continuously flowing, nonlinear, and difficult to model well mathematically.

This means, for the present analysis, that it is not necessarily the case that *either* greater well-being causes more generosity *or* the other way around. It could be both; it probably is both. These are not mutually exclusive possibilities, of which we must select only one. The relationship between generosity and well-being is not like a simple shot in a game of pool, in which the motion of the cue ball exerts force on, say, the solid-red three ball, which is then knocked into a corner pocket. The direction of influence between generosity and well-being need not be only one-way—indeed, it is very unlikely that the direction is only one-way. Since both generous practices and states of well-being can change across the continuous flow of time and action—unlike more fixed or stable features of social life, like people's sex, race, or early childhood experiences, which do not change—we have no good reason to think that they cannot causally influence each other. In fact, we have good reason to believe that they do so, and we are quite sure that they do.

Well-being Causally Influencing Generosity

Let us consider first the ways that greater well-being in people's lives likely causally influences more generous practices. This is the response of the causal skeptics. They are not hard to think of. Some of them very likely include the following causal mechanisms:

1. *Positive Mental Outlook.* People who are happier, healthier, and more purposeful in life will, all other things being equal, tend to have a more positive, hopeful outlook on life and the possibilities for doing good in the world than those who are less happy, healthy, and purposeful, and so will be more generous in various ways.

2. *More Energy.* People who are happier, healthier, and more purposeful in life will, all other things being equal, tend to have more energy to spend on matters beyond their own personal concerns than those who are less happy, healthy, and purposeful, and so will be more generous in various ways.

3. *More Money.* People who are healthier (though not necessarily more happy or purposeful) will, all other things being equal, tend to have more money to spend on matters beyond their own personal concerns than those who are less healthy, insofar as health problems tend to consume money and may curtail people's ability to work in the paid labor force, and so will be more generous in various ways.

4. *Social Network Connections.* People who are happier, healthier, and more purposeful in life will, all other things being equal, tend to be better connected to and more engaged in a wider range of social relationships in a broader variety of institutional settings than those who are less happy, healthy, and purposeful—and those social ties will provide more opportunities to engage through invitations and requests in generous practices, and so they will be more generous in various ways.

These kinds of explanations for how greater well-being in life may facilitate higher levels of generosity make great sense. We have good reason to think that they help to explain the significant association between generous practices and life well-being that we observed in the previous chapter. Our account in this book does nothing to deny them. We accept these explanations as part of the larger picture of complex causal dynamics. But, we also suggest, they are only *part* of that picture, only one side of a complicated, two-sided dynamic that we need to better understand.

Reasons to Doubt One-Directional Causal Models

One of the reasons that we might suspect that the direction of the causal explanations just noted (well-being → generosity) accounts for only *part* of the picture is a set of questions that crop up as we pause and ponder the matter more carefully. Let us consider them briefly here.

First, if greater well-being, as the supposedly only "independent variable," accounted entirely for the significant associations observed in the previous chapter, then why were four particular forms of generosity (giving blood, donating organs, lending possessions, estate giving) not significantly associated with greater well-being? If giving 10 percent of one's income and volunteering are the results of being happier, healthier, and more purposeful, then why are giving blood and lending possessions not also caused by that as well? The same logic explained in the causal mechanisms just named should also apply to giving blood. Happier and healthier people should give blood more, because they have a more positive outlook and more energy and social ties. But they do not give blood more, according to our findings. However, our theory about the key differences between practices and one-time or irregular acts *does* explain this difference. Yet that explanation assumes in this case that it is generosity that at least partially causes greater well-being, not only the other way around. If we are not able to acknowledge the causal influence operating in both directions, then we have difficulty answering this question about these inconsistent effects.

Consider too that not all forms of generosity require being healthy. Yes, an unhealthy person may not be able to volunteer to spend his Saturdays building a Habitat for Humanity house. But that same somewhat unhealthy person *can* write a check to support Habitat financially. And that same person, who is in only fair health, can also practice most forms of neighborly generosity, such as watching over a house for neighbors who are away or having friends or relatives over for a visit. Only those people who are in truly very bad health would be unlikely to be able to practice *any* form of generosity, and among the whole population they are relatively few. Furthermore, in fact, some of the most generous people can actually struggle with personal finances and health difficulties, yet they practice generosity anyway. Mother Teresa, for example, suffered from heart problems, spiritual desolation, and perhaps clinical depression. News stories sometimes report relatively poor people who give away a great deal of money without fanfare.[4] And many Americans return from service trips to the Global South deeply moved by the amazing expressions of generosity and hospitality they received from people they met there who live on very little. These cases may be exceptions that do not fit the general tendency among Americans. But they at least caution us against making potentially simplistic assumptions about a high income or quality of health that is required in order simply to be a generous person.

As a matter of fact, some empirical evidence suggests that Americans who volunteer are, when it comes to very specific measures of chronic health conditions, in fact *not* privileged over those who do not volunteer. For instance, according to one national study of 4,582 adult Americans, those who volunteer are no different than those who do not in the average number of medical prescriptions taken daily, number of doctor visits and hospitalizations in the previous year, or the percentage suffering specific diseases that might curtail volunteer activity.[5] Nevertheless, these same volunteers reported feeling better and enjoying higher levels of mental health than the non-volunteers. Something more complicated seems to be going on here.

By the same logic, not all forms of generosity require a big income. Most people possess different kinds of resources, not simply money, which they can share generously. People living on modest means, for instance, can and often do volunteer their time generously for causes they believe in. And practicing relational and neighborly generosity is not dependent upon secure financial resources as a precondition. So we should not overstate the importance of having a lot of money as a prerequisite for being a generous person. As a matter of fact, certain features of having a lot of money may actually make it more difficult to share time, finances, and attention in relationships—as wealthier people are also often more busy and distracted.

Furthermore, having a positive mental outlook on life does not necessarily, much less automatically, mean that people will be generous as a result. Such a psychological state could arguably also work against generosity. In theory, someone's happiness and health could give rise to a positive, optimistic outlook on life in a way that was actually self-satisfied, content, and fairly indifferent to the needs of the world. Simply having a positive outlook could very well find expression in such non-generous ways.

Finally, we might doubt the one-directional-causation models of the causal skeptics for this reason. Evidence from multiple studies of the determinants of human happiness show that about 40 percent of the difference in how happy or unhappy people are is explained by the effects of intentional activities in which they engage, which tend to influence happiness. About one-half of people's happiness seems determined by a genetically determined happiness "set point" that is fixed, stable, and largely immune to influence. About 10 percent of people's happiness appears to be shaped by the particular life circumstances they enjoy or suffer, such as income security, marital status, religious membership, and so on. But the first portion—about 40 percent—of the difference in people's level of happiness is determined by activities in which they can intentionally engage, such as exercising regularly or counting one's blessings rather than focusing on one's problems. And among the kinds of intentional activities known to increase happiness are many involved in practicing generosity, such as intentionally helping others, working to be mindful of one's abundance, and becoming involved in a meaningful cause.[6] If generosity is entirely driven by one's prior level of happiness and health, then we should not expect to see fully 40 percent of people's happiness determined by activities in which they can intentionally engage (or not). But since this significant proportion of differences in happiness is influenced by intentional activities, it seems clear that generosity should have at least some causal capacity to influence well-being.

For these reasons and based upon much of the theoretical logic and empirical evidence reviewed in what follows, we proceed with the belief that generosity and well-being are mutually influencing. Greater well-being can causally encourage more generosity. But practices of generosity can also causally enhance people's well-being. Part of making the case for this bidirectional model of causation involves spelling out specific causal mechanisms by which generosity can increase human well-being. It is to this task that we turn next.

ANCIENT WISDOM ON GENEROSITY

To generous souls every task is noble.

—*Euripides*

No act of kindness, no matter how small, is ever wasted.

—*Aesop, "The Lion and the Mouse"*

Nine Interrelated Causal Mechanisms

Generous practices do not improve human well-being magically. The causal connection is not inexplicable. Generous practices enhance human well-being by means of specific causal mechanisms that can be theorized, studied, and understood. The following pages suggest the most likely causal mechanisms by which generosity increases well-being.[7] Most of them are closely related to each other and interact in complex ways in the real world. But for present theoretical purposes we state them conceptually as distinct mechanisms. Let us begin with a very simple, understandable, yet powerful causal mechanism:

1. *Generosity often fosters and reinforces positive emotions and reduces negative emotions in givers, which tends to lead to greater happiness and health.*

The fact that treating others with generosity leads to positive emotional responses in the generous is well established by many studies. Marc Musick and John Wilson are sociologists at the University of Texas at Austin and Duke University, respectively, who study helping behaviors. Here is what they say about helping others and positive emotions:

> Doing our duty, living up to our responsibilities, meeting our obligations, are intrinsically rewarding behaviors. Furthermore, helping others, or working on behalf of a cause, provides a sense of mission, giving purpose and significance to our lives. Doing volunteer work. . . allows us to use personal skills and strengths in which we take pride.[8]

Furthermore, positive emotions have been clearly linked causally to greater well-being. Duke Medical School researcher Harold Koenig says it well:

> Altruistic behaviors that involve helping others without expectation of reward are associated with fewer negative emotions and more positive emotions. It is difficult to be angry, resentful, depressed, or fearful when one is showing selfless love toward another person. Such loving acts neutralize negative emotions that stimulate physiological responses known to adversely affect immune, endocrine, and cardiovascular functions.[9]

Take, for example, the generosity involved in proactively forgiving other people. This form of generosity, and the positive feelings it evokes in generous forgivers, have been shown by studies to reduce stress, tension, and sadness, and to lead to lower heart rates, lower skin conduction levels, and lower blood pressure. By contrast, those who ungenerously hold grudges are more angry, feel less in control of their lives, and, partly as a result, exhibit symptoms of unhealthy physical conditions.[10] It is hard to confirm that worse health causes an ungenerous, unforgiving disposition. All of the research shows the causal effect working in the other direction. Thus, the psychologist Allan Luks observes about generosity and positive emotions, "We *feel* a connection, a vicarious experience of the other person's problems, a recognition of him or her as a fellow being. These feelings which are transmitted to our bodies produce the good, relaxing sensations that seem to lie at the heart of healthy helping."[11] The empirical evidence and theoretical logic supporting this claim are strong.[12]

In our own interviews with Americans, we find ample support for these rewards. The people who practice generosity by forgiving others and making peace with the hardships in life are better able to overcome negative emotions. By giving more attention to what they *do* have rather than what they lack, they minimize damage from their troubling experiences. The most vivid example of someone we interviewed whose generous lifestyle offsets negative emotions is "Tina Kennedy," a single mother of three in Northern California.[13] Tina is on social welfare, having suffered a spinal injury in childbirth, and as a result is no longer able to work long hours on her feet as a cosmetologist. After giving birth to one of her children, Tina learned that the child's father had decided to leave her for another woman, one of her good friends. She recalls that time as a particularly dark chapter in life. It was not easy, but she did find a way to move past the pain and forgive her boyfriend, her good female friend, and the doctors responsible for her injury. Rather than letting bitterness take root, she remains thankful for what she has. "I had to regroup, regroup, re-evaluate things, where you put your priorities and things of life. But overall, I'm blessed, and that's why I keep my strength. I have life to be thankful for, you know?" Even though she could easily be overwhelmed by her health, financial, and romantic setbacks, she still generously reaches out to other people, by providing aid to extended family members and volunteering much of her time to local schools.

Another woman, "Marlene Davis," in Nevada, has been separated from her husband for almost twenty years and is coping with poor health. When reflecting on the more difficult aspects of her life, she says, "And I'm still here. Even with being, I'm a diabetic, type two.... If I get a little low, then the first thing I can do is look around me, and when I look around me...

and you see you're not as bad as you thought you were." By incorporating her own problems into the bigger picture and remaining sensitive to the hardships that others also face, Marlene refuses to let the negative dictate her outlook. "There's a lot of wrong in this world, there really is, and there's a lot of wrong that's been done to me," she continues, "but I'm not going to stay on that to make myself feel sad because of that." Instead she finds joy by generously investing her time and money in her local religious congregation.

Other studies suggest that many people find that being good to others, even while not expecting to receive any benefit in return, proves to be rewarding emotionally.[14] Merely the act of providing help to others has been shown to improve helpers' moods and self-evaluations.[15] Insofar as generosity relieves the sadness that people can feel about the misfortunes of others, still other research shows that the generous helping of other people improves people's emotional states.[16] One multi-nation study, for example, conducted by scholars at the Harvard Business School, investigated the causal relationship between spending money on other people, rather than on oneself, and greater feelings of happiness. The results, it reported, revealed evidence for a cross-cultural "psychological universal: Human beings everywhere may experience emotional benefits from using their financial resources to benefit others."[17]

In our interviews, "Dale Steinecker," a resident of Illinois in his fifties, talked about this emotional benefit from helping other people as having a sense of "inner peace":

I think there's an inner peace that you receive from it, if nothing else, knowing that you have been able to help somebody. You may never know 'em. You may never see 'em, but at least you have a feel-good feeling, I guess, from the idea of helping somebody.

Dale does not need to interact directly with the recipients of his generosity to experience this "feel-good feeling." As with most of the generous people we interviewed, it is enough to know that his resources are being put to good use in the lives of others. Dale is just one of many generous people we studied who experience this type of peace and happiness as a result of giving money away.

Furthermore, research on volunteers' self-reports about their own experiences of being generous to others confirms these findings. In one national study, 89 percent of volunteers agreed that "volunteering has improved my sense of well-being," and 73 percent reported that "volunteering lowers my stress levels." Volunteers also reported less frequent negative emotions, including anxiety, loneliness, helplessness, and hopelessness. Americans who volunteer specifically through their jobs also reported more positive attitudes toward their colleagues and employers as a result of their volunteering. Eighty-one percent say that "volunteering with work colleagues has strengthened our relationship," and 76 percent report that "I feel better about my employer because of their involvement in my volunteer activities."[18] In short, those who are practicing generosity directly report that it makes them feel better, and improves their affective states, which has positive consequences in their lives.

A second causal mechanism explaining how greater generosity produces improved well-being is closely related to this influence of positive emotions, but operates at a more biological level:

2. *Generosity often triggers chemical systems in the brain and body that increase pleasure and experiences of reward, reduce stress, and suppress pain, which tend to lead to greater happiness and health.*

Here we address the fascinating link between subjective human experience and body chemistry. When people act generously, it often triggers the release of chemicals in the brain and body that enhance pleasure and happiness and reduce stress and pain. These include oxytocin, dopamine, serotonin, vasopressin, endorphins, and prolactin. These biochemical responses appear to be activated by the kind of positive emotions just mentioned, and contribute to them as well.[19] We know that people's brain and hormonal functioning have big influences on their subjective experiences and mental states. But it is also true that people's subjective mental states and experiences can influence their brain and hormonal functioning as well. Brains not only regulate emotions and experiences, for instance, but behaviorally shaped emotions and experiences can and do trigger chemical events in the brain—events that can have real consequences for happiness and health.[20]

In recent decades, psychologists have called the neurologically induced well-being effect caused by generosity the "helper's high" and "helper's calm."[21] Economists have labeled it the "warm glow" that follows generous behavior.[22] Social work scholars refer to "helper's therapy," which heals those who help as much or more as those helped.[23] And neuroscientists increasingly find that the "reward areas" of the human brain "light up" when people give generously to others.[24] This all points to a complex set of neurobiological processes that are triggered in the brain by people's generous practices and the positive emotions they tend to produce.

Until recently, we knew little about these neurological processes and their connection to generosity. Even today the science of this area is in its early stages. But an accumulating body of neuroscience research is making increasingly clear how generous practices and attitudes work through the brain to enhance human well-being. Experts in this area note that, "the neurobiology of affiliative [positive socially bonding] behaviors has been well worked out, including the neural pathways, brain regions, and neurohormones and neurotransmitters involved. In addition, it is clear from epidemiological and clinical studies that positive emotions, affiliative behaviors, and salubrious [healthy] activities. . . are associated with better health outcomes." The connection between the two appears to work through "several neural and neuroendocrine pathways that mediate the effects of positive emotions and affiliative behaviors on immune response and health."[25] This connection between generosity and healthy biochemical responses is worth examining further.

Consider the mammalian hormone, oxytocin. This is a chemical associated with behaviors and feelings of social bonding, sexual arousal, maternal care, increased trust, reduced fear, and increased empathy, among other things. Experimental studies have shown that increasing the amount of oxytocin in people's neurological systems significantly increases their generosity, empathy, and love.[26] But the relationship may work both ways: increased feelings of empathy for others and generous practices also appear to be capable of increasing the oxytocin released in people's brain systems. Experimental research, for instance, shows that simply watching an emotional video designed to elicit empathy in viewers significantly increases the viewer's levels of oxytocin, compared to those who watched an emotionally neutral video.[27] Another study showed that interactions of physical touch with intentional acts of interpersonal trust were followed by a significant increase in oxytocin levels in the body, which were also related to increased reciprocity among actors.[28]

Consider also the neurotransmitter dopamine, which operates in the human central nervous system to regulate rewards and learning.[29] Dopamine is known to be implicated in human social bonding, affability, and prosocial behavior.[30] Research suggests that an altruistic orientation is associated with increases in dopamine. The authors of one study, for instance, observe that, "the linkage between the reward and altruistic attitudes provide the neuro-chemical substrate and 'hard wiring' needed to drive acts that benefit others even at the expense of reducing one's own [reproductive] fitness." Noting this significant association between human selflessness and levels of dopamine, the authors conclude, "we [humans] 'feel good' and are rewarded by a dopamine pulse when doing good deeds."[31]

As far back as the 1980s, the psychologist Allan Luks was pioneering the scholarly connections between voluntarily helping others and volunteers' increased personal well-being. In a national study, Luks found that volunteers reported much higher levels of health, happiness, calmness, and self-esteem and much lower levels of stress, fatigue, helplessness, and depression. He attributed those differences to the effects of endorphin neurotransmitters operating in response to helping experiences. Endorphins are pain-reducing peptides that interfere with the sensitivity of brain neurons to the transmission of information about pain. They are produced by the pituitary gland and released into the bloodstream, and make their way into the spinal cord and brain by way of hypothalamic neurons. Endorphins function something like an opiate, muffling pain—in fact, the word endorphins is short for "endogenous morphine," that is, something like morphine that is produced naturally by the body itself. Thus, the more endorphins, the less pain people feel. Endorphins can be released by "good stress," such as running for exercise, which produces the well-known "runner's high." They can also be produced by excitement, pain, meditation, eating spicy foods and chocolate, laughing hard, and orgasms. According to Luks, generously helping other people is another means for stimulating the release of endorphins. At the time that he wrote, Luks could not explain why or how helping increased endorphins, nor the exact psychobiological mechanisms by which the process worked. But we know more about it today as a result of subsequent research, which in recent decades has confirmed the argument of Luks's original hypothesis.[32]

Another neurotransmitter, serotonin, seems to play a role in the generosity-happiness connection. Linked with general feelings of well-being and happiness, lower levels of serotonin are associated with negative moods, hostility, and greater susceptibility to depression. Those with higher levels of serotonin tend to have better moods, greater social support, and a diminished incidence of depression, suicide, and mortality.[33] Serotonin, understood to be involved in the neural substrate of moral judgments, sociality, and the reduction of aggression and negative feelings, also encourages generous behavior. Intact levels of serotonin suppress the desire to harm others while increasing empathy, thus promoting prosocial and altruistic behavior.[34] In other words, people with adequate levels of serotonin are less hostile and do want to prevent or alleviate the suffering of others. This suggests that serotonin encourages generous behavior, or acting for the benefit of others, and this empathetic action indirectly increases oxytocin levels. Studies to date have not researched whether the causal arrow moves in both directions (that is, whether people's generous practices may help increase serotonin levels), but findings and models in related areas suggest that it very well may. More research is needed to confirm this, however.

At the same time, the *lack* of generosity can stimulate *negative* neurochemical processes. Take the hormone cortisol, for example, which is secreted in the human body by stress. While cortisol's short-term effects may be functional for human behavior, its longer-term consequences are known to be detrimental to health, creating "wear and tear" on the body.[35] Cortisol has been identified as an important mechanism by which life stress leads to declining physical health.[36] So, consider this for present purposes: one recent experimental study showed that greater generosity with money is associated with lower levels of cortisol in the body. In this study, people who were stingy in giving money secreted higher levels of cortisol. This was due, the research suggested, to people's own negative emotional responses, such as guilt or embarrassment, to having behaved in a miserly manner. The study thus concluded: "Stingy economic behavior can produce a feeling of shame, which in turn drives secretions of the stress hormone cortisol."[37]

Perhaps, then, it is not surprising that many ungenerous people we interviewed felt embarrassed about not giving their money away. For example, one middle-class homemaker in Nevada, "Maria Berry," told us, "When we go to church I don't like to give my money to them" and acknowledged that "sometimes I feel embarrassed." Another woman, "Stacy Spiegel," from Connecticut, enjoys a well-compensated career in upper management, but chooses to give no money away. She says that she actually would prefer to be more generous and struggles to justify her stinginess, and says she is "self-centered in that respect." She became especially flustered when talking about her alma mater:

> My college will call for money, and I don't give. And, like, they were good to me in school, you know? And it's like, I don't know, I know it's not right. But it's like, I don't know. So I'm not as generous as I should be, you know?

Stacy believes she is wrong for not giving to her alma mater—"I know it's not right," she admits. And as she sought to put together an answer that could better account for her lack of generosity, she stumbled over her words and sounded anxious, as she was unable to come up with an explanation. It is this kind of stress, embarrassment, and guilt experienced by ungenerous people that has consequences for their long-term physical health. So, once again, the connection between generosity—or lack thereof—and human well-being seems to be explained in part by the responses of body chemistry.

Other neuroscience studies have used Functional Magnetic Resonance Imaging (fMRI) technology to examine the real-time operation of brains as people have engaged in various kinds of generous activities. These studies show that the parts of the brain that are activated when someone receives a concrete, gratifying reward or pleasure (such as from food, sex, drugs, or money) are the same that are also engaged when one behaves generously. One study, for example, shows that when people give monetary charitable donations, it activates the brain's (mesolimbic) "reward system" in the same way that is observed when people win monetary rewards for themselves. The researchers conclude that their "lines of evidence indicate that human altruism draws on general mammalian neural systems of reward [and] social attachment."[38] A different study shows the same area of the brain that registers concrete rewards from consuming food, drugs, and money is similarly activated when people make financial contributions to charitable causes. The authors thus argue that, "monetary payoffs to oneself, observing a charity getting money, and a warm-glow effect related to free choice [in giving]. . . all activate similar neural substrates."[39] In yet another experiment, women were presented with modest amounts of money that were sometimes taxed, sometimes increased, and sometimes the women had the option of giving the money to a local food bank. All subjects in the experiment found pleasure in receiving money. But about half of the women gained more pleasure from giving money away than receiving it. Giving money away, in short, has similar causal neural effects in the brain as receiving more money for oneself.[40] Generosity and altruistic behavior can be quite pleasurable.[41]

Although our own sociological research interviews did not tap directly into these neurological processes, we did find overwhelming evidence of a reported "giver's high" and the "warm-glow effect." For example, "Susan Traber," a woman in her early fifties, purposively gives away 10 percent of the income that she and her husband earn from their small business. She enjoys giving money to various religious and local organizations in her home state of South Carolina, explaining:

As you're getting more and more blessings and all [earning money], you feel really good about it, so you want in turn to bless somebody else. . . . It makes me feel good to be able to help other people. So yeah, givers gain. I enjoy being able to help other people.

"James Caruso," a New York City professional who regularly contributes to various charities, is another example of someone who experiences the warm glow of generosity. His regular charitable contributions, he says, make him feel "more upbeat."

Well, I don't feel as if I'm losing something. I mean, obviously, you know, you give a check for a little, just say, 150 dollars to a charitable organization, and you can see in the checkbook that there's 150 dollars less, but that's not the way I view it. I view it as doing something positive, and I think that people should accept the challenge to try to make the world better than what it has been.

So, we asked, how does that giving make you feel? "Well," he reported, "for the most part I would say that it makes me feel more upbeat and more positive, recognizing that you know it's going to be used for a positive purpose."

Volunteers often experience a similar high from devoting their time to others. "Christina Heffner," a twenty-something accountant in Washington, DC, volunteers her time tutoring low-income children: "I really like the volunteering, it makes me feel like a better person. It makes me feel warm and fuzzy when I know I can help other people. And these kids, they know my name, they give me hugs, they're like, Christy, we're so glad you're here. So it makes me feel really great."

For Christina, the "warm and fuzzy" feeling is not just the result of knowing that she's using her time to help others, but also due to the fact that the children she helps express gratitude and affection. Like many volunteers, she is appreciated by others for her work, and that feels good.

Though many generous people like Susan, James, and Christina talk about giving without hesitations, others express more ambivalence toward giving. For the latter group, the warm glow is a personal benefit that can counteract stinginess. Take "Cynthia Fountain," a fifty-something woman in South Carolina whom we will discuss more in Chapter 5. Although she says that giving away about 10 percent of her income feels good, she also admits to having a "greedy side."

It makes me feel good when I [give money]. I guess if I had a choice I would probably be a greedy person and keep it. But I know that I'm supposed to do it and I feel good when I do it, so I guess my greedy side is probably only about 25 percent.

Again, these mixed desires are not uncommon, but generous people like Cynthia generally see a greater good in giving money away, and experience the personal benefit of the warm glow, which in turn works to override the "greedy side" of their human nature, of which they are not proud. Unadulterated altruism, in other words, is not a necessary condition for generous behavior or for reaping the benefits from such behavior.

In addition to this research on the warm-glow effect of giving, a variety of other studies have increased our understanding of the neurological basis of human moral thought and judgments, which are clearly related to generosity. These studies, consistent with everything noted above, identify specific regions of the human brain that are engaged in the process of moral cognitions, such as those engaged in generous practices. They, too, suggest strong neurological linkages between feeling empathy for others, engaging in generous or altruistic behaviors, increased self-perceptions of personal agency, feeling affirmation and pride from having "done the right thing," and the secretion of the kind of healthy neurochemicals described above, including oxytocin, serotonin, and dopamine.[42] One leader in this area of research, Paul Zak of the Claremont Graduate School, concludes that, "Human beings have a physiologic moral compass," grounded, he says, in neurobiology. This means that not only does "happiness come from leading a virtuous life," as Aristotle argued, but also, according to Zak, that "virtuous societies will be happier."[43] And Zak's larger research program clearly shows that generosity is one of the key virtues that leads to happiness.

These neurobiological processes do not simply make people feel good in the short run. They also involve biological mechanisms that boost immunity and health over the long term. For example, the systemic reduction of stress and biochemical blocking or reducing of the negative effects of stress through practices of generosity enhances health and well-being in many ways. Many of the neurohormones and neurotransmitters discussed above help to boost the immune response of the body. In addition, endorphins have been causally associated with pain reduction, better body temperature regulation, healthy blood pressure regulation, and the control of fear.[44] Some research suggests that the processes we have described can also have direct healing effects on headaches, backaches, obesity, sleeplessness, infections, acid stomach, lupus, asthma, cancer, coronary artery disease, cerebrovascular disease and stroke, and general recovery from surgery.[45]

Once again, this logic is also confirmed by the testimony of generous people collected in social-scientific studies. For example, in one national study on generosity in volunteering, 84 percent of volunteers reported that "volunteering improves physical health," 68 percent of volunteers say that "volunteering has made me [personally] feel physically healthier," and 27 percent report that "volunteering has helped me manage a chronic illness."[46] Given the great intrinsic value of good health, the massive costs expended on health-care today, and people's desire to find ways to improve their own health, these are very important findings. Human bodies have natural, built-in mechanisms so that by simply doing good for one another through various forms of generosity, physical health and subjective happiness are improved.

Generous practices also have other positive psychological consequences, including the following:

3. Generosity increases personal agency and self-efficacy, which tends to enhance happiness and health.

Practicing generosity typically requires and promotes the exercise of personal agency in the world, which is a fundamental aspect of living as a flourishing person.[47] Increases in agency tend to promote greater mental, emotional, and physical well-being. By contrast, lower levels of personal agency tend to diminish health and well-being. By "agency," we mean the exercise of one's natural human powers and capacities to make things happen in the world, to affect or prevent changes one wishes to see happen. Generosity itself, by definition, represents a form of agency exercised, that is, purposeful interventions of giving intended to convey valuable things to others in order to enhance their good. Contrasting with the agency expressed in generosity is an outlook that says, "What I do does not matter," "I cannot make a difference in the world," and "Events and outcomes are beyond my control." That kind of disempowered anti-agency is bad for mental, emotional, and physical health.

Generosity increases the personal agency of the generous giver in various ways. First, engaging in generous practices usually requires getting "on top of" the resources that one has to give away. Many people are disorganized, scattered, and out of control when it comes to their own money, time, and attention, reflecting a relative lack of agency exercised as the owner of those resources. Being generous with that money, time, attention, energy, and so on usually requires becoming intentional, getting organized, taking stock, setting priorities, and following through with decisions about allocations. And that in and of itself is already a form of personal agency exercised, a significant step in the right direction.[48] This is particularly true of the people we interviewed who give away a tenth or more of their household income. Take "Tammy Philpot," for example, an upper-middle-class stay-at-home mom in South Carolina whose household gives 10 percent of its income to its religious congregation, in addition to various nonprofits. She maintains the family finances with finesse:

> I use computer software and I've got all of our accounts set up on Microsoft Money and I balance them all every month. I've got one account that requires a lot of hoops to jump through. Like I've got a checking account with $25,000 in that we can earn five percent interest on, which is a lot these days. But I have to jump through a whole bunch of hoops, like doing a certain number of debit card transactions and a certain number of this, and spin around five times, and so it actually requires a good bit of attention to maximize our interest earnings. But I do that every month.

Tammy's organization and readiness to negotiate the various hoops she has to jump through are uncommon among most of those we interviewed, but less so among the more financially generous. In such families, following through on the decision to give, say, 10 percent of their income requires real planning.

Those who are generous also tend to think more carefully about their spending habits and choose to minimize unnecessary consumption, so that they can put their savings to service in more productive ways for the good of others. "Matthew Duhamel," a chemistry graduate student who earns a modest income as a lab assistant in Indiana, gave up his daily Starbucks coffee in order to give more money to World Vision, a charity that works to alleviate childhood poverty.

> I think it's easy to maybe purchase something you don't need or spend money on something, like getting a coffee or something like that, which ultimately aren't as important as giving, it's easy to sorta slip into that if you don't plan your giving. . . . I used to have only one sponsored child through World Vision, and at one point I was like, "Oh I really would like to sponsor another child, but is that really financially possible?" Then once you start to break down your finances and see where your money is going, it is easy to identify things like a coffee a couple times a week that can add up to being able to do something like that.

Matthew's desire to be a generous person forced him to increase his mindfulness about his finances. In this he exercised greater agency, something we know tends to boost health and happiness.

Emotionally, many people are also driven by insecurity and fear when it comes to money, time, and other resources. These people's experiences are often controlled by their supposed lack of money, time, and energy. How much of these resources that they do or do not have can literally govern how they think, feel, and live. For example, one especially stressed respondent, "Danny Ramirez" (whose story we spend more time on in Chapter 4), captured this fear about lack of time well:

> Modern life is just fast-paced, everything. Everything. It's just go go go go go, everything automated, everything's supposed to be designed to make our lives easier, but I feel that it just makes it harder. We're always in a hurry to be everywhere. For me that's what it does. Everything's designed to make it easier, but, in actuality, I think it just makes it that much more hurried. If you really think about it, you're always trying to get somewhere.

Danny works about forty hours a week as a factory supervisor, but the job tires him out and does not leave him with enough energy or time, he says, to volunteer or look into organizations that ask him for money. During the weekend afternoons and evenings we spent with Danny and his family, he spent most of his time in his room playing video games and watching television. Similarly, "Shane Little," an army veteran enrolled at a state college in Oregon, feels helpless—that is, lacking agency—when it comes to making changes in his life.

> I can never get ahead and I absolutely hate that. I have a tendency to flirt with women, and I wish sometimes that I could stop that. Sometimes it feels like I can't. Or maybe it's sometimes I don't want to, I don't really know. So that's obviously caused some problems in the marriage, and that's something that I wish I didn't do and causes arguments and whatnot.

Others do not feel out of control and do not suffer from a lack of agency when it comes to using their resources. They are simply disorganized, even reckless. For example, "Shelly Martinez," a retired teacher in Georgia who complains about her modest household income, explains how she and her husband impulsively purchased a large SUV they had wanted, which cost more than $40,000.

Once the kids left, then we finished paying off some accounts that we had and all that, I was always asking my husband, "Come on, let's buy a new car!" "No, it's not time yet. It's not time yet and it's not time." All of a sudden, he just says, "You know what? Are you ready to go buy a new car?" Not that we had extra money or anything, but it was just, I said, "Yes."

When we asked her husband, Rodrigo, a handyman, if he was happy with the purchase, he tells us, "Yeah, we're happy, just sometimes I don't have any work and then it's kind of hard to make that payment." As empty-nesters with only a financial obligation to themselves as a couple, Shelly and Rodrigo seemingly have little need for monetary organization or planning. But this lack of structure leads to impulsive and risky purchases and, in the case of Shelly and Rodrigo, eliminates the possibility of generous financial giving.

In most such cases, to become generous with these resources first requires getting in emotional control of them, taking emotional charge of one's own stock of goods and how one intends to use them. Giving away some of what one owns for the good of others often entails making an emotional break from those objects' control over oneself, over one's life and feelings. Rather than being driven *by* them, one must instead become freed up to *use* them for one's own intentional purposes. That means becoming the master of one's money, time, energy, attention—ultimately, of one's life—rather than being mastered by them. And to undergo that shift—from being anxiously controlled by them, to instead being in control and the master of them—involves another powerful assertion of personal agency.

Practicing generosity strengthens people's sense and exercise of agency in other ways. Expressing generosity, for instance, often involves undertaking various kinds of healthy challenges, projects, and investments. Such undertakings are in and of themselves good for the agents who do them. Studies show, for instance, that simply practicing generosity enhances self-esteem in givers, and is associated with a greater sense of self-efficacy (that is, the view that one is able to effectively make things happen in the world).[49] Our interviews confirm this. "Troy Musser" in Illinois believes he can have an impact on the world around him: "I believe in that ripple effect. We have to affect our own family, our neighbors, our communities, and I think that if we do that in a positive way, it will ripple out." In Washington, "Shannon Johnson" believes she has the potential to make a difference in the lives of the children she works with as a volunteer soccer coach:

I think I have the power to influence individuals. I've done some volunteer soccer coaching and I think everyone has somebody they look back and they remember this kind of role model. And I'd like to think that some of the kids I coached that they would remember you and say "Hey remember, she was a good person."

Other research reveals that volunteering generously builds self-confidence in volunteers in ways that carry over in their effects into other spheres of life.[50] Practicing generosity also often involves learning and exercising new skills and abilities that, research shows, can actually improve "one's chances in the paid labor market by increasing one's stock of human capital."[51] Scholars furthermore suggest that generous practices, such as engaging in voluntary community service, reflect and reinforce a kind of "ability signaling"—that is, they tell oneself and the world that one is capable and competent to take on and achieve goals and interests in the public sphere.[52]

This generosity–agency connection is demonstrated in a remarkable study by University of Maryland psychologist Kurt Gray, the findings of which indicated that "the very act of doing good increases agency." Gray conducted three controlled experiments that compared the physical abilities of people doing good deeds with those engaged in acts of neutral value. He found that the randomly sampled group of good-doers proved literally physically stronger and more tenacious than those doing neutral tasks. In his simplest experiment, people drawn randomly from a crowd at a subway station were asked to hold a five-pound weight out horizontally from the side of their bodies as long as they possibly could. The length of time they held the weight out was recorded. After doing so, each person was given one dollar. Half who were randomly selected were then asked to give their dollar to UNICEF, and all of them did. At that point, everyone was asked to again hold out the five-pound weight for as long as they possibly could. After controlling for differences in body strength reflected in the original times, it turned out that those who had donated the dollar were able to hold out the weights the second time for significantly longer periods of time than those who had kept their money.

Gray's other two experiments also validated the hypothesis that those who do good subsequently exhibit greater bodily strength. Reflecting on his findings, Gray argued, "Self-perceptions can be quite powerful, causing people to act in ways that confirm their self-perceptions. Importantly, the perceptual association between moral deeds and agency may have physical effects because many such associations are embodied, extending beyond mind to the body." In sum, Gray concluded, "doing good does more than just make us feel better: It gives people the personal strength to act more effectively and better achieve their goals."[53] And that, he suggests, provides a possible explanation for why generosity toward others correlates with greater personal well-being. Once again, then, we see that the mental orientations typically involved in generous practices translate into greater personal agency. Marc Musick and John Wilson, quoted above, agree: "Doing volunteer work. . . allows [people] to develop [new]. . . aptitudes and thus an enacted sense of [empowered] self."[54]

As before, generous people are often aware of these agency-enhancing effects of their own generosity. In the same survey mentioned above, 97 percent of Americans who volunteer believe that "through volunteering, one person can make a real difference." The vast majority of volunteers in the US also believe that volunteering can change lives, create goodwill, give people hope, and unite communities. Four out of ten also believe that volunteering can further the cause of social justice. Ninety-seven percent of American volunteers also believe that volunteering is an important service to their community; 96 percent think that volunteering can help create a stronger, healthier America; and 73 percent of US volunteers report that they have learned valuable things about themselves through volunteering.[55] Precisely those kinds of outlooks and experiences reflect robust expressions of personal agency of the sort that tend to work toward greater mental, emotional, and physical health.

This all also relates to the next causal mechanism by which generosity produces enhanced well-being:

   4. Generosity often creates positive, meaningful social roles and personal self-identities for generous givers to live out, which tends to lead to greater happiness and health.

This causal mechanism is fairly straightforward. Flourishing human life requires living a meaningful existence. Most meaning in human life does not float down out of the sky into people's minds and hearts. Meaning, rather, is largely acquired by living in and out of personal and social roles and identities. These operate in powerful ways to tell us who we are, where we came from, what we are supposed to be doing, and what life is all about.[56] Therefore, people who occupy weak self-identities and fewer positive social roles tend to be less healthy and happy. By contrast, people who enjoy many positive, meaningful social roles and personal self-identities are better positioned to enjoy greater personal well-being. Such social roles and self-identities provide people with solid groundings in the world, reducing anxiety and disorientation. Research shows too that these meaningful roles and identities also enable people to cope with stress and difficulties in life.[57] All of this has positive causal consequences for health, happiness, and purpose. For this reason, Musick and Wilson observe that the "health benefits [of volunteering] should be attributed to the performance of meaningful social roles, which in turn lead to a stronger sense of self-efficacy."[58]

How exactly does greater generosity create positive, meaningful social roles and self-identities? The answer is straightforward.[59] When people practice generosity, they usually come to understand themselves as enacting particular formal or informal social roles and identity. A person who volunteers through an organization thus becomes, for example, "a volunteer at the shelter" or "a volunteer at the museum." They are able to tell other people and themselves, "I am an after-school reading tutor once a week" or "I'm a regular helper at the animal shelter." Those are social roles that in most contexts have positive meanings, which can become part of someone's personal identity and sense of self.

Similarly, even when donors of money do not occupy officially organized programs and categories recognizing their generosity, people who are generous financial givers can still occupy the informal social role of, and so think of themselves as, "strong supporter of my church" or "college" or "hospital" or whatever they support. Even if people around them do not know they are, they themselves can know that they are "a good steward," "a faithful sponsor," "a good citizen," a "caring person," "philanthropically generous," or whatever other role, identity, or category seems to fit. In most cases, those self-images and social roles are positive, meaningful, and affirming—which tends to enhance people's happiness and health.

Our own interviews are replete with examples of generous people who fill meaningful social roles. This will become very apparent in Chapter 5, so for now, here are only two examples:

> I am my church's clerk, which means I do all the business, I write the minutes up for the business meetings. But we've done a lot of things in the past. I've done library volunteer work at the schools and I did a lot of volunteer work when the kids were younger at their various schools. Lunch buddies, tutoring, that kind of thing. [Tammy Philpot, South Carolina]

> Maybe one of the things that I enjoy the most is financial counseling, I have done it through church. It's mostly helping people get their budgets in line

and work their way out of debt, to get themselves in a better personal financial situation. [Alan Bradshaw, Indiana]

Research on volunteers' self-reports on their own experiences confirms the influence of this causal mechanism. In the same national study of US volunteers referenced above, 92 percent say that "volunteering enriches my sense of purpose in life," and 85 percent say that "volunteering is an important part of who I am."[60] In another study, 72 percent of volunteers said that they volunteer in part because it enabled them "to support a cause they cared about," and 69 percent said "because it is the right thing to do." Another 39 percent said they volunteered at least partly in order "to feel useful and needed."[61] In yet another study, 69 percent of a sample of American volunteers rated volunteering as very important or even one of the most important things in their life, when compared to other activities in their lives.[62] This suggests that practicing generosity often plays a crucial role in the lives of people who do so, providing them with a sense of personal self that is located in the social world of action and identity in a positive, meaningful, and rewarding way. And that has positive consequences for happiness and health.

A somewhat related yet distinct causal mechanism has to do with generosity helping people to get outside of themselves and move beyond their own concerns and problems:

5. *Generosity tends to reduce maladaptive self-absorption, which tends to produce greater happiness and health.*

Too much focus on oneself is not healthy. People can easily get so caught up in their own lives that they focus most of their attention on their own perceived needs, problems, worries, inadequacies, failures, losses, and uncertain futures. That is not good for physical health, nor does it increase happiness. Quite the opposite: too much self-concern, self-absorption, and self-obsession are physically unhealthy and depress levels of happiness. For example, people who subjectively perceive themselves to be unhealthy, and focus on that, tend subsequently to become somewhat less healthy in actuality; while people who rate themselves as healthier than they actually are, tend then to become somewhat more healthy.[63] Self-perceptions and self-ratings can actually influence bodily well-being, to some degree. And the wrong kinds of self-perceptions and focusing can do so for the worse.

More generally, when people concentrate too much on themselves, they are often focusing on negative concerns, and that only tends to make the problematic things on which they are concentrating get worse. In a fascinating book entitled *The Curse of the Self: Self-Awareness, Egotism, and the Quality of Human Life*, Wake Forest University psychologist Mark Leary describes how the natural human ability for self-reflection easily degenerates into obsessive, self-destructive, egocentric tendencies, actions, and habits.[64] These can involve nurturing destructive emotions, trusting distorted perceptions, overestimating potential problems and losses, ruminating about past failures and future worries, basing poor decisions on biased information, indulging addictions, and more. As a result, people find that they cannot sleep well, cannot get past slights and hurts, and cannot help but damage their current relationships. Our interviews with ungenerous people confirm this. Self-absorption and a fixation on the negative are, for example, exemplified in many quotes from our quite ungenerous interviewees. One, for example, complained, "My household situation stinks. I hate living in an apartment, I hate it. . . I hate my job." Another, when asked if he was living the life he wanted to live or would rather make big changes in his life if he could, replied that he wanted to own more things:

> Well, financially if I had more money. Me, I am the type of person who, I guess you could call it a little bit materialistic, meaning like cars, nice cars, like I'd love to have a new car. A nicer house, meaning fix it up, have money to have the life that I would want to have.

Still another reported:

> I don't have a whole lot to complain about, but as far as the "average" person, your average person hasn't [unlike me] had to go through back surgery and hasn't had to be forced out of a job that they loved dearly and wanted to do. So, it sucks. I hate it. I still get angry over it, and yeah, I feel I've gotten screwed over by somebody else.

People of course sometimes do have real problems and real reasons to be unhappy. Positive thinking cannot simply remake the world for people. At the same time, the self that is not properly focused and balanced can easily become a curse to itself. Happy and healthy selves, by contrast, usually learn ways to transcend themselves, to put themselves into perspective, to constrain, reframe, and re-narrate self-destructive tendencies rooted in this kind of self-absorption.

Stated differently, people are often better able to cope with themselves the less they focus on themselves.[65] Getting outside of oneself is an important part of putting one's life into perspective, even forgetting about one's own pains and problems. More often than not, it is good for people to take their eyes off of themselves and focus instead on others, especially others in need who they can help. Such a change of focus and concern can have powerful effects in the person shifting attention. This is even true when it comes to bodily matters, such as the matter of pain management, for instance. Research shows that one effective way for people to reduce the pain they feel is to distract themselves from it by simply focusing on other things.[66] Some of the pain we feel is in fact amplified in our minds. A more functional, adaptive, effective way to deal with such personal pains and problems in many cases is to get the focus off of ourselves.

Generous practices do just this. Take, for example, people who might otherwise be concerned with how little money they have, but turn their attention to helping other people who may have much less. Generous practices direct people's awareness away from their own felt needs, worries, and pains and instead toward helping to care for the needs and worries and pains of others. Our interviews also confirm this. Dale of Illinois, for instance, finds satisfaction in his generosity and thinking of others before himself.

> I mean, you hear this from guys at work all the time that are so discontent, hate being in this job, hate being around people, just having such a hostility toward everything. And I think it comes back to their frame of mind, that if they would only move over into the view of, "What can I do to be a blessing to somebody else?" rather than, "The world owes me this, or the world owes me that." Because if people's got that attitude, they never are gonna be satisfied.

Others spoke of more specific plans about caring for others. "Stan Guthrie" in Georgia has a dream of raising money for the American Heart Association in his first year of retirement. Rather than pursuing self-absorbed leisure, he aims to raise funds for an organization that tackles the difficult problem of heart disease. He is thinking of what he can do to make a difference for others.

> This is what I'd love to do in retirement and I've talked to the American Heart Association about it. When I retire, I want to spend one year, and I've even got plans out, about how we'll get a car from one of the local dealers or whatever, go into [big cities nearby] and coordinating it in any way, like

when there's a basketball game one night in Atlanta and baseball the next, getting sponsors, and getting a hotel to put us up, getting sports memorabilia, gloves, bats, autographed baseballs, basketballs, and storing them someplace for a year, then having a huge auction.

If nothing else, generous practices heighten people's awareness that they live in a big world full of both beauty and suffering, goodness and problems, which can help to put their own lives into healthy perspective. Such understanding tends to be mentally, emotionally, and therefore physically good for people.

Another way to explain this is that generous practices have the capacity to reduce the "relative deprivation" that people feel when they compare themselves to abstract ideals or to references beyond their capacity to emulate or achieve. When people want their existence to be ideal, real life can turn out to be somewhat miserable. When people focus their attention on those who they think have more than they do, that easily generates envy, frustration, and disappointment.[67] No matter how wealthy, able bodied, or fortunate anyone is, it is always possible to find someone better off than oneself, and thus become dissatisfied with one's own life in comparison. That is because, except at the farthest extremes, most measures of health and happiness are relative to other positions. And, until someone has learned gratitude and contentment, it is easy to focus on other positions that are better than one's current state, which only generates discontent. Generosity provides powerful ways to help people break these kinds of maladaptive, dysfunctional self-absorptions and losing comparisons, so as to appreciate and enjoy all of the goods that they actually do possess.[68]

Of course, this causal mechanism can degenerate into feelings of superiority, paternalism, or condescending pity on the part of the generous giver, who then seems to benefit by transcending his own self-absorption. There is the risk of an attitude that conveys, "Pity these horrible wretches, I am glad that my life is so much better than theirs!" But there is no necessary reason why this must be so. That kind of response is often actually based on either a deep fear (that perhaps one's life will someday also become horribly wretched) or a deep sense of guilt (why do I have so much when others do not?)—neither of which are healthy or reflect genuine generosity.[69] However, it is possible for people practicing real generosity to do so with authentic solidarity, and reciprocity with and love for those to whom they give. Superiority and paternalism are not inevitable. And avoiding those is entailed in the kind of authentic generosity that promotes genuine, long-term well-being in both the givers and those who receive.

The next causal mechanism is again roughly parallel to the former, but involves a specificity of transformation that is well worth noting separately:

6. *Practicing generosity requires and reinforces the perception of living in a world of abundance and blessing, which itself also increases happiness and health.*

People's perceptions of the sufficiency of what they possess are only loosely correlated with the objective amount they do possess. There is of course a minimum of resources needed for people to live healthy, functional lives. But above that, how much people do and do not have, and how adequate they think that amount is, start to become highly subjective. We know that very wealthy people can still feel highly insecure about the amount of money they own, whether it is sufficient, and how they should handle it.[70] And people with very modest incomes can live with a great deal of contentment, feeling thankful and blessed for what they have. The relative sufficiency of material goods is certainly not all "in the mind." We still live in a material world with real physical and nutritional demands and constraints. But the mind nevertheless plays a huge role in the meaning people make of the relative sufficiency of their resources.[71]

One way to think about this is to observe the following. Different people who are in possession of the exact same amount of income, wealth, property, time, energy, attention, and affection can assess their situations radically differently. One person might evaluate her condition with great gratitude, satisfaction, enjoyment, and security. Another in the same circumstances may respond with insecurity, worry, and dissatisfaction. In the end, a great deal of how much is felt or believed to be enough, sufficient, or abundant comes back to subjective feelings and beliefs. And that is largely a matter of assumptions, expectations, and perceptions—which are cognitively and culturally relative. This means that it is possible for people occupying the same objective situations to understand themselves as either living in a world of abundance, blessing, sufficiency, and overflow, *or* living in a world of scarcity, deficiency, vulnerability, and insecurity. The actual facts about the objective worlds they inhabit do not determine those understandings. Rather, one's cognitively and culturally mediated assumptions, expectations, and perceptions determine them—and real consequences for human well-being depend on which of those two worlds one lives in.

People who live in perceived-and-believed worlds of scarcity, deficiency, vulnerability, and insecurity will, as a result, be less happy and healthy than those who live in a world they understand to be one of abundance, blessing, sufficiency, and overflow.[72] Here again, human emotions and experiences—which can be profoundly shaped by one's own assumptions and outlooks—can powerfully influence well-being. Worry is bad for human health and happiness; so is stress. These are known medical facts. Chronic disappointment, anxiety, resentment, envy, and restlessness of the kind that often accompany living in perceived worlds of scarcity, deficiency, vulnerability, and insecurity are also bad for health and happiness.[73]

Put differently, there is more than one way to be impoverished. Some people live in poverty because they do not have the income to buy adequate food, shelter, clothes, and medicine. But some people who have a lot of money can live in a different kind of poverty. Theirs is a poverty of anxiety, of imagined scarcity, of vulnerability, of dissatisfaction.[74] Such people suffer an impoverishment, amid real abundance, of believing that they do not have enough, that what they have may be lost, that the unknowns of the future are threatening. Such people find it hard to relax, to celebrate, to truly enjoy, to be thankful, to share. How can one enjoy when one is fundamentally worried? How can one share, when one does not even have enough for oneself? One has to protect oneself and one's family. One has to hold onto everything one has. The world beyond one's private self and family is essentially a threat.[75]

Such an outlook, that kind of impoverishment, living in such an imagined world of scarcity, deficiency, vulnerability, and insecurity, is *not* good for one's health or happiness. Such beliefs corrode health and happiness. They trigger biological systems in the body—such as "fight or flight" mechanisms—that cannot be sustained over time without damaging the body. They tighten up and close off one's social relations. They put up walls, avert worthy risks, and minimize possible threats, none of which promotes human flourishing.[76] The following quotes from our interviews with distinctly ungenerous people, specifically in response to questions about living in abundance, illustrate this outlook:

Well you got people bombing each other and blowing crap up, how can that not [feel] insecure? Who are these people looking at abundance? You got kids starving to death right next door, not literally next door, but you know what I mean. You got people living on the street, how is that abundant? I don't understand that. I mean sure this is the land of milk and honey and all that, but the people in charge have ran this country into the frickin' ground, so I don't see how that's, they got frickin' blinders on. [Kyle Jones, South Carolina]

It was a place of abundance, I think it's now turning a bit scarce. How do I say, you're going to have to screw someone else eventually, I think. Some other family, some other person. [Brandon Tribble, New York City]

I think now at my age [mid-40s] I feel a little bit more insecure about stuff and that there's really not a lot and that people have to be willing to help each other because of that. The resources aren't there as they think they are and that may be because of my upbringing. Because I think when I look back at my own life I think wow, I've had a pretty easy life. My parents have helped me out. And then now that my parents are older and now I'm the one who is the so-called breadwinner of the family, it's sort of like, you know there's not a lot out there and there's no one there that really takes care of you. That you do kind of have to be careful and watch out for yourself. [Corrine Cizek, Michigan]

Such answers differ from the responses of generous people, who generally express contentment, anticipate having enough, and are markedly more optimistic about their future well-being. They say things like, "We have more than what we actually need. We could all live with less," and "I think my outlook is one of looking at the blessings and all that you've got. I think we all should embrace an attitude of gratitude. If you can get up, you can breathe, you can walk, you can talk, hopefully you can work, what's not to be grateful about?"

Practicing generosity often has the power to overcome those life-corroding tendencies and outlooks exemplified above and lead to better health and greater happiness. How so? In most cases, in order to start practicing true generosity, people have to come to terms with whether they believe they live in a world of scarcity or of abundance. The deeply emotional, existential issues we are discussing here have to be confronted and resolved. Generosity will always be reluctant, anxious, and hesitant when it comes out of a believed world of scarcity. And that means that it probably will not last very long or be very useful. But the moral challenge of generosity can also push people to confront and overcome their emotional, existential fears about insufficiency, their psychological perceptions of scarcity as a mode of life that governs their world. Sometimes this is a gradual process. Other times it can be dramatic.

No matter how it happens, the testimony of those who have shifted in their minds, spirits, and emotions from an imagined world of scarcity and insecurity to one of abundance, blessing, sufficiency, and overflow is almost always the same: it is *liberating*. It removes a weight, a burden, a nagging fear. It sets one free to appreciate and enjoy what one has, rather than being burdened with the wish that one had more or worry about losing it. This kind of personal transformation shores up the personal security grounded in believing that, whatever the future holds, one will always have enough. It makes every bite more tasty, every sensual enjoyment more pleasurable, every good more blessed, every sunset more beautiful, every embrace more warm, every day more a gift. And it often also makes one want to share what one has with others—that is, to become a lot more generous. This is the experience and testimony of people who have undergone the paradigm revolution from an understood world of scarcity to one of abundance.[77]

"Denise Powell" articulates this experience well. Three years prior to our interview with her, her husband was incarcerated, which was an upheaval in the stay-at-home mom's life in Oregon. Finding herself in financial straits, after more than two decades away, she reentered the work force and began to forgive her husband and piece her life back together.

> So I've gone through six months of unemployment, and finding a job here or there. You don't get much in the unemployment check when you haven't worked for twenty years. So some of those things, you survive it, you can survive it, and you can survive some pretty nasty things. So you know, I'm confident that we'll get through it. Even in an economic downturn, we're getting through it. There's not really a whole lot of choice. But I used to worry, all the time, about things that I could not change, and you learn the futility of that, and you're a whole lot healthier when you don't do it.

After confronting her new reality and coming to peace with having fewer resources than before, Denise is on a path to greater well-being. She has the newfound fortitude of someone who trusts that there will always be enough, someone who can survive life's pitfalls. It is due to this perspective of abundance that she gives 5 percent of her income (twice the national average) to her religious congregation and various international aid nonprofits.

Again, the mental, emotional, and physical ramifications of such a transformation of expectations, outlook, and appreciation can be significant. The human body and spirit are simply built in such a way that they tend to thrive when they experience the liberation, enjoyment, gratitude, confidence, and openness that accompany life in a perceived world of abundance. And those same bodies and spirits wither under the anxiety, stress, preoccupations, hoarding, and self-protection that accompany imagined worlds of scarcity and threat. Practicing generosity often entails at some point an existential confrontation that is involved in the personal paradigm shift away from living in a world of scarcity and instead into living in a world of abundance, blessing, gratitude, enjoyment, security, and sharing. Therefore, practicing generosity in this way tends to promote happiness, health, and purposeful living.

Many of the mechanisms discussed so far have focused on psychology and bodies. But other important causal mechanisms by which generosity increases happiness and health have more to do with social relationships. They include this one:

> 7. *Generosity expands the number and density of social-network relational ties, which tends strongly to lead to greater happiness and health.*

Many practices of generosity involve extending and strengthening the ties that generous people have in their social networks[78]: reaching out to and through social relationships that would not exist without the generous practices. Generosity, in short, tends to build relationships.[79] It is well known that having extensive social-network ties tends strongly to enhance people's well-being. A large body of social-scientific research has clearly established that social-network ties have a positive effect on both mental and physical health and happiness.[80] The more people an individual knows, the greater the chances that that person will enjoy exposure to a broader and deeper range of helpful information, access to more useful resources, and greater support in difficult times. By contrast, the more socially isolated people are, the fewer opportunities, new ideas, and sources of help and advice they will enjoy. Social networks are one of the major ways that human social life works. Those who are poor in social-network ties simply do not do as well in life as those who are rich in them.[81]

Practicing generosity usually has the effect of expanding and strengthening the social-network ties of the generous givers.[82] Volunteering almost always has this consequence for volunteers. Practicing neighborly generosity does too. Even giving money away generously tends to stretch financial givers into new social worlds that enhance their overall social-network connectivity, because giving money generously often requires either being involved in one or more local organizations—such as a religious congregation or voluntary association—that embeds the giver in the organization's webs of social relationships; or it requires researching and contacting non-local organizations that one believes in and wants to support. Furthermore, people who give money generously oftentimes also want to follow up on their donations, to find out more about how their money did good things in the world. And that, too, often helps build new social ties in life.

Research on volunteers' self-reports about their own experiences confirms these findings. For example, in one national study, 90 percent of volunteers in the US agreed that "volunteering is a great opportunity to socialize," and 89 percent said that they have "developed new friendships as a result of volunteering." Volunteers are also significantly more likely than non-volunteers to report that they have a "very good" capacity to enjoy socializing with others and to develop rich interpersonal relationships. Eighty-eight percent of volunteers say that volunteering provides opportunities for social networking and even career development.[83] Indeed, 22 percent of the volunteers in one national survey said that they were motivated to volunteer in part to network professionally.[84]

Those are strong testimonies to the power of generosity to expand social-network relational ties, which our interviews repeatedly confirm. As a PTA board member, a committee-member of a public housing initiative, a high school tutor, a museum docent, and a coordinator of local disaster preparations, "Mary Ann Birch," an Oregonian homemaker in her early fifties, is not only well-known for her spirit of volunteerism throughout her community, but she also knows many people as a result of her efforts. "Just about everywhere I go locally I run into somebody I know," she reported. Occasionally, Mary Ann's friendships and relationships led to unique leadership opportunities, such as the opportunity to volunteer for a presidential primary caucus. "The precinct captain couldn't do the [presidential primary caucus in 2008]," Mary Ann recounted, "so she talked me into leading it. That was kind of cool. It was packed." This volunteer work no doubt expanded her existing social network. Still, one does not need to be as engaged in the community as Mary Ann is to enjoy the social benefits of volunteer work and some, like "Yolanda" from Texas, even leverage charitable events to create annual traditions with friends. With her close and health-conscious group of friends, who, as Yolanda puts it, "still have what we consider girls' night out," Yolanda participates in "our yearly thing where we all get together and we run the 5K for Susan G. Komen Breast Cancer. We do that every Mother's Day weekend, that's just a tradition for us."

Relational generosity is another way to expand and deepen network ties. The "Bradshaws," an Indiana family with a modest income, enjoy the generosity of hospitality in hosting out-of-town friends, family, and acquaintances: "We have an open house, if someone needs somewhere to stay, they can usually stay here. We have a revolving door full of guests in and out, on a fairly regular basis." In other cases, giving money generously can result in hosting new dinner guests, as the "Harris" family recalls: "In fact, we had, just this Tuesday, we had a couple and their three kids here that are missionaries in Brazil, we support them on a monthly basis. They came and ate dinner with us." Their financial generosity not only connects this Texan family with their dinner guests, but also, indirectly, the Brazilian people with whom the missionaries work.

Conversely, our interviews with ungenerous people revealed more limited social-network ties and fewer meaningful friendships. For instance, "Adam Berry," a Nevadan husband and father of two in his forties, admits to having "very few friends." Only at his wife's insistence and against his financial goals and hopes "to get into a bigger house and everything," his household donates about $30 a month to an international charity for children. Regarding his friendships, or lack thereof, he explains, "I don't really have a big social life. I kind of come to work, come home. I have a few friends, but most of them are through work." He puts minimal effort into maintaining and cultivating these relationships: "There might be times I don't talk to them for a month, and maybe a text or email, and that's about it." Likewise, in the following exchange, "Ruby Jones," who gives pocket change here and there and declines volunteer work when asked, is disconnected from social groups beyond her immediate family: "I don't belong to any groups or communities. Honestly, no. Even where my family lives, my family is kind of out there and sometimes you just don't feel like you belong even there." As a stay-at-home mother in her thirties living in South Carolina, Ruby's energy is devoted to, and depleted by, raising three small children. While many stay-at-home moms are an integral part of the civic fabric, when they live generous lifestyles, Ruby is detached from her local community and has few social interactions with adults other than her husband. And though her extended family offers some relationships, she does not feel a sense of belonging with them.

On the topic of generosity and relationships, another observation merits attention: *generosity tends to promote happier and more meaningful relationships between spouses, family members, and friends*. Generous people are generally more compassionate, forgiving, in tune with others' needs, empathetic, and more likely to see the world in terms of abundance. These are traits and skills needed for successful close relationships. Generous people are also less stressed and better able to avoid depression and anxiety. That kind of mindset also promotes healthy ways of relating to loved ones. Financially generous people in our interviews also consistently have more knowledge about and control over their finances. Because money is a major cause of marital problems, financial givers who talk things out with their spouses in greater detail and see money going to worthy causes tend to have happier marriages (this is not true when only one spouse makes the decision and practices giving, and we have at least three households in the sample that fit that bill). For generous people, money simply seems less problematic in their lives, regardless of their income. Conversely, ungenerous households, as discussed above, are generally less knowledgeable and secure about their finances and tend to experience money as a point of conflict, as an asset to be used for mass consumption and furthering the individual family's desires. Often that is associated with more household conflict and division. Consider, for example, the case of "Rob and Rachel Gardner," who are quite generous with their money, are in their early sixties, and live in Texas. Rob says: "Rachel and I are coming up on our thirty-eighth wedding anniversary, so we've had a good, strong marital relationship through the years. We try to focus on at least a date night a week, and work together, do things together on weekends. We pretty much carve out that time for ourselves on a regular basis."

"Does someone take the lead in money matters?" we asked.

"Well, our income is pretty much fixed for several years. The discretionary money, we decided how to spend it together. We make decisions together and talk about it. Like, hey, you know, there's a campaign going on to give to this particular orphanage, what do you think our gift ought to be? We'll throw out numbers to each other and say fine, that's good, let's do that."

"Rhonda Guthrie," a woman from Georgia in her early fifties, also a generous financial giver, says this about her marriage: "I'm in love with my husband. We have a lot of fun. You'll see when you meet him. There's not anybody that doesn't like him 'cause he's always laughing and talking and really we do enjoy each other's company. We enjoy our grandkids. We enjoy our daughters and their husbands."

So, we asked, how much agreement is there about money matters between Rhonda and her husband?

"We're in total agreement. We both know how much money we have in the bank and in savings. We know what our bills are. We know how much we can spend, how much we have for fun, or how much money, what all of our bills are. I mean, we're just in agreement on it."

By contrast, consider the way these people, who do not generously give away money, talk about their family lives. "Faith Little" from Oregon, in her late twenties, reported on her marriage this way: "It's been a good marriage, kind of a little bit ornery, but. . . About money? A lot of married couples argue over money. It's like one of the big things. We've had our squirms, our squirms here and there, but we've never ever really argued, like seriously had enough of each other and talked about divorce or anything like that over money." "Liz Kalon," a thirty-something woman from Southern California, and also in a marriage that gives away no money, mentioned that, "I have had rough times with Bill, but we have gotten through it. That would be it. [Laughing.] He is my problem. By rough times I mean we went through a, when we moved in here, we had pressure, because we had to do stuff to the house. Money, credit cards went up. . . I dunno, we just argued." We do not mean to suggest with this evidence that the correlation between family generosity and amicability is perfect, or even extremely strong. We do, however, note a general tendency in our data associating family practices of generosity and better quality family relationships.

Another causal mechanism by which generosity enhances well-being is through the cognitive development that it often fosters:

8. *Generosity tends to promote increased learning about the world, which often leads to greater happiness and health.*

Living generously not only introduces people to new social settings and communities of people, which expands the breadth and density of their social networks; it also often provides new learning experiences and exposure to sides of life and society that would have otherwise remained unknown. That is educational and generative. And expanding one's horizons in such ways, being exposed to new information and new possibilities in life, tends to enhance human well-being. Boredom is replaced by fresh stimulation. Repetition is displaced by new challenges. Stasis is pushed aside by further insights and understandings. The brain is stirred. The emotions may be provoked, desires clarified, the imagination stretched. Once again, volunteers' self-reports on their own experiences confirm these findings. In one national survey, 82 percent of American volunteers reported that they "have learned valuable things about the world through volunteering."[85] In another survey of Germans, 27 percent said they volunteered in part to expand their experience of life and 20 percent said it offered them an opportunity to acquire new skills.[86]

How did the respondents in our interviews talk about the link between generosity and increased learning about the world? Ungenerous people generally reported a sense of boredom in life—"Right now I'm in stagnation," as "Brandon Tribble" in New York City put it. But generous people tend to speak with greater enthusiasm about the world around them and point to how giving generously expands their knowledge and encourages mindfulness. In the course of determining the best uses of their money, financial givers come to learn about needs and opportunities in the world that they never knew existed. They find out, for example, a little more what life is like in the inner city, what it takes to build a new wing of a building, why and how wildlife needs to be protected, or how museums preserve their collections. In addition, people are sometimes made aware of volunteer opportunities that increase knowledge because of their financial generosity. A mailing sent out to donors, for instance, alerted "Mary Ann" to the possibility of becoming a volunteer docent at a popular art museum. Her training gave her the opportunity to learn more about art and how to give tours.

> The training was fun because I got to learn about art. And we would go in approximately once every two months and have a lecture on the new art and then some idea of how to give tours, and then basically there was an email sent out: there's tours on these coming days, who can volunteer for them? Or we had some open times to volunteer where you would just wear an "ask me" button, especially for big tours, they just want people to wear "ask me" buttons and just walk around for a couple hours and you just sign up for stuff like that.

Not surprisingly, volunteering one's time to an organization, even without giving money, has a similar impact. Volunteers at the soup kitchen learn what homeless people actually are like when you sit down and talk with them. Volunteers at the neonatal intensive care unit who simply cradle and rock infants in the hospital learn about medicine, health care, and the fragility and strength of life in ways they otherwise would never have known. As a tutor at an after-school program in a low-income neighborhood, Christina, a Washington, DC, accountant in her twenties (mentioned earlier in this chapter), partners with people beyond the scope of her Beltway sphere of upper-middle-class professionals. In addition to learning first-hand about the shortcomings of public schooling in impoverished neighborhoods, she also attends educational seminars about how her organization's work influences the local community. "We have to go to sessions and learn," she explains, "educational classes about the community and what we're doing for the community and how in the past the funds we've raised or the programs we've done have done this and that and the other." In these kinds of ways, those who are relationally generous in helping their friends, family members, and neighbors are more likely to learn a new thing, from how complex people's emotional lives can be, to how to properly turn on the pilot light of a hot-water heater.

In short, being a generous person puts people "out there" in the world in ways that those who are more likely to only take care of themselves never experience. And that kind of extension, exposure, research, and helping has highly educational consequences, informally and formally. That building of one's knowledge and experience base also enhances one's own depth, complexity, and resourcefulness as a person, which in turn leads to enhanced well-being in various ways.

The last causal mechanism we will consider returns us to very simple bodily functions of exercise and movement:

9. *Generosity tends to increases givers' physical activity, which usually leads to greater happiness and health.*

We know that sedentary, inactive lifestyles do not promote health, happiness, or purpose in living. Sickness and mortality are significantly associated with a lack of exercise and activity in life. And physical sluggishness can be related to apathy, aimlessness, and sometimes depression. The more people, especially older people, get up and out of their homes and engage their bodies in physical activity, the more likely they will be to be vigorous, in good spirits, and living with purpose. Sometimes all that people need to feel better emotionally and physically is to become more active, to get out and about, to exercise their bodies.

Many generous practices do that. They get people out of their homes, meeting, talking, and working alongside other people. Some forms of generosity—such as joining in neighborhood cleanup days, helping organizations move provisions, organizing after-school sports programs for kids, or helping Habitat for Humanity build a new house—can require real exercise, genuine workouts. Others entail less sustained physical activity, but nonetheless get those involved up and moving, or at least walking around and interacting with other people. For some Americans, simply spending one day a week visiting at the local nursing home, volunteering as a docent in the local museum, or doing some office work at the local organic food co-op provides an important, routine way to stay minimally active. What otherwise might become a true "couch potato" lifestyle is routinely interrupted by physical activity. We know that even minimal activity enhances people's health and happiness. Once again, multiple studies have shown that volunteers, including among the elderly, tend to be more physically active than non-volunteers.[87] Ninety-three percent of volunteers in one study, for instance, report that volunteering keeps people physically active.[88] In another study, 46 percent of volunteers said that they volunteered specifically in part in order "to stay socially, physically, and mentally active."[89]

Our interviews with generous people confirm this research. For example, volunteering as a parent chaperone for his son's Boy Scout troop keeps "Markus Birch" active and complements his time spent at a sedentary desk job. "We go camping or hiking," he tells us, and with much to explore in his home state of Oregon, it is not difficult to "Get out in the outdoors, once a month through the whole school year and then some bigger things in the summer." Others, like "Ken Walker," a Michigan resident in his forties, find that their volunteer work allows them to spend ample time outdoors, walking and interacting with others. Ken admits that his role as a volunteer soccer coach for a traveling team is mostly that of an administrator; he tells us, "I'm not a soccer guy, but I make the kids enthusiastic and make them work hard and run fast and all that stuff, and my assistant coach is really the soccer mind. I manage the minutes of the game and the rotations and the substitutions and he just advises them in practice." We also have good reason to believe that people who engage in greater relational, neighborly, and even financial generosity are also likely, as a result, to be made less sedentary, more physically active people. And that tends to enhance their health and happiness in life.

Imagining Ideal Types

It should help to make these causal mechanisms more concrete and

JEWISH WISDOM ON GENEROSITY

Good will come to those who are generous and lend freely, who conduct their affairs with justice. They will have no fear of bad news.

—Psalm 112: 5, 7a

I was young and now I am old, yet I have never seen the righteous forsaken or their children begging bread. They are always generous and lend freely; their children will be blessed.

—Psalm 37:25, 26

One man gives freely, yet gains even more; another withholds unduly, but ends up impoverished.

—Proverbs 11:24

A generous person will prosper; whoever refreshes others will be refreshed.

—Proverbs 11:25

Cast thy bread upon the water: for after many days thou shalt find it.

—Ecclesiastes 11:1

comprehensible if we use our imaginations to picture four "ideal-type" people who represent the extremes of generosity and well-being.[90] Most Americans do not live at these extremes. These are only ideal types offered for purposes of theoretical illustration. But they should help to bring the ideas presented above a bit more down to earth.

Maddock and Grace

Imagine first the ideal type of extremely generous persons for whom all of the above causal mechanisms for enhancing well-being are operating. Let us call them "Maddock and Grace." These two people give 10 percent of their income to causes and organizations they believe in. Maddock also volunteers a few hours a week at a local community organization. Grace in particular works intentionally to attend to the emotional and material needs of her family members, friends, and neighbors. Grace also gives blood regularly and is an organ donor, and recurrently thinks about the good that might do others. Maddock has taken the time to make sure that some of his assets will go to his alma mater to support programs he cares about after he has passed away. We have many good scientific reasons to believe that Maddock and Grace will be relatively healthy, happy people who live their lives with purpose and interest in personal growth. Why and how?

Maddock and Grace both recurrently enjoy the good feelings they experience from knowing that they are helping other people, doing the right things, living up to their own moral standards. He feels good when he exchanges personal letters with poor children overseas whom he supports with monthly pledges. She feels good knowing that she helps her religious congregation to thrive with her financial support. He enjoys tutoring disadvantaged children at the community center, watching them learn and grow over time. They both feel emotionally connected to their spouses and children, which provides a deep feeling of satisfaction. They are both happy to live in neighborhoods where residents often help each other out. When Grace drives by the local hospital, she is gratified knowing that her own blood is helping to heal, perhaps even save the lives of, sick people. Maddock is happy to think about his college growing stronger in the future as a result of his planning and financial support.

Whether they know it or not, Maddock and Grace enjoy the positive effects of a variety of good hormones and neurotransmitters that their positive experiences and feelings regularly release into their brains and bloodstreams. Oxytocin, dopamine, endorphins, serotonin, vasopressin, and prolactin are flowing freely, while cortisol is inhibited. As a result, Maddock and Grace often feel quite happy, relaxed, contented, and able to handle the stresses in their lives.

Maddock and Grace have learned from the kind of lifestyles they have constructed for themselves that they can make a difference in the world. They have made decisions to be generous, taken actions, and enjoyed seeing the good consequences that have resulted. Maddock is actually starting to daydream about setting up his own foundation to support the tutoring of inner-city children. Grace is contemplating becoming involved on the Board of Trustees of the local museum she supports and visits regularly. In addition to the family, occupational, and religious roles that Maddock and Grace play, they are also known as solid community boosters, compassionate volunteers, reliable neighbors, trustworthy counselors, and all-around good people to their family, friends, and neighbors. They like that, and hope it sets a good example for others to follow.

Maddock actually makes a lot of money, and has inherited even more from a wealthy grandfather. Grace earns a modest income, but is thankful for the job she enjoys and the provisions in life that it makes possible. Maddock feels incredibly fortunate, even blessed, to be in a position of commanding considerable financial resources. He definitely feels like he owes the world something significant in return, that he wants to "give back," and is happy to fulfill that responsibility with a good spirit. Grace sometimes struggles with being able to pay her bills. But when she steps back and thinks about all that she has, all of the good opportunities and enjoyments and relationships and experiences, she feels a deep contentment and confidence about a life she is living well. Both Maddock and Grace have seen a lot of needs, challenges, and problems in the world that are often troubling. But both also feel part of some larger groups that are having a positive impact addressing some of those difficulties. And, while that hardly makes everything better, it is still somehow deeply rewarding and life-affirming.

Maddock and Grace of course have some of their own personal problems and neuroses. But they have learned pretty well to manage them, and so they function well in life. Both, for example, have learned various ways of gaining better perspective, counting blessings, remaining hopeful, and proactively addressing their problems. Through their various forms of giving to other people, both are constantly reminded that the world is a very big place, that their lives are relatively minute in the larger scheme of things, that they actually have it relatively well in life, and that, all in all, things will turn out fine. Those kinds of outlooks often help Maddock and

Grace to be able to step back, take in big breaths, let out big sighs of relief and relaxation, and not get too worked up about their particular personal issues.

Maddock and Grace both have a lot of friends. A lot of different kinds of people tend to like them, want to talk with them, and enjoy spending time with them. They know people from the community center, from church and temple, and have a few good friends at work. They are on friendly terms with their neighbors, and enjoy tasty neighborhood cookouts and fun block parties a few times a year. Both Maddock and Grace have been through some difficult interpersonal struggles with various members of their families. But they have also worked them through, confronted real issues, and are generally appreciated and often turned to by members of their extended families to discuss matters of importance. That can sometimes get tiring, but being valued parts of mostly functional extended families is also gratifying. Neither Maddock nor Grace ever finds himself or herself lacking advice or information to help them solve their problems. They know so many different kinds of people that no matter what challenge or puzzle comes up, they always have someone they can check with to get a reliable answer. Some of the people they know have also been instrumental in helping them deal with certain health crises, computer problems, and job transitions in the past.

Maddock has to protect his free time, which he likes to spend working in his backyard vegetable garden, because he has so much else going on in life. Grace makes sure not to miss her one favorite television show each week, the watching of which is often threatened by her other activities and commitments. Both Maddock and Grace are quite busy. Sometimes they wonder if they are too busy. But when they think it over, they have a hard time imagining what they would cut out of their lives. Life can be pretty intense, but it also feels richly good, genuinely rewarding, and truly replenishing. All of the various ways that they are involved in the world give them a sense of purpose and energy that usually rejuvenates them. On some days, they wish they could just sit at home and do nothing. Actually, on some days they do just that. But, overall, they know that life is short and they are happy feeling that they are living it to the fullest.

Part of what is energizing for Maddock and Grace is the continual flow of new people, ideas, insights, and learning experiences. It can actually get overwhelming, but neither of them are bored. Grace has learned a lot recently about problems in the social welfare system of her state, as a result of her tutoring work and some discussions with parents that resulted. Part of her finds it unsettling. But Grace also feels somehow more in tune with the realities of the world she lives in, which she supposes is a good thing. Recently Maddock learned a bit about how to build a deck, by helping a neighbor on a project. That was unusual for him, because, with his income, the most natural thing for him to do is simply to hire a contractor to build such things for him. This was actually the first time he ever used a circular saw in his life. It was kind of fun. Afterward, Maddock's neighbor offered to come over and help him clean up his pool for the swimming season. That got Maddock to thinking about hosting a neighborhood Tahiti-themed pool party.

Maddock thinks he would like to get on the treadmill at the club after work more often than he does, and Grace would like to miss fewer aerobics classes than she does. But both of them are actually in pretty good physical shape. They are often out and about town, going on walks with friends to talk about life, and occasionally helping the youth group at their religious congregation or community center with car washes or service days. And, although they do not think about it much, both Maddock and Grace actually enjoy the pleasures of the various activities in which they are engaged more than the treadmill or aerobics classes.

All things considered, Maddock and Grace are quite happy people. They are doing good things in life and are glad for it. Every now and then, they simply sit in wonder at the privileged lives they lead, amazed by just how good chocolate tastes, how much they love their dogs, how precious their own family members and health are. As it turns out, Maddock and Grace will live long and happy lives. So many things about their lives—at the center of which stands the virtue of generosity practiced—work together to foster bodily health and satisfaction in life. Nothing is ever easy. But all things considered, life is good. They enjoy it and want to share it with others.

Mort and Lilith

Next we turn to an imaginary ideal-type pair of people located on the highly *un*generous end of the spectrum. Let us call them Mort and Lilith. Mort earns a good salary as a middle-level manager, and Lilith gets by as an accountant. Neither of them gives away money to any cause or organization, however, even the few of which they are members. Mort goes to church somewhat regularly, to hear about God's law and justice—but the preacher hardly deserves five cents a week from him, Mort thinks, considering what a hypocrite he is. Both Mort and Lilith spend and save nearly all of their money, such as it is, on themselves, believing that one has to enjoy some of the finer things in life. Not to mention retirement is not too far away and neither feels very confident that they have saved enough for the day they can quit working. They certainly do not count on Social Security to be solvent in their old age.

Neither Mort nor Lilith volunteers in any way for anything. If they are going to do work, they want to be paid. In any case, no organization that asks people to work for free should be trusted, they think, since they are probably either naïve, or intent on scamming people. Mort and Lilith do not like the idea of being taken advantage of; they take care of themselves.

Mort and Lilith also do not reach out to family members facing difficulties. Most people pretty much get what they deserve, they think, and the best thing for anyone to do in hard times is to just buck up and deal with it. Besides, Mort and Lilith have enough problems of their own without having to worry about other people's messes. Mort's marriage fluctuates between boredom and tension, and Lilith is divorced. Although they both live in what most people consider nice neighborhoods, these two are also suspicious of their neighbors, most of whom they do not particularly like. Mort is certain that one of his neighbors has stolen some tools from his backyard. And Lilith has a habit of looking out her windows every hour or so when she is home to make sure nobody in the area is doing anything nefarious. The neighborhood kids are such a pain—loud and destructive. Nothing like a good fence and a mean dog to keep kids off one's property.

Neither Mort nor Lilith have ever given blood, not that they have ever really considered it. Once Mort was asked at work to give blood, but he thought it sounded too painful and said no. If people need blood, Mort and Lilith suppose, they should buy it on the open market. They probably should have not gotten sick in the first place. Nor are Mort or Lilith organ donors. They fully intend to be buried with all of their body parts intact when they die. The very thought of death itself is morbid, in fact, so it's all best pushed aside. Besides, death only creates trouble in families, where survivors will argue about the inheritance. Mort refuses even to think about it. Lilith, however, has lately been pondering the idea of giving all of her possessions to a distant niece, who is already well-to-do, just to spite the closer family relatives who annoy her.

Mort and Lilith are pretty cynical people—"realists," as they see it. The world is such a hard place, people are so disappointing, nothing ever changes. "Life's a bitch," as Mort likes to say. You pretty much need to look out for yourself, and don't expect too much. Just looking at how their kids are turning out reinforces that approach. Mort is really too busy, he thinks, to keep up with what all his kids are up to, but he is pretty sure that the oldest is into trouble. Lilith's interactions with her kids consist mostly of arguing and yelling. As they see it, you do everything for your children, and all you get back is ingratitude and laziness.

Mort and Lilith also both have enough health concerns to keep them preoccupied. He struggles especially with chronic back pain, and she with migraines and acid reflux. Mort smokes a pack of cigarettes a day and drinks too much (at least that is what his wife says). His doctor constantly hassles him about losing weight, too. Lilith smokes cigarettes as well, and sometimes marijuana too, when she needs to relax and the kids are away with their father. Frozen dinners and Chinese take-out are standard fare in the evenings. That is easy to get and clean up, which leaves the rest of night free for watching television. Of course, most of what's on is crap, they say, but Mort and Lilith watch it anyway. The news, reality shows, the comedy channel: it's all somehow both depressing and amusing. Both spend a fair amount of time on the computer, surfing the Internet. Mort has spent years studying fishing boats, but never gets around to actually buying one—a habit of indecisive daydreaming that his kids make fun of. Lilith has a variety of chat rooms she is into, one of which involves a fair bit of cyber-flirting with some guys who sound interesting. That gives her a supply of rewarding cheap thrills.

On occasion, especially when he's sick of his wife, Mort will skip television and head off into the den to pay bills. There are far too many bills. By the time you get done paying for the basic things in life, there's no money left over to do anything fun, he thinks. Everyone is just out for a buck. What else would you expect? If only his boss would give him the raise that is overdue, Mort thinks, he might have some extra money. He would be able to finally buy the fishing boat. As for Lilith, personal finances are a mess that she prefers not to think about. Her desk at home is a wreck of papers. She does enough careful work with financial numbers all day long, she thinks, that she does not need more of them in her personal life. As long as she can cover her credit card minimum charges and not fall behind with her utility bills, that is enough. She is annoyed, however, that her ex-husband is falling behind again in his child-support payments, and needs to be harangued for them.

Mort does not have as many friends as he used to. He is very busy, it seems. He is happy to leave his work colleagues behind at the end of the day. His wife is often off shopping with her friends. There are a few people from the old days that Mort likes well enough, but others from college who are still around he just cannot respect. Not many of them reach out to him anymore, anyway. He used to get invited over more to watch football or to play tennis, but those calls have stopped. No big loss, Mort thinks. Lilith's situation is similar. She lost a lot of her former friends with the divorce. Most of the "friends" she now has are online. Her kids tire her out when they are at home, so she prefers down time by herself when she can get it. She has been invited a few times by people at work to go on a camping trip or a retreat, but she said, no thanks, she's just too busy.

Recently, Mort needed his house painted. He did not know who to ask for a recommendation for a good painter, most of whom, he has heard, are unreliable. He ended up hiring someone on a cold-call out of the Yellow Pages. Mort was not happy with the job when it was done but, being a responsible person, paid the bill anyway. If you want something done right, you have to do it yourself, Mort likes to say. But he also has no intention of going up on any ladders in the hot sun. Lilith is helping her oldest son, Bobby, apply to colleges. But she does not really know where Bobby should go, or even how to go about thinking about choosing a college. They all claim to be excellent and they are all expensive. "Just go to a state school," she finally tells Bobby, "don't fail out, don't get anyone pregnant, and I'll be happy."

Every so often Mort goes through a bout of depression. It is like a black haze just settles in over everything. His wife tries to help, but she just does not get it. He muddles through. Enough coffee, donuts, bourbon, time alone to ruminate, and a few peeks at a favorite porn site or two help him to carry on. When he is honest with himself, Mort knows he's a pretty lousy person, that his life does not amount to much. And it actually feels good, he has realized, to admit that to himself. At least he's being honest and realistic, he thinks, with pride. Then again, everyone else is pretty lousy too, so what's the difference? Lilith, on the other hand, thinks quite well of herself. All of her ex-husband's carping and her kids' criticisms are their problems. People are so negative, she cannot stand it. She's not such a bad person.

Mort doesn't know it, but his wife is having an affair with another man. She will leave Mort in a few years, and he will spend the rest of his life angry about it. After she leaves, Mort will also be transferred, demoted actually, to a branch of his company halfway across the country. If he thinks the weather is lousy where he lives now, wait till he gets there. He will spend a good part of his remaining years watching television, with an occasional lunch at Hooters and a regular Friday evening at a nearby gentlemen's club for fun. He enjoys spending what money he has on simple pleasures. His kids and grandkids will visit occasionally, though more often than not those are pretty awkward occasions. In due time, Mort will develop cancer. Very few people attend his funeral. Lilith, for her part, lives a reasonably decent life well into her eighties. Most of her time and money are spent on doctors. But she eventually gets her mortgage paid off and finally retires from the job she has come to hate. She loves her grandchildren, but they all live far away and do not call much. Her final years in a nursing home prove to be not very pleasant.

What is the point? We do not mean to imply by constructing these ideal-type characters that Americans who do not compare to Maddock and Grace must therefore be equivalent versions of Mort and Lilith. For one thing, most real Americans occupy a broad middle ground of relative, not absolute, generosity or lack thereof. Our purpose here is not to label people by implication, or to cast aspersions on less-than-totally generous people. Moral judgment or wagging fingers is not the issue. Rather, we have constructed these ideal-type characters to help visualize by illustration how the causal mechanisms spelled out above can operate in people's lives, in both hypothetical and real ways, to produce genuine differences in health, happiness, and purpose. Maddock and Grace may seem romanticized and valorized, and Mort and Lilith caricatures of pathetic lives. But they are, again, only imagined cases at the far ends of the generosity spectrum to help us think analytically. Of course, there really are some people out there who *are* like Maddock, Grace, Mort, and Lilith. But most of the rest of us represent less extreme cases. The take-away here, then, is simply this: the causal mechanisms described above actually are often operative in most people's lives, one way or the other, depending in part on how much generosity toward others they practice. This point is, for present purposes, not a matter of moral admonition, but rather a simple observation of the workings of some elementary biological, psychological, and sociological facts. If we want to understand generosity and its positive effects in people's lives, we need to understand how these causal mechanisms work.

Caveats

We want to be clear: not every act or practice of generosity necessarily improves happiness, health, and purpose in every participant's life. Many generous practices do, it seems. The general causal tendencies at work for the entire American population are evident in findings of analyses of empirical evidence. However, general causal mechanisms can affect individual people differently. Some people may be more susceptible to generosity's well-being-enhancing effects than others. All of the mechanisms examined above also interact differently in specific cases with particular people's health conditions, family settings, geographical and neighborhood contexts, socioeconomic status, general outlook on life, lifestyle practices, risk behaviors, and more. Human bodies and social life are complicated. Nothing is necessarily predictable or guaranteed in any given instance, even if the overall pattern of associations and causes is pretty clear for the population. We are dealing here, in other words, with probabilities, likelihoods, and tendencies that apply to most people, not with universal laws or formulas that work for everyone.

Furthermore, certain kinds of generous practices can themselves become unhelpful, perhaps even toxic. Giving generously of oneself is one thing. Not taking care of oneself because one is so "generous" is quite another. Generosity can be expressed by some people in misguided, unbalanced, and even pathological ways. When it is, we have reason to think that generosity does not build health, happiness, and purpose in life. For example, common sense and some studies suggest that volunteering for too many hours a month actually becomes counterproductive to one's well-being, and therefore also likely lessens the value of one's contribution as a volunteer.[91] Living as a generous person in social settings that are dehumanizing, filled with interpersonal conflict, or even simply poor matches with one's gifts and interests can also harm rather than help one's health and happiness. And practicing generosity out of a powerful sense of unrelieved guilt, personal inferiority, or yearning for basic social or self-acceptance will also likely not provide the positive well-being effects that we observe in this book to be normal.

At the same time, we should recognize that such dysfunctional cases appear to be relatively rare. There are people who cannot take care of their material needs because they give away too much money to others, who burn out by volunteering too much, who always take care of the emotional needs of others and ignore themselves. But they appear to be a small minority of the population. If "dysfunctional generosity" were much more prevalent than that, then we would not be observing the kind of positive generosity and well-being effects we noted in the previous chapter. But we do observe them, so it appears that most expressions of American generosity are adequately sensible, balanced, and healthy.

Summary and Conclusion

These nine causal mechanisms, and perhaps others, help to explain why it is that more generous people tend to be significantly more happy, healthy, and purposive people.[92] It is not just that generosity is caused by some greater original well-being. The well-being itself is also caused in part by practices of greater generosity. In multiple, complex, and interacting ways, bodies, brains, spirits, minds, and social relationships are stimulated, connected, and energized by generous practices in ways that are good for people. Thus, as a result of the generous practices themselves, those who live more generous lives also tend to enjoy greater well-being in life. This is why, for example, 96 percent of Americans who volunteer say that volunteering makes people happier, 95 percent say that volunteering improves emotional health, and 94 percent believe that volunteering builds self-esteem.[93] They are correct, and that insight about volunteering extends more generally to other forms of generosity.

The evidence presented in this book, however, suggests that, for

CHRISTIAN WISDOM ON GENEROSITY

Remembering the words of the Lord Jesus, for he himself said, "It is more blessed to give than to receive."
—Acts 20:35

Whoever sows sparingly will also reap sparingly, and whoever sows bountifully will also reap bountifully.
—Saint Paul of Tarsus, 2 Cor. 9:6

Helping a person in need is good in itself. But the degree of goodness is hugely affected by the attitude with which it is done. If you show resentment because you are helping the person out of a reluctant sense of duty, then the person may receive your help but may feel awkward and embarrassed. This is because he will feel beholden to you. If, on the other hand, you help the person in a spirit of joy, then the help will be received joyfully. The person will feel neither demeaned nor humiliated by your help, but rather will feel glad to have caused you pleasure by receiving your help. And joy is the appropriate attitude with which to help others because acts of generosity are a source of blessing to the giver as well as the receiver.
— St. John Chrysostom

Peace is not the product of terror or fear. Peace is not the silence of cemeteries. Peace is not the silent result of violent repression. Peace is the generous, tranquil contribution of all to the good of all. Peace is dynamism. Peace is generosity.
— Archbishop Oscar A. Romero of El Salvador

generosity to enhance one's well-being, it must be *practiced*. Single, random, irregular acts of generosity may be good to perform and may be beneficial for everyone involved. But to have the kind of clear, significant effects on well-being observed in the previous chapter, generosity needs to become a practice, a routine, a regular part of life. For it is practices of generosity, not simply one-time events, that tend to trigger the kind of mechanisms examined in this chapter. Generosity changes people through processes of formation, not isolated behaviors. And formation requires time, repetition, and practice. Those are the conditions in which people's lives are actually shaped for the better. That itself explains, we think, why some behaviors that are truly generous—such as giving blood on occasion, being an organ donor, or writing wills that facilitate estate giving, and so on—are not so clearly associated with greater health, happiness, and purposeful living as others we have seen. These acts of generosity are often not regular, not practiced recurrently, but often only done once or twice and then forgotten. That often is not enough, apparently, to generate the paradox of generosity.

So what does all of this have to do with pool tables and soccer games, again? Our point in using these images above was to emphasize the multiple, complex, and interactive nature of causal forces in social life. Nothing is simple, and we do not have to choose between well-being explaining generosity versus generosity explaining well-being. The causal explanation works in both directions. Not only that, but there are also many causal mechanisms at work in the process. We have in this chapter, for the sake of conceptual clarity, separated out and described nine distinct causal mechanisms by which generosity tends to enhance human well-being. But clearly these mechanisms operate in the empirical world in complex, interactive ways. The brain chemistry at work in the second mechanism partly presupposes and then partly produces the positive emotions at work in the first. Increased personal agency and self-efficacy are often related to enacting positive social roles and personal identities. Transcending maladaptive self-absorption is often related to a changed psychology that focuses on abundance and blessing instead of scarcity and insufficiency. And increased physical activity, developing social networks, and learning new things about life and the world also often work together as well. The nine distinct mechanisms do not operate in isolation from one another in real life. Instead, they often interact with and reinforce each other in complex ways across time, depending on particular larger life situations, in ways that enhance the well-being of the generous. This works much more like a soccer game unfolding before the eyes of the fans than pool balls shot with a cue and bouncing around a table.

It is important not to overstate the power of generosity to enhance people's happiness and health. Gross exaggeration of the facts does not help anyone. Generosity is not a magic bullet that can solve all problems. Generosity's salutary effects can also be neutralized in some circumstances, such as when the giving experience itself becomes exhausting or destructive. So generosity is by no means a panacea for all problems—that much is clear.

At the same time, we should not neglect or underestimate the power of generosity to enhance the well-being of those who give. In many ways and for many reasons—as we have seen in this chapter—generous practices can indeed significantly improve the happiness, health, and sense of purpose in life of those who practice it. That is a scientific fact that is worth knowing and appreciating. In some cases, the evidence is impressive. Consider the findings of the following studies, which show that, in given periods of time, *volunteers are less likely to die* than non-volunteers. One longitudinal study, for example, has shown that volunteering by the elderly reduces mortality more effectively than either physical exercise or church attendance taken alone. Volunteering also reduces mortality almost as much as the effects of not smoking cigarettes.[94] Another study of older Americans also concluded that, during a seven-year time period studied, those who volunteered were 28 percent less likely to die than non-volunteers.[95] Yet other researchers have shown that generously giving to others protects overall health twice as much as aspirin protects against heart disease.[96] Those are mighty powerful effects of one form of generosity that illustrate the larger theme of this book: namely, paradoxically, those who give in fact receive back in many beneficial ways.

We might summarize the larger meaning of the observations of this chapter like this: generosity tends to nurture love in the giver, and love stands at the heart of human flourishing, so generosity naturally tends to promote human flourishing. Social scientists do not often write about love.[97] But that is odd, because love is so central and important in human personal and social life. Love may not seem like a very "scientific" term, but that does not diminish its importance in human life. Without love, where would any of us be now?[98] We know, in fact, from both developmental psychology and our own human experience, that people only flourish when they are loved by others. A person growing up in the context of purely instrumental, rational, exchange-oriented relations would and could not be a happy, healthy person. He would be stunted, perhaps psychologically and relationally pathological. Love creates the conditions for real life, growth, learning, and thriving. Anything that happens in human life that produces any good in the world that does not involve love—such as, say, competition—must itself presuppose a deeper existence of love for setting the context within which it takes place. Otherwise, it does not promote human flourishing.

In this sense, it truly is better to give than to receive. Philosophers and religious teachers have claimed as much, and so does modern science.[99] Generous giving generates happiness, health, and flourishing. The negative side of that fact, of course, however, is that people who are not generous, who refuse or shrink away from giving generously, tend to be shaped in ways that move away from human flourishing. We will see this illustrated, more concretely, in the lives of ordinary Americans in later chapters.

CHAPTER 3 | Generous and Ungenerous America

IN ADDITION TO THE primary paradox of generosity—that by giving we in fact receive—we have noted in earlier chapters that there is a related second paradox worth noticing. This is that very large numbers of Americans, despite (we presume) wanting to enjoy happy, healthy, purposeful lives, fail to practice the kinds of generosity that actually tend to lead to happiness, health, and purpose in life. Something gets in their way. Like children whose fingers are caught in "Chinese handcuffs," they pull hard to take care of themselves, but that simply keeps them stuck. However, by relaxing and freely letting go of some of their resources instead, the evidence suggests, such people can escape the trap of ungenerous living.

When it comes to generosity with money, time, skills, and relationships, we know that relaxing, letting go, and giving away is not often automatic or easy. This is especially true in American culture, which from all sides constantly pounds home messages of scarcity, discontent, insecurity, and acquisition. These messages may serve to grow the consumer economy, but they are often not good for the consumers. So, given the omnipresence of these cultural messages, real generosity requires learning something different, something that may not feel natural for many people. It often requires real personal change. A better understanding of how generosity works can aid that learning and change. But in the end, we believe, actually living generously results from an existential confrontation with what is ultimately humanly valuable and important in life and the world. Even so, knowing some of the facts about generosity can help. That is one reason we wrote this book.

But just how generous or ungenerous are Americans? And in what ways are we generous or not? This chapter reviews the findings of the Science of Generosity Survey. What we see is that many Americans are indeed generous. Then again, many others are not. Sizeable proportions of Americans give away money, volunteer, go out of their way to take care of their families, friends, and neighbors, give blood, are organ donors, and more. At the same time, large proportions of Americans do not volunteer in any capacity. How one evaluates the state of volunteerism and generosity in the US depends on what one is expecting. In any case, to get a better handle on the relative generosity of Americans, the following pages review some basic facts.

Financial Giving

According to data collected by the Science of Generosity Survey, about 3 percent (2.7 percent) of adult Americans give away 10 percent or more of their income (Figure 3.1). This number is calculated by dividing the amount respondents reported giving away by their reported total salary.[1] What does this tell us? If we think that giving away 10 percent of one's income is an exceptional feat, then this number is a bit impressive. But if we think it is a good baseline measure of true financial generosity, then the vast majority of Americans are falling below the bar. For purposes of this book, suffice it to say that giving 10 percent of one's income is a good marker associated with enjoying better health, happiness, and purpose in life. Viewed this way, the vast majority of Americans (97 percent) are forfeiting the chance to enhance their well-being by practicing real generosity with their money.

This 2.7 percent *may* underestimate the actual percent of adult Americans who give 10 percent or more of their income. Some other surveys reveal somewhat larger percentages than that. For example, the General Social Survey (GSS) finds, in the most recent year it asked this

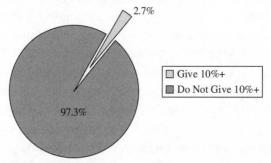

2.7%

□ Give 10%+
■ Do Not Give 10%+

97.3%

FIGURE 3.1 Percent of Americans who give 10% or more of income (reported $ given / income)

Source: Science of Generosity Survey, 2010

question (1998), that about 8 percent of Americans give away 10 percent or more of their income. Research by the Barna Group reports that only about 4 to 7 percent of all Americans give away 10 percent or more of their income. At the same time, a study by long-time church-giving researchers John and Sylvia Ronsvalle suggests that, while a much higher percentage of American churchgoers *claim* to tithe, only about 2.6 percent of them actually give 10 percent of their income, a number nearly identical to ours—and church-attending Americans tend to be much more financially generous in giving than those who do not attend religious services.[2] It is not possible to know the precise amount of giving for all Americans, and gathering the detailed data to calculate these numbers precisely gets tricky. But we are on solid ground when we estimate that somewhere between 3 and 8 percent of Americans give away 10 percent or more of their income.

We think the true number is closer to 3 than to 8 percent, however, for this reason. Estimates for larger amounts tend to ask respondents the percentage of their incomes that they give—which people typically overestimate for various reasons, including social-desirability bias (confirmed by what we see in Figure 3.2). But our estimate of 3 percent is based upon a sum total of giving carefully calculated by asking respondents to report specific dollar amounts for thirty-six possible different giving categories, which tends to produce more accurate results, and comparing that to their reported incomes.[3] We also must remember that these survey data were collected in the midst of the Great Recession which began in 2008, and is only showing signs of abating as this book is published. So our numbers should be understood as representing generosity at a time of relative economic stress for many Americans. That likely helps to explain some of our numbers, which are a bit lower than those of previous studies.

When asked to calculate these numbers in their *own* minds, Americans typically report much higher percentages of giving. In

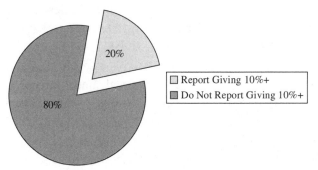

FIGURE 3.2 Percent of Americans who report "Giving 10% or more of income"
Source: Science of Generosity Survey, 2010

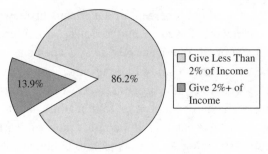

FIGURE 3.3 Percent of Americans who give less than 2% of income
Source: Science of Generosity Survey, 2010

response to a straightforward survey question that directly asked respondents whether (by their own reckoning) they do or do not give away 10 percent of their income, 20 percent of Americans answered yes (Figure 3.2). Clearly, some people (about 17 percent of Americans) tend to be much more "generous" with *themselves* when it comes to thinking about how much money they give away, compared to what seems to be real when it is directly calculated (Figure 3.1). This tells us a few things. First, a decent proportion of Americans believe that giving money away is a good, socially desirable thing, and so give themselves the benefit of the doubt when it comes to thinking about how much they do give away. Second, a proportion of Americans seems to be not very good at estimating how much money they are giving away. Some at least, when they think about it in general terms, believe that they are giving away more than they actually are. This does not surprise us at all, based on what we have learned in our interviews with Americans about their generosity.[4]

We can assess Americans' financial generosity by lowering the standard and seeing what percentage of Americans do not give even 2 percent or more of their income. Findings from the Science of Generosity Survey show that at least 86.2 percent give away less than 2 percent of their income (Figure 3.3). This, again, is calculated by dividing the sum of the amount of money they say they give away in thirty-six possible categories of types of giving by their reported annual income—which we have reason to believe produces accurate results. Assuming so, we see that most Americans, about six out of seven, do not give away even 2 percent of their income. That suggests a relatively stingy lot of people, financially speaking—though, again, we should keep in mind the effects of the Great Recession on these numbers.[5]

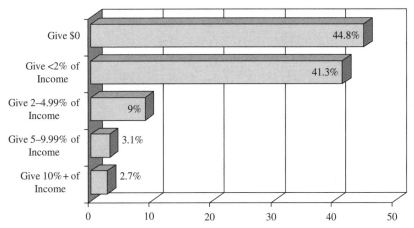

FIGURE 3.4 Percent of Americans' financial generosity by proportion of income given away

Source: Science of Generosity Survey, 2010

Figure 3.4 shows the percentage of Americans who give certain percentages of their total incomes by categories. Nearly half of all Americans (44.8 percent) give away not one dollar, by their own admission. Another 41.3 percent gives away some amount of money but less than two percent of their income. Nine percent of Americans gives away between 2 and 5 percent of their income, 3.1 percent gives away 5 to 10 percent of their income, and 2.7 percent (as we saw above) gives away 10 percent or more. Again, the vast majority give away relatively little of their financial means in voluntary charitable donations.

Some readers might assume that the percent of income that Americans give rises gradually with increases in their actual income. It stands to reason that the more money people make, the greater the percentage of it they should be able to give away without cutting too much into their own basic needs and wants. But this is not the case. Making more money in America is not associated with giving money more generously. Figure 3.5 shows that the average percentage of income given away by income brackets does not increase at all from the lowest income category (less than $12,499) to the highest category ($90,000+). In fact, the percentage given actually drops slightly, from 2.2 to 1.1 percent of income given away. Earning a higher income in the US, in other words, does *not* translate into giving larger proportions of that income away. People who objectively could give more money away in fact do not, at least until they move up into the highest income bracket. This we find in our own data, but it is also a well-established fact confirmed by many previous studies.[6]

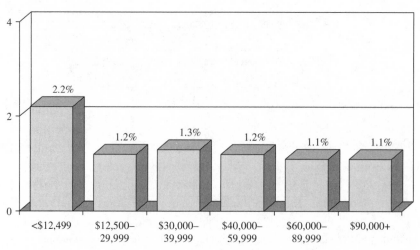

FIGURE 3.5 Percent of income contributed in all charitable giving by income category (adult Americans)

Source: Science of Generosity Survey, 2010

We can look at the financial generosity of Americans in yet another way. Suppose we took all Americans and distributed them on a line from the least financially generous to the most generous. Imagine then that we clustered them into twenty groups of 5 percent of Americans each, again from the least to the most financially generous. Then suppose that we calculated the percentage of all dollars given by Americans for each of the twenty groups of 5 percent. That is what is represented in Figure 3.6. There we see that the least generous half of Americans (50 percent, on the left side) gives away almost none of the total dollars given—only .41 percent of all dollars given away, to be precise. At the other extreme, we see that the most generous 5 percent of Americans gives a whopping 57 percent of all of the money given away in financial charitable contributions. Between the least generous 50 percent of Americans who give almost nothing and the most generous 5 percent of Americans who contribute well more than half of all the money given, the balance of the money (43 percent) is accounted for by the remaining 45 percent of relatively generous givers. And most of that is given by the few highest-end groups of givers. For example, adding together the money given by the 20 percent of the most generous Americans (the four 5-percentiles on the right) shows us that they give 86 percent of all of the money voluntarily given away in the US.

If you have ever heard of the "80/20 Rule," when it comes to voluntary financial giving, the actual rule is in fact more like the "86/20 Rule."

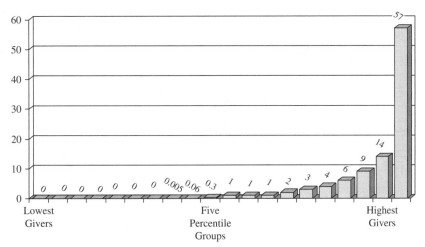

FIGURE 3.6 Percent of total dollars contributed by adult Americans grouped in five percentiles by increasing levels of generosity

Source: Science of Generosity Survey, 2010

In short, a quite small group of Americans gives away the vast majority of the money that is donated in voluntary financial giving in the US. Stated differently, while some Americans seem to be quite generous with their financial resources, the vast majority contribute very, very little to the overall giving that takes place in the US. If the top 10 percent of most generous Americans were to stop giving money, the entire sector of society and the economy based on voluntary financial giving would simply collapse. In other words, there is a huge amount of room for growth in financial generosity for many Americans.

Volunteering Time and Talent

Financial giving is only one form of generosity in which Americans might engage. What about others, such as volunteering for or through an organization? Research shows that about one-quarter of Americans volunteer in any given year. Figure 3.7 shows that 24 percent (23.6 percent) of respondents to the Science of Generosity Survey reported volunteering in the previous year. Corroborating that, roughly, the Corporation for National and Community Service estimates that 26.8 percent of Americans volunteer.[7] That is good. But it also means that three-quarters of Americans do not volunteer. Of course, many Americans have a lot of valid reasons for not volunteering. Not everyone can or ought to be a volunteer. But there is also no doubt that there

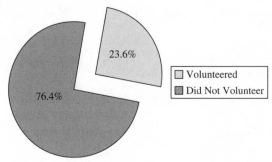

FIGURE 3.7 Percent of Americans who volunteered in the previous year
Source: Science of Generosity Survey, 2010

are many Americans who could volunteer, who would be helpful to others by volunteering, and who would benefit themselves by volunteering, if they did. But they do not. Why they do not volunteer will require further research. Meanwhile, according to one study, one in three Americans who do not volunteer say they do not do so simply because they "are just not interested."[8]

What about the number of hours that Americans spend volunteering? Figure 3.8 shows the number of hours people in the US volunteer per month. Again, 76 percent simply do not volunteer any hours. Ten percent volunteer 1 to 10 hours per month and 11 to 39 hours per month, respectively. Finally, less than 4 percent (3.8 percent) volunteer more than forty hours per month. Once again, here we see that a small group of relatively generous Americans devotes a lot of time to volunteering. The vast majority, however, volunteer not at all.

Relational and Neighborly Generosity

In Chapter 1, we saw that the Science of Generosity Survey measured generosity of more informal kinds. One focused on care and self-expenditure in relationships, which we called "relational generosity." This involved people taking the time to take care of other people, investing themselves emotionally in the needs of others, working to be sensitive to the condition of other people, and so on. Another focused on behaviors of taking care of neighbors, friends, and family, which we called "neighborly generosity." This included watching over houses and property for people who are away, taking care of others' children, and having people over to one's home for a visit. None of these requires having large amounts of money, as we might think is necessary for generous financial giving. People who are living on a shoestring can be generous in these ways. In that chapter,

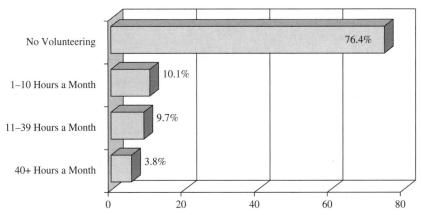

FIGURE 3.8 Percent of Americans' volunteering average number of hours per month
Source: Science of Generosity Survey, 2010

in keeping with the larger patterns observed there, we saw that more relationally generous Americans and those with higher neighborly-generosity scores are also healthier, happier, and living with more purpose.

But just how relationally generous are Americans? And how much neighborly generosity do they exhibit? Since relational generosity was measured using a multi-question scale, we calculated the numbers here as those who on average scored "strongly" on this set of questions. We estimate that 25 percent did score strongly (not shown in a figure). The remaining three-quarters scored less-than-strongly on relational generosity. Scoring less-than-strongly on this scale does not mean that three-fourths of Americans are positively ungenerous when it comes to relationships. They simply did not score on the high end of the scale. Some of them are moderately generous relationally. Some of them are very ungenerous relationally, again by their own admission in their survey answers.

Figure 3.9 shows the percentages of Americans who reported "never" to a number of measures of neighborly generosity. These numbers are not astoundingly high. Sizeable chunks of Americans appear to be exercising different forms of neighborly generosity. Still, significant proportions of Americans are not. About 9 percent say they never visited with family relatives in person during the previous year, and 13 percent never had friends over to their homes for a visit. Thirty percent did not help friends or neighbors with a job they were working on, 34 percent never watched over a house or property of a friend who was away, and 42 percent had never helped care for anyone else's children during the previous year.

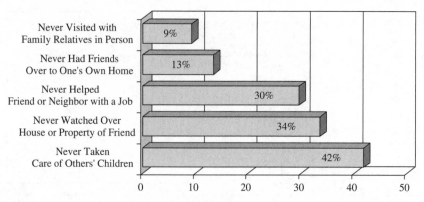

FIGURE 3.9 Percent of Americans never performing acts of neighborly generosity

Source: Science of Generosity Survey, 2010

In some cases this may reflect not an unwillingness to do these things, but rather a lack of opportunity. Some Americans do not have neighbors or family members. Others may not have friends. Some may live in neighborhoods where residents simply do not ask favors of each other. And some Americans may live in situations where no children are around. Even so, we think that some of these facts themselves are revealing when it comes to practicing generosity. And we think that they do not fully account for some of these substantial cases of never practicing these forms of neighborly generosity. Our position here is not one of condemnation. Rather, we simply observe that at least some Americans probably have the opportunity and ability to increase their practices of relational generosity, and thereby enjoy the health, happiness, and purpose benefits that tend to come along with that.

Giving Blood, Donating Organs, and Estate Generosity

According to the Science of Generosity Survey, about 12 percent (11.5 percent) of Americans gave blood in the previous year, 2009 (Figure 3.10). Federal statistics put the percent of Americans who give blood in any given year at less than 10 percent.[9] These people provide the American healthcare system with an absolutely indispensible source of life for millions of its patients who need blood transfusions. Giving blood is all the more impressive because it is essentially anonymous to those who benefit, it takes time and can hurt, and it is often not rewarded with monetary compensation. At the same time, this means that almost 90 percent of Americans—the vast majority—do not give blood. This is not because there is no need for more

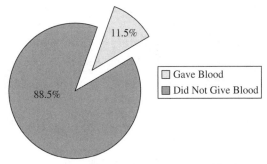

FIGURE 3.10 Percent of Americans who report giving blood in the previous year
Source: Science of Generosity Survey, 2010

blood, or that the demand for donated blood is fully satisfied. Oftentimes, in fact, the healthcare system suffers blood shortages. Rather, despite the need, the majority, most of whom we know are eligible to donate blood, simply do not give. Again, some Americans are generous with their blood. But many others could become more generous.

More Americans are organ donors, however, according to Figure 3.11. There we see that 43 percent of Science of Generosity Survey respondents claim to be organ donors. This comports roughly with the 38 percent of licensed drivers in the US who are said to be registered organ donors.[10] At the same time, as we noted in Chapter 1, becoming an organ donor is not itself difficult. Oftentimes the opportunity is presented to people when they first obtain or renew their driver's license. All they need to do is to check a box in the paperwork and they have become donors. Being an organ donor in the vast majority of cases also does not affect the donor anytime during her lifetime. The consequences might only become triggered after death. We know that donated organs save the lives of many sick people. We also know that there is a major scarcity of most organs that people might donate. Many sick Americans die while waiting for a donated organ to become available for them. In light of all of that, although the organ-donation glass can be viewed as not quite half full (at 43 percent), it can also be viewed as half empty, with somewhat more than half of Americans not being registered as organ donors. Again, there is certainly room for improvement, a greater opportunity for generosity of this kind to increase in the US.

What about being generous by designating a favorite nonprofit as a beneficiary in one's will? Not many Americans are generous in this way. Figure 3.12 shows only 4.6 percent of Americans have a nonprofit organization not related to their family as a beneficiary in their will. Of course, most Americans do not have wills in the first place. So this precludes their donating to worthy

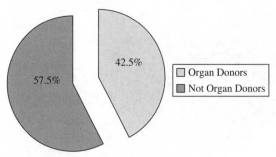

FIGURE 3.11 Percent of Americans who are organ donors
Source: Science of Generosity Survey, 2010

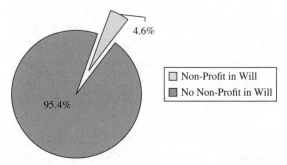

FIGURE 3.12 Percent of Americans who report having a designated nonprofit named as a beneficiary in their will
Source: Science of Generosity Survey, 2010

causes or organizations upon their deaths. But, at least for Americans of any positive net worth, that itself reflects a lack of proactive forethought for generosity as a legacy to leave of one's completed life. Nineteen out of twenty adult Americans do not behave generously when it comes to this form of giving. Again, for some, especially the poorest of Americans, estate giving may simply be an irrelevant idea. Their problem has more to do with debt than with where to give their resources. But estate giving, however modest, could become a more important expression of generosity for many Americans.

Willingness and Reluctance to be Generous

In addition to these behavioral measures of generosity, the Science of Generosity Survey also asked respondents how *willing* they would be to engage in four different kinds of generosity. Examining their answers provides yet another view on American generosity. First, the survey asked respondents how willing they would be "to give money for an issue of

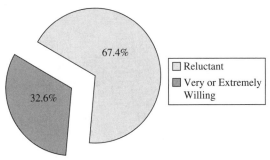

FIGURE 3.13 Percent of Americans reluctant to give money for an issue of concern to them (less than "very" or "extremely" willing)

Source: Science of Generosity Survey, 2010

concern to them." Answers ranged on a five-point scale, from extremely willing to very willing, somewhat willing, not very willing, and not willing at all. Figure 3.13 shows the percent of Americans who stopped short of saying that they were very or extremely willing to give money for an issue of concern to them. These we call "reluctant." There we see that 67 percent of Americans are reluctant to give money to address issues that concern them. Thirty-three percent, by contrast, are very or extremely willing to give money. In short, about two-thirds of Americans do not reflect high degrees of readiness to be generous with their money, *even when it comes to issues that personally concern them.*

The same kind of question was asked about respondents' willingness to volunteer for an issue of concern to them. Figure 3.14 shows that 63 percent of Americans were less than very willing to volunteer their time and talents for a matter that concerned them. Again, nearly two-thirds of American adults admit to a reluctance to being generous in volunteering. Remember that this question did not ask about actually committing to volunteering, merely an attitudinal readiness to volunteer in theory. Even so, most Americans do not seem enthusiastic about volunteering.

The numbers change somewhat when respondents are asked about giving blood. Fifty-three percent of Americans said they would be very or extremely willing to give blood if they were able to do so (Figure 3.15). Slightly less than one-half were not especially willing to give blood. Since we know that only 11.5 percent of the same survey sample actually did give blood in the previous year, something must explain the gap between the theoretical willingness and the action. In any case, more Americans at least profess a readiness to give blood than to give money or to volunteer. Finally, only one-quarter (25.9 percent) of Americans said that they would

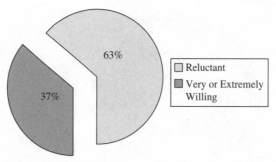

FIGURE 3.14 Percent of Americans reluctant to volunteer for an issue of concern to them (less than "very" or "extremely" willing)

Source: Science of Generosity Survey, 2010

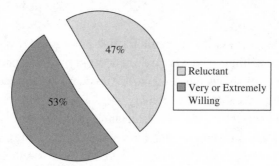

FIGURE 3.15 Percent of Americans reluctant to give blood if they were able (less than "very" or "extremely" willing)

Source: Science of Generosity Survey, 2010

be very or extremely willing to include a charitable donation in their will, to engage in estate giving. Three-quarters were reluctant to say they might do that (Figure 3.16). Again, this is complicated by the fact that many Americans do not ever think about writing wills for passing on their possessions. And some people may simply not want to think about their own deaths. Even so, the large proportion of American adults who professed not to be very willing, even in theory, to dedicate some of their resources upon passing away to a worthy cause in the form of a charitable donation does not reflect a particularly robust level of generosity on this measure.

Conclusion

If Americans want to become happier, healthier people who live with greater purpose, suffer less depression, and enjoy more personal growth, one way they might better accomplish that is to learn to be more generous.

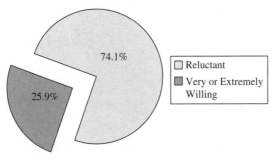

FIGURE 3.16 Percent of Americans reluctant to include a charitable donation in their will (less than "very" or "extremely" willing)

Source: Science of Generosity Survey, 2010

The scientific evidence shows clearly that more generous people are doing significantly better in their lives in many important ways. And we have a solid grasp of the kinds of causal mechanisms that link greater generosity and higher well-being in life. What this chapter has shown is that Americans have not "topped out" their capacity to live in the kind of generous ways that we expect could increase their happiness, health, purpose, mental health, and growth. Only a minority of Americans are living clearly generous lives, however you measure it. The majority of Americans thus enjoy the opportunity to dramatically increase their generous practices. Doing so would not only be good for the people to whom they are generous—it would also be good for themselves. What may stand in their way we will address further in the next chapter.

CHAPTER 4 | Understanding Ungenerous
Americans

OUR INTERVIEWS WITH UNGENEROUS Americans clearly confirm the
findings of our statistical analyses in Chapter 1: compared with their
more generous counterparts, ungenerous Americans are not as happy,
healthy, or imbued with as much purpose. Ungenerous people are less
likely to believe they can accomplish much in life and seem largely uninterested in personal growth. As a group they are less physically healthy
and more pessimistic about their problems. They are also more likely to
experience symptoms of depression and anxiety disorders. Furthermore,
fewer of the ungenerous manage to carve out personally satisfying purposes in life. But the biggest difference between generous and ungenerous Americans we find in our interviews concerns their happiness. Our
data suggest that miserliness does not lend itself to an overarching sense
of well-being, contentedness, and being at peace with oneself, others,
and the world. In general, the less generous people are, the less happy
they are. The ways these differences are expressed can sometimes be
obvious and sometimes subtle. In either case, what we repeatedly hear
expressed by our interviewees is that an ungenerous life is also one that
is compromised, underwhelming, and often anxious and unhealthy. That
is as reliable and empirically verifiable a finding based on our interview
data as the paradox's flipside: namely, that generous people tend to lead
more happy and fulfilling lives. The absence of generous practices has
the capacity to shape people negatively, just as much as the presence of
generosity affects them positively. In what follows, we will see that most
ungenerous Americans view themselves as holding basins collecting
more and more resources, without realizing that their concave lifestyles
drain and hollow out whatever health, vivacity, and happiness they might
otherwise have.

How Ungenerous Americans Think about Generosity

What do we mean by "ungenerous" people, and how do ungenerous Americans make sense of the idea of generosity? Of the thirty people we interviewed who do not lead generous lifestyles, most are ungenerous across the board with their money, time, relational care, and other resources. Four people we interviewed volunteer significant amounts of time but give very little money away, even though their households accrue sizeable incomes. "Elaine Woods" of Southern California logs long hours as a volunteer for various causes throughout her community, but her reasons for volunteering depart from the standard motivations of more generous people:

> I think I'm a bit of a control-freak, and I think I tend to gravitate toward things where I can have control. I do a lot of volunteer work in the schools and in Scouts because I feel like I can have control of what I'm doing there.

Rather than freely giving her time, volunteering is about attaining a greater sense of control. "The thing that prevents me from giving more [money] is feeling like I'm not able to, but I'm not sure I'm [being] rational." Realizing that her sense of deprivation does not accurately reflect her household's upper-middle-class position, she acknowledges that her sense of not having enough to give is illogical. But because she somehow believes that she does not have enough money, she does not give money away. Even though Elaine scores high on measures of generosity in terms of volunteered time, she does not follow the normal patterns of the generous when it comes to well-being, because her volunteer work is mostly a form of self-validation and she feels uncomfortable giving any money away or moving into situations she cannot control. And her volunteer work, it turns out, is unfulfilling: "I feel like I'm generous with my time, but not with myself—if you can identify a self inside." Among those whose incomes exceed the median, we find that giving money away specifically is a crucial component for experiencing the paradox of generosity. It is not enough to give of only time, if money is also available but withheld. This is particularly true among those for whom money is a source of felt insecurity and a perpetual reminder of a fear of scarcity.

Another issue here concerns dynamics of marital relationships. Most ungenerous Americans we interviewed are partnered with someone who is similarly ungenerous, or else they are the sole head of the household.

As exceptions, we did interview four wives and one husband who are married to generous spouses, yet they themselves have little desire to give away time or money. In fact, they all despise their spouses' liberality. Both sides of the paradox of generosity are seen in their households. "Rose Steinecker" in Illinois, for example, told us that her husband controls the family's finances. She has a credit card, but does not have access to the checking or savings accounts—"He's the decision maker on the finances. He brings the bacon in." She explains, "I think my husband's just a giving, he's got a giving heart," and then admits, "I mean, if it was just me, we probably wouldn't be giving to anybody, you know?" As with Rose's husband, "Dale," who experiences what he calls an "inner peace" as a result of his financial generosity, the generous spouse takes charge of financial generosity and usually experiences greater well-being as a result. Deprived of financial control, and upset with her husband for giving their money away to others while giving her limited access, Rose's unhappiness seems to be a response to Dale's generosity, an indication of the fact that the same generous practices that allow one person, Dale, to flourish may result in the limited happiness of another, Rose. Generosity, of course, is not a surefire precursor to global well-being—generous practices can and do sometimes harm not only recipients, but also personal relationships.

As another example, "Martin Cizek," whom we profile in Chapter 5, is quite generous, and yet his wife, "Corrine," detests generous financial giving, and will occasionally sign up to volunteer only to back out at the last minute. Martin is happy, mentally healthy, constantly looking for opportunities to grow, and leads a purposeful life. But Corrine, as we will see learn later in this chapter, is unhappy, tormented by personal demons of depression and anger, and believes that she is not able to enjoy the life she should be living.

The relatively few cases of those who give time but not money and the miserly partners in discordant marriages shed light on how the practice of generosity matters most when it comes to well-being. Even though these people are generous in one dimension, either by way of household financial giving or volunteering time, closer study shows that they tend to resemble ungenerous people in their overall well-being. What seems to us to most importantly separate generous from ungenerous Americans, a factor that moves generous people toward greater well-being, is the active practice of purposefully giving away moderate portions of dearly held resources. That is the basis upon which we categorize people as generous or ungenerous. The ungenerous tightly hold on to their resources out of self-protection and the fear that they may not have enough in a time of need. The generous are willing to share some of their resources with others.

Not surprisingly, ungenerous Americans do not think of generosity as a moral obligation. They instead think it's a "nice thing to do" if a person or family wants to give some of their income or time away. It may even provide some good karma. For example, "Shane Little" from Oregon says:

> In my opinion, I don't feel it's a moral duty. Although I think it's in the best interest of everybody if they did. Again, what goes around comes around. But again, if you choose not to, then that's your own decision and I don't think anybody should be required to.

In some ways, "karma" seems to be a softer version of the utilitarian tit-for-tat that some ungenerous people idealize and draw on to support their autonomous inclinations. Karma, in their minds, functions like capitalism—what is good for the goose is good for the gander. Citing karma as the reason to practice generosity assumes personal pleasure as the yardstick to measure the worthiness of actions. It also relieves the ungenerous of responsibility for other people.

According to Shane's wife, "Kimberly," the couple would like to be generous with their resources, but, she says, they cannot afford to give money away. When asked if she would be willing to volunteer instead of give money, she admits that she would rather not. "When I'm not working, I'd rather be with my family, I know that probably sounds a little selfish." Like many ungenerous Americans we spoke with, Kimberly, who already feels stretched thin by the demands of her taxing and low-paying job at a big-box store, prioritizes her family. Her broader community is beyond the purview of her concerns. "Adam Berry" of Nevada also acknowledges that he does not have a desire to be generous, since the workday takes a lot out of him and is overwhelming enough; self-indulgence becomes his default mode of life. "I think it's just because I get home and I'm so wrapped up in my own life, that's why. I just don't even think about it." Another, "Truman Wright," avoids giving time or money simply because "I don't want to be bothered." Several ungenerous people in our study admit that their refusal to act generously violates what it means to them to be a good person. They regularly refer to themselves as "selfish," "a scrooge," or "an asshole."

Other relatively ungenerous Americans sometimes do give smaller amounts of money, usually one-time gifts under $50 to friends raising support for a race or a good cause, or to the local police department, for example. Many of these do not give for generous purposes, but rather have strong ulterior motives. For example, "Bill Kalon" of Southern California is a warehouse manager and has $3.50 automatically deducted from his biweekly paycheck and given to the United Way. "I don't even think about it," he says, at first not even remembering this donation. Only after a few minutes of talking about financial generosity does he remember. So why does he bother to give $84 away each year? "Honestly, to be 100 percent honest, it's kind of frowned upon to not do that at [my company] as a manager person. . . It's because [my company] wants to be one of the leaders in contributing to United Way. . . I'm not even sure why they do it." If his company were not involved with United Way and sending subtle signals of pressure to give, would he give money anyway? "Nope," he says, "Probably not."

There are yet others who have a strong libertarian streak, like "Randall Weir" in Northern California, who actually warn of generosity's ills and believe that people who give anything away are delusional and weak. "When people act like they need to take care of somebody else, when it's not part of their responsibility, it's like, they want to be nice [but] it gets to a point where I get worried, I get concerned," he told us. "I think that's destroying the human spirit, the spirit of 'I'm going to take care of my own things.'" A strong believer in self-sufficiency, Randall scoffs when we ask him if he considers himself to be a generous person: "Yeah, sort of like I roll over and get stepped on kind of a thing?" Are there any circumstances, we asked, in which someone else might merit his generosity or the generosity of others? His reply:

I'm sorry, but living in the middle of the Sahara, you're gonna die! That's why I don't go to the Sahara. And if I was there, I would book my ass out of there in whichever way I could. . . . I'm not going to grow a family there. I'm not trying to be cold-hearted, I'm trying to be helpful to solve their issue. . . . If somebody's living in a place where there's constant, repetitive, overwhelming community lack of food, you know, come on. Make a better choice. Do something about that. Move closer to water. Move away from the desert. They need to fix their own problem. I'm not going to move their own furniture, they've got to do that themselves.

Randall does not envision himself as "cold-hearted." He is "trying to be helpful" and encourage people to achieve autonomy, which he believes to be the greatest human good. Like more generous respondents, he believes the world is a place of abundance. But he rejects the assertion of generous people—that they have plenty for themselves and thus should be generous toward others. Randall believes instead that every individual should be able to track down the resources needed to survive, and that help from others can only diminish the capacity of those in dire straits to achieve their own flourishing. Although he adamantly refuses to give away any of his $60,000 salary, he does volunteer for his son's Boy Scout troop, but his motives there are not generous either. Rather, he volunteers "because it's fun stuff to do. I'm not out to change the world for Jerry's kids or something. I just don't care [about that], I guess."

Personal autonomy, self-preservation, and rugged individualism are key and sacred concepts in the vocabulary of the ungenerous people we interviewed. Generous giving does not make sense because, as expressed by Adam, Shane, or Kimberly, one's own individual autonomy is of primary importance in life; or, like Bill, they are only interested in giving money when it serves a direct personal interest. Still others, like Randall, believe that generosity toward others undercuts the ability of the beneficiaries to support themselves.

As we show throughout this chapter, there are deeply rooted cultural and sometimes psychobiological reasons why a practice of generosity proves difficult for many of our respondents. We are in no way suggesting that ungenerous people can simply will themselves to be more generous with their resources and thus experience greater well-being. The reality is far more complex. Our analysis points to the importance of context and socioeconomic inequality when considering the social forces that encourage or impede generous practices.

What, then, do ungenerous lifestyles actually look like? And how, in turn, might the meanings that ungenerous people ascribe to generosity shape how they see the world and their place in it? Finally, how do these definitions of humanity and visions of the good life translate into understandings of well-being? To begin answering these questions, we turn our attention to an in-depth look at two of the ungenerous families in our study.

Case Studies

No single case study of an ungenerous household can represent all ungenerous Americans. But such case studies can showcase some of the more important themes our analysis turned up—themes which are crucial to understanding what it means to have one's life shaped by a lack of generosity, but often are difficult to grasp unless they are seen in the contexts of people's larger lives. The "Arnolds" in South Carolina, for example, represent the pursuit of self-interest at the cost, paradoxically, of actual happiness. And our discussions with the "Ramirez" family, more constrained in their finances than the Arnolds, reveal a cyclical pattern of anxiety and apathy. Taken together, these two case studies offer exemplars that provide insights into the entire collection of interviewed ungenerous Americans. In what follows, we first recount the experiences of these two families, and then turn to different voices in our study to examine how other ungenerous people experience and talk about their physical health, mental health, personal growth, and life purpose. We then consider the extent to which these ungenerous Americans are leading happy, fulfilling lives or not.

The Arnold Family: "It Comes Down to Money" and "The Switzerland Attitude"

Devotion to self-interest is the most pervasive thread woven throughout our interviews with both Doug and Michelle Arnold; it is a thread intertwined with the fear of falling off the middle-class track of security. This clearly gives rise to a complex of stress, anxiety, insecurity, and banality, not the happiness they say they would like to enjoy. Their vision of "the good life" is mostly confined to the scope of personal financial security. Unable to separate their personal happiness from having enough money to buy a lifestyle of leisure and modest luxuries to counteract the dulling grind of work in which neither experiences much purpose, they shortchange themselves when it comes to the possibility of a different and richer life. It is only a slight exaggeration to say that life's purpose for the Arnolds is not to be searched for or made, but consumed. They simply want to take care of their own without the interference of others. In exchange, they are willing to return the same courtesy and refrain from asking for help from anyone else. They do not expect people to help them, so why should they use their resources to help others? "Live and let live" is their functional motto of life. Doug and Michelle freely admit that they do not want to give away anything generously. They are content to keep their resources to themselves.

Doug and Michelle Arnold aspire to home ownership in a safe beige cul-de-sac of two-story houses, with a landscaped backyard and a deck on which to sip some wine in the evenings, a weekend home by the beach, and public schools that keep out children from the poorer neighborhoods. What forty-year-old Michelle, a reserved brunette with manicured eyebrows and a curvy figure, wants most out of life is "some financial happiness and some financial freedom at the end. . . as long as we can say we were happy at the end." This pursuit of "financial happiness" has been a driving force for the Arnolds from the start of their relationship, but they have yet to find the security and happiness they seek. Now in his early forties, Doug, a broad-shouldered man with a graying goatee, recounts floundering in his twenties. He was working at a ski lodge, got married young, and then divorced. When he started dating Michelle, "both of us were kind of going nowhere and I was about to hit 30 and I think that in my mind, when I hit 30 I needed to probably settle down and get serious." Michelle agreed: "We just weren't going anywhere, so we said, 'if we're ever going to own a house and have kids, and do the things we want to do, we gotta move. So we literally threw a dart at a map and South Carolina is where we ended up." Doug and Michelle traded in their young, aimless lifestyle "to be more career-oriented," because, as Doug says, "it comes down to money." So they packed up and left their families and dead-end jobs behind in the Midwest. "We threw our shit in the back of a U-Haul and put my car in the back and threw the cat in the front seat of the truck and drove. I mean we had nothing." To make ends meet while they were looking for work, they maxed out their credit cards. "It was more survival at that point in time. I think we're [now] a little bit smarter about that."

Two years later they married, because, Doug says, "we figured if we could move down together, we could probably stand each other." Michelle confirms this as true. She takes a practical, good-enough approach to their marriage: "I'm sure we have our ups and downs. We're good. Overall, I mean, we get stressed out occasionally, take it out on each other like everybody else." Doug and Michelle share a strong sense of autonomy— each person can decide what they want themselves—but whereas Michelle can be tightly wound, Doug has a laid-back demeanor. Their personality differences are most perceptible when it comes to financial decisions— something they fought about constantly in their early days of marriage. "He's a 'You can't take it with you' and I'm a 'Horde it all away for a rainy day,'" Michelle explains. Money continues to be a source of stress, but for the most part they get along and rely on one another for support and daily banter. Both confess that they are emotionally bonded with each other and only a few other people; they generally prefer to keep their distance from most people. "Her and I are very close, almost friendship-wise," Doug says, "and it's my thought anyways, I don't think that we have a lot of ties with a lot of different people that we rely on. We don't like to rely on others—I think we rely on each other and family or just us, the four of us [including two children] down here. I think that not having any family down here has made us more cohesive." But when we ask Doug if he could be happy without Michelle and their daughters, he says, "Probably, I don't mind, yeah, I'm pretty independent. I don't mind being alone."

They settled in a comfortable South Carolina exurb along with a rotating crop of fellow white-collar transplants, a local community that embraces and shares the Arnolds' strong streak of individualism. The fabricated names on bronzed placards—Granite Tides and The Arcadian Lakes—embellish the various subdivisions of track homes, signaling exclusion. This is a neighborhood catering to those who aspire to personal solace without the infringement of responsibility to others who live beyond its gates. Built just before the housing bubble burst, the Arnolds live in Sunset Canyon Ridge, a decidedly middle-class development. In earlier decades, before working professionals like the Arnolds moved here for a shot at upward mobility, this land grew tobacco, and stark distinctions of race and class divided the community. The days of plantations and share-cropping may be long gone, but the older farmsteads, double-wides, and Ma-and-Pa ramshackles that occasionally dot the area landscape offer faint reminders of a distinct Southern heritage, reminding the newcomers that not all who live here have had the privileges of the white middle class. In the end, though, these fixtures are not enough to save their community from the exurban fate of catering to highly mobile people willing to relocate for a better job, safer neighborhoods, and nicer schools. Many crave familiarity and feel burdened by demanding hours—they do not want to be bothered or have their stability threatened by confrontation with difference, poverty, or people in need of care or assistance, especially in a community in which they lack roots.

In the mornings, a long stretch of single-lane asphalt carries Michelle and other workers in a steady stream of traffic to cubicles in the nearby city. "I'm not big on the commute," she explains, "but it's worth living out here on the weekends for the calm and quiet." Self-admittedly an "extremely type-A personality," Michelle likes her job as a human resources manager only insofar as it puts bread on the table—"It's definitely not the direction I ever started out in. 'I'm gonna be an HR manager' that was never like 'Woohoo, that's what I'm gonna do with my life.' It just sorta happened, and it's pleasant enough, pays the bills." She works full-time and sometimes spends the night out of town on business trips, but she is devoted to family, "specifically immediate, nuclear family, they're always first."

The Arnolds purchased a home on their block because the neighbors there were like them: working professionals with children. "This street is its own little community. We've done misfit Thanksgivings together because we're all transplants. None of us have family in the area." The Arnolds' cul-de-sac offers a sense of family and refuge from the larger world, but sometimes causes problems—problems they mostly try to avoid. Michelle recounts a messy extramarital affair between neighbors that resulted in divorce and separation. It was stressful, but true to her "to-each-their-own" mentality, she tried to remain as uninvolved as possible. "I've managed to maintain the 'Switzerland attitude' throughout the whole thing, of I'm not taking sides." This approach transcends her neighborhood friendships, as she is content to keep to herself and dedicate her resources to herself and her family. The Arnolds mostly keep to themselves. In the evenings, Michelle tells us, they put daytime work away, make dinner, help the kids with homework, bathe and get the kids in bed, and then "I'll curl up with a book, he'll watch TV. We're pretty much homebodies." Sometimes on the weekends the whole family goes camping nearby, to visit the beach. When asked what has made her the happiest in the past two or three years, Michelle gushes about a back-yard deck that she and her husband just had installed: "We go out there on a Friday night, we light the little torches, and we sit there with a glass of wine, and it's our grounding force of peace. It's quiet back there."

They also enjoy the "small-town feel" in their community. "We wanted that feel of, where the kids went to school they would know everybody," Michelle says, "you'd bump into people when you walked around." Though they do feel connected to the community, at the same time, their oldest daughter does not attend the public school at the end of their street. As Michelle puts it:

> We don't want her to go to that school, their test scores are just horrendous, they have way too many behavior issues. They bus kids into that school from [a poorer part of the county], where their test scores, if you have bad test scores for two years in a row, you can opt your child into an alternative school. [Our local public school] is an alternative school for [that other, poorer school] and that's just not happening for me.

As far as she is concerned, everyone should stick with their local neighborhood schools. She realizes it sounds harsh, but why should her daughters pay the price for equality and desegregation? Her child should not suffer because other people's children attend underachieving schools. Thankfully, since Doug works from home, he can easily drive their daughter to and from an out-of-town school, one that does not bus students in from low-resource schools.

For the most part, Doug enjoys his job and the flexibility it offers. The work suits his competitive streak and extroverted nature. He also appreciates the mutual self-reliance of business relationships between companies and their customers:

> I like the way it works. Between the customer and a company there is always a mix of, you need your customer to pay your bills for the company, and I think that is always a struggle with different companies. So I think the way business works, everybody's got their place. The customer supports you, but then this person has to pay their bills somehow too so this person has a job and they're doing something, so there's someone [else] almost below them.

Everyone does their part and seeks out the necessary support in a complex division of labor and exchange. This business-relationship metaphor extends beyond Doug's work; it also shapes the way he understands people to be related in a society and their responsibilities or participation. Communities ought to operate much like supply chains. There are no free lunches because no one should *need* a free lunch. "Everybody's got their place." This helps explain why he chooses not to give generously. Generosity is not necessary in his model of reality, because he believes people can autonomously provide for themselves. So, when we asked, "If your girls grew up and didn't give away a penny, didn't volunteer, just lived their own lives, would you be fine with that?," it is not surprising that Doug replies, "It wouldn't bother me." If people want to be generous, that's fine, in Doug's book, but nobody has a moral obligation to help others. "If you want to, that's terrific, and thank goodness people do, but I don't think it's anything that you should feel guilty about." Instead, people should live exactly as they wish:

> I don't judge people by stuff that happened. Like I guess the best [example of this] is Tiger Woods. I don't judge him for what he's done. It's his life. Do I think he's any different of a golfer because of it? No. Do I think Bill Clinton's any different because of Monica Lewinsky? No. It's just a person. It doesn't affect what he did in his administration. Private life is private life.

Privacy is an important concept in Doug's lexicon, the keystone of a society that anchors the values of self-sufficiency and autonomy.

These essential characteristics give people the opportunity to pursue a self-interested approach to happiness. The other side of this logic, as we shall shortly see, is that everyone but the most disempowered should fend for themselves and take care of their own problems. Beyond that, individuals ought to be given full freedom to live out their private desires without fearing collateral damage to others or the public sphere. Material possessions or personal indiscretions seem to have little bearing on a person's ability to be a professional leader or citizen. The decisions made in private life, after all, rarely bleed into the professional or public life. Also, so long as loved ones are not adversely affected, Doug does not worry about problems in the future that he might have had a hand in creating. Consider, for instance, his thinking about the possible problem of global warming and climate change:

> I don't pay attention a lot to that. But in the big picture of, "Is the ice all gonna melt in Antarctica?" Yeah sure, it probably is. Am I going to be here? Probably not. Are my kids gonna be here? Probably not.

How one uses shared natural resources does not matter, at least not for the current user. Here, Doug is thinking pragmatically for the short run: he realizes that there may be trouble down the line, but he is not worried, because he does not think that he or his daughters will suffer the consequences of our current course of action, as many scientists describe it. This way of thinking fits well with his "live and let live" mentality, in which people should and do simply solve the problems they find themselves in. Later generations may well find themselves in a seriously troubled world, but that will be *their* problem to solve, not his to worry about now. In the meantime, until we have reached a point of crisis, people may continue living as they wish. Along similar lines, we ask what he thinks about the 28,200-square-foot home of the former US Senator John Edwards, outside of Chapel Hill. Are there any limits, keeping that in mind, to what people should possess?

> If he has the money to build a house that size, well all the power to him. If I had money to buy a Porsche, yeah probably [I would]. So do I think it's too much? No, I mean, it's all what your means are, I guess.

There is no such thing as too much for Doug, in short. In his mind, individuals can behave as they see fit and take whatever is there for the taking, without voluntarily restraining themselves or feeling guilty. It does not matter how many five-million-dollar mansions or Porsches anyone has—people are completely entitled to their own self-defined, materially focused happiness, no matter what that might involve. The possibility of voluntarily living a more modest life and giving away some of one's resources generously is simply not on Doug's radar of possibilities. Autonomy is nearly absolute and consumption limited only by what someone can financially afford. Reading between the lines, Doug seems either to believe that faithfulness to self-interest takes precedence over the good of others as a matter of principle, regardless of consequences, or else he is blind to the possibility that individual actions can and often do negatively influence the lives of others.

It makes sense, then, that Doug expects others to be uninterested in helping him if he were ever in need. He and Michelle, for example, feel uncomfortable asking friends to babysit their kids. Likewise, he should not be expected to provide them help. If good friends were thinking about getting a divorce, we asked, would he be willing to spend time talking with them and providing support? "No, because I wouldn't ask someone to do that for myself." So, we probed, if they wanted your help, you would just say, "I have to go now"? His reply: "Um, yeah, I probably wouldn't drag that out. No, I wouldn't. And maybe that's just I'm not that close, I'm probably not that close to someone and I feel like that's overbearing." But with such little reliance on others and limited responsibility to care for others, what sort of meaning in life does this autonomy support? Doug told us that he doesn't think he has a purpose in life. However, he does think that a happy life involves "being comfortable and providing for my family." Still, he leaves these goods and goals unexamined. He does not search out a higher truth or grounds for living. We ask him, does he ever have any thoughts or ideas about "higher values or transcendence or life beyond just sort of living, being adequately comfortable with family, or not?" "No," he says, "I don't think that far into it, that deeply into it." He continues:

> I don't feel like I have a calling or a drive. I don't consider myself very religious at all. That kind of calling stuff, I don't feel the need to join the Peace Corps. World hunger does bother me and stuff like that does bother me, it's just that I don't feel like that's [what I'm] here for.

So it is not that Doug is flatly insensitive to bigger problems in the world—rather, he just does not have "a calling" to do anything about them. Interestingly, his example of joining the Peace Corps is an intense, all-or-nothing, two-year commitment, implying that a life of really caring about such concerns would have to be radically different from his current life path. Michelle is also content with a life of modest accomplishment, of taking care of her own and not stepping on too many toes. When we broach the topic of personal growth, she acknowledges that it probably is not worth the effort. "I think I should improve, but I think realistically will I? Maybe a little. But I don't put a ton of effort into it."

Despite their "live and let live" mentality and limited sense of purpose and interests in self-growth, it is clear that neither Doug nor Michelle is completely hardhearted. Doug is bothered by world hunger, even if he has no desire to actually do anything to alleviate hunger. When directly asked, he and Michelle sometimes give twenty or fifty dollars to aid in humanitarian relief after natural disasters or to support a friend collecting funds for a cause. Given that Doug does not think generosity itself is an important virtue, we press him to explain why he gives this money away.

"Just to take a hard line," we asked, "So what? It didn't happen to you. If it had happened to you, you would take care of yourself."

Doug replied, "It must be my soft side." [Both laugh.]

We continued, "what do you mean by 'soft side?'"

> I think I do have a side to me that is, I have some compassion. I may come off like I don't have compassion, but sure it bothers me. The tsunami [in Indonesia] was a horrible thing. Pictures of that stuff make you feel bad. So, sure, I have compassion with innocent people caught up in situations like that.

So Doug feels compassionate when the people in need are not responsible for bringing hardship upon themselves. Michelle mostly agrees with Doug when it comes to generosity. If someone earns a nice living and decides not to give a cent away, that would be morally fine. She herself does give some money away, usually to show support for acquaintances who are raising funds for various causes. But even then, she gives begrudgingly: "I wouldn't say that I hate doing it, but I wouldn't say that I'm excited about donating it." Like Doug, she says she has a "soft spot," but only for people caught up in troubles that she deems beyond their control, like tsunamis and earthquakes. "I do feel bad and we do donate small amounts to stuff like that to try and help. When it's natural disasters, I think I view it differently because it's entirely out of their control. You couldn't control, you could technically control, I guess, where you live, but come on, like you're ever going to predict what's going to happen where." Because she bases her compassion on whether or not someone can control their situation, it makes sense that there are limits to her empathy. She actually feels embarrassed by her limited empathy and believes that she is out of the bounds of what is socially acceptable on the matter:

Q: Would you say that you are a naturally empathetic, or sympathetic, person? Or are you not naturally prone to empathize with other people's feelings, needs, or problems?

Michelle: I would say no I'm not [laughs].

Q: Not. What do you mean? Why is that funny?

Michelle: Because this is all tied, you're so sympathetic. Because I'm not, I just, I'm not. I know I should be, it's the right way to be.

Q: What is it the right way to be?

Michelle: I don't know 'cause you're just supposed to be kind and sympathetic, and that's just not me. I mean to be that way, but I'm kind of like, "Oh, look, you're okay." And I move on.

Q: So what are examples of that?

Michelle: Whether it's somebody being upset about something. I'm okay to a point, of listening to you, and saying, you know, patting your back, "It's gonna be okay, it's all gonna, you're gonna get through it somehow." And then I hit that point where I'm like "Okay, I don't really want to hear it anymore." And I just, I get that from my mother, 'cause my mother was pretty much the same way, of "I'll give you a shoulder to cry on, and then pick yourself up by your panties and move on." Because just sitting here wallowing in it isn't gonna do anything.

Michelle endorses an autonomous chutzpah—people should not rely on others to solve their problems. "Pick yourself up by your panties" is a statement of the tough-love she offers to those she cares about. She admits that she does not have much patience for troubled people, but wants to be helpful and is practical insofar as "wallowing in it isn't going to do anything." She maintains a tough line for others, and for herself, but holding herself to these standards can come at a cost. In college she was diagnosed with stress-related stomach ulcers. And at other points in life, she has suffered stress-related insomnia. The consequences of her self-reliance and refusal to rely on others or to be relied upon, then, can be costly.

Given their valorization of autonomy, and a belief that their generosity should be limited to small amounts and offered only to those who demonstrate extreme need, it makes sense that neither Doug nor Michelle understands why some people purposefully give large sums of their incomes away. They have some family members who give 10 percent of their income away for religious reasons, and know of some people in South Carolina who do the same, but they think the idea is absolutely ludicrous. They cannot understand why anyone would do that. They do think it is fine if someone individually chooses to be moderately sacrificial in their giving, but no one should feel expected or compelled, only prompted with a guilt-free ability to opt out of doing so if one wishes.

> Doug: I think that's your own personal preference, if it's part of your budget, it's part of your budget.
>
> Q: Why is that?
>
> Doug: I just don't think that's relevant. That's like me joining a golf club. I don't think it's any different than joining the YMCA. I don't think that's a proper approach. I think asking for a donation is a little different than requiring you to do that.
>
> Q: So there's something about the individual, totally free choice of giving that matters?
>
> Doug: Sure. When you're required to it, that wouldn't be charity, would it?

Again, we see the business-model mentality crop up here, but this time generosity provides the exception to the rule. Doug frames much of life as a fee-for-service producing eventual equilibrium. This is true even when it comes to the personal care of others, such as the hypothetical divorcing friend—he would not expect someone to listen to him, so why should he listen to others? The same applies to giving money. Being required to do anything in that regard desecrates the essence of generosity. This outlook functions to give Doug a way out of feeling guilty about his lack of generosity.

Apart from their belief that giving is unnecessary and should never be a prerequisite of membership in a group, the Arnolds also believe that even if they wanted to give, the resources just are not there in their family budget. Even though they together earn about $115,000 per year, they clearly live in a subjective state of relative deprivation, imbued with a constant sense that there is not enough money for the things they need and want. Truth be told, they do not have a very good grip on the extent of their resources. "I can be very impulsive," Doug admits, and "not hugely interested in [budgeting]. I don't necessarily like to do it. Michelle doesn't necessarily like to do that either." According to Michelle, she and Doug have a rough idea of their budget each month. "We know generally what we should spend in a month, and how much free money we have at the end of that month," she explains. "We know how much leftover we have as, 'Okay, we can play with this much.' " When it comes to financial giving, they do not look at their accounts and think objectively about what they could give away. Instead, they rely on their intuition about what the numbers might be. "I guess it's what I feel comfortable with our weekly budget, what I feel like I can give out of the budget," Doug says. "It's like an intuitive, 'I think I'll give fifty bucks,' if the occasion arises." This budgetary "flexibility" and "intuitive" purchasing and giving style, however, we know are not optimal ways of managing money. Such practices leave the Arnolds unsure and vulnerable. They actually have little in their savings account and routinely borrow money with high interest rates. "Do I like owing people money?" Doug asks, and then answers his own rhetorical question: "No, I can't stand it. I guess it's just that I almost feel like it's a necessary evil at times."

This approach to money can result in some ways of looking at life that the Arnolds come to regret with time. For example, when Doug learned that Michelle was unexpectedly pregnant with their second daughter, his mind first jumped to thinking about the costs: "The second one was definitely not planned. So that one was kind of a, um, in fact, we had just moved into here [the new house] and I remember sitting here and both looking at each other, and I got daycare figures going in my mind on what it's going to cost?" Finances have been vexing at other points in life for the Arnolds. Most recently, in the year previous to our interviews, both of the companies that Doug and Michelle worked for were restructuring, and thus both Doug and Michelle were very worried about the possibility of being laid off. Michelle recalls it being particularly nerve-racking:

> We thought both of us were losing our jobs, and it was a big stress. We started making the lists of, "Okay, these are the necessities, and this is what we'll cut first, and this is how we'll do it." You know, we stressed for a while, we argued for a while, and then we figured out we'll get through it somehow. If it means we sell the house, then we'll figure it out.

Such a possibility would be stressful for anyone, and like many, the Arnolds do not leave much wiggle room for unexpected misfortunes. This may be somewhat surprising given the fact that Michelle is not a stranger to stress. "When I was in college," she recalls, "I got diagnosed with an ulcer from literally being a ball of stress my whole life. And the doctor was like 'You need to figure out a way to put it all away because you can't live like this.'" Since then, she says things have improved, but she still finds herself worked up in stressful circumstances. Usually these problems center around financial security. Last year she completed an online advanced degree to try to earn a pay raise.

> I would say finishing my master's degree was huge, because that was a constant draining juggle of life, basically. It was working, coming home, dealing with the kids, and then I would go online at nine, ten o'clock at night until two or three in the morning, and then sleep for a couple hours and then get up and do it all again the next day.

Though she has more free time now and a bigger paycheck, the chronic sleep deprivation made for a very difficult stretch of life. Doug also faced job-related chronic stress.

> The previous company I worked for went through a bankruptcy. It was very stressful for a couple of years with that. Going through a bankruptcy, going through a selling, we went through a number of different upper-level management situations, and I kinda just flew below the radar screen the entire way. Then we got bought out by the company I'm with now, and they got rid of probably 70 percent of the reps from my old company, cause they had their own set of reps. So I kinda tried to fly below the radar. I think that probably taxed my, it put some years on my body, just worrying about, getting through that and with the family and the house.

Doug tells us that he had a back-up plan in case he did lose his job. It involved working two jobs: "I'd probably have to, I can go back into my previous business even if I wanted to, and I'd probably just do that [two jobs], it's just a lot of hours. Keep the house, and then just get two jobs." Scaling back does not seem to figure into the realm of possibilities. Rather than lose his footing in the stability of home ownership, Doug would rather work an extra job to make the ends of his current lifestyle meet. This stressful possibility may in part explain his lack of generosity—understandably, the fear of losing it all is constantly tucked into his subconscious.

Not far from the Arnolds' home are plots of packed dirt in an unfinished neighborhood of the large new homes often referred to as "McMansions," a graveyard of the broken dreams from the burst real-estate bubble involving subprime lending and worse, reminding those with eyes to see of the consequences of borrowing on a faith in ever-expanding and eventually impossible prosperity. But that kind of sometimes-unwarranted faith can be difficult to shake. Doug and Michelle know that well. They regularly and unhappily borrow money at high interest rates to appease their quest for better and more. What they have at any time, whatever that may be, is simply not enough: there is still more to be had and they want it. More comfort, more leisure, more to balance out the daily slog of jobs they both find unfulfilling. Thus, after recently installing their new deck as a place of evening retreat, the Arnolds now want a pool to enhance their ability to wind down in private and retreat from others. "But you have a neighborhood pool, right?" we ask. Doug replies, "We have a neighborhood pool, but we want a pool on our property." Why do they need a private pool? "Because it's private, it may be more private." But, we point out, their yard is not very big and it slopes steeply up. "Yeah," Doug concedes, "this isn't the best spot for a pool. I don't think in this backyard it will work. I think in our next house it will." And that is in addition to the beach house Doug and Michelle plan to purchase. Not entirely satisfied anymore with the occasional weekend trip to the beach, "We eventually would like to own a place down there," Michelle says, "We figure probably that's about another five years away." They also have some new cars in mind. Because they are always looking to save for such future luxuries, it is no wonder that Doug and Michelle believe they do not have the money to give generously to anyone or anything at present.

Lowe's, the chain of home improvement stores, expresses with its brand slogan the sentiment that the Arnolds and countless other Americans assume: "Never Stop Improving." For the Arnolds, the idea is to never settle into or be content with what you have. One always needs to look to the future for better and more. Satisfaction with what one already has is not acceptable; there must always be room for improvement. There is a good side to this, of course. But the outlook also gives the Arnolds permission to indulge (and worry a lot about) their own desires without being responsible to or for anyone else. When there is always room for "improvement" in what one possesses, the threshold of the kind of wealth that might justify even a modicum of generosity moves farther away with every step up. People like the Arnolds will probably never reach a point of having enough to give more away.

Continually clamoring for more and clinging to material security, the Arnolds are building a fortress to protect their assets and reduce the possibility of intrusion by others who may be in need or could benefit from a share of their resources. This is a continual work in progress built by tightening their grip on resources. At the same time, their efforts are relentlessly buffeted by an anxiety over possibly not having enough, which drives them to seek even more material goods that they hope will provide happiness: a private pool, a beach house, new cars, and so on. But the happiness that the Arnolds desire is fragile and, according to research and folk wisdom alike, also an illusion. It actually exposes that which it seems to seek to hide—namely, the anxieties of the relatively privileged people who pursue it. And to some extent, they are delusional in holding opposing ambitions of happiness. The Arnolds want a close-knit community but they are unwilling to spend much time helping their friends solve problems and they refuse to let their daughters attend the local schools that bus people in. They want to feel comfortable financially, but they stretch their dollars to the max and keep a tight budget with little room for error. Michelle tells us that her stress ulcer days are over, but she still is worried to the point of insomnia. They say the deck makes them happy, but they want a pool and beach house, too. They want to take care of themselves and think people should take care of their own, but they refuse to see how vulnerable this logic left them when they both faced the possibility of unemployment.

Meanwhile, the kind of happiness the Arnolds want for themselves remains and always will remain at a distance, held beyond their reach by the need to obtain an online degree, survive the current company restructuring, build the pool, buy the next car, and so on. Happiness is something to continue working toward, something not yet reached, beyond the horizon's line-sight—not something to realize in the present. The compass points that guide the Arnolds' thinking are material success, financial security, personal opportunities, and some comforts in life, but we know that none of these will guide them to true satisfaction and fulfillment in life, just a hunger for more. Happiness will remain elusive.

The Ramirez Family: "The World's Just Going Down the Drain"

On the other side of the country and a notch in status below the Arnolds, "Danny and Sylvia Ramirez," parents of a precocious five-year-old girl, rent a three-bedroom house in a mostly Latino service-industry workhorse suburb east of San Diego. Off the interstate exit heading toward the Ramirez house, the homes are new, with tiled roofs and young palm trees. These residents enjoy local "lifestyle centers" of frozen yogurt shops and upscale home improvement stores offering gracious parking lots with crisply painted lines. This part of town is something like the West Coast equivalent of the South Carolina exurb in which the Arnolds reside. But after traveling a few miles away from the arterial freeway that connects the vast expanse of Southern California, markers of affluence trickle off and then disappear at the suburb's extremities of crumbling strip malls and the tightly packed residential areas, one of which the Ramirezes call home.

The 1970s ranch-style homes in their neighborhood were designed as single-family units, but many (including the Ramirez family, who live with Sylvia's mother and uncle) split the rent with extended family members or others to make ends meet. Here, life is not easy, with high rents, uncomfortably close living quarters, and an unemployment rate of nearly 12 percent at the time of our interviews. With storage warehouses within eyesight and jagged cracks in the asphalt from the hot sun and earthquakes, their neighborhood block has a gritty feel to it, even though there is little obvious disrepair. The Ramirez family hates it here, especially Sylvia. "Are you scared yet?," Sylvia asks, as she fumbles with the double-locked steel screen door, "Yeah, you see what I mean now, right? This is not a nice place to be. You locked your car, right?" Sylvia, in her mid-thirties, has prominent cheekbones and long black hair that swings along her lower back. In the phone conversations to set up these interviews with the family, Sylvia made it clear that she was unhappy here—"Why would you want to come here? It's like living in Mexico." "Illegal aliens," the term she uses to refer to her neighbors, are the bane of her existence. California would do well to adopt Arizona's controversial immigration policies, she thinks: "I wish that we had to drive through fifty checkpoints here in California, too." Sylvia appears to be Latina and her married name has Latino roots, but she makes no mention of this. Sylvia is part Native American, which she lists, along with being overweight and a mother, when we ask her to describe herself in her own words. When it comes to possible personal changes, she would most like to lose weight. In general, she holds herself in low esteem. When asked how her closest family and friends would describe her, she says, "Annoying. I don't know. Crabby, annoying." She counts two friends, her husband, and her mother as people with whom she is close.

During the interview, it becomes clear that Sylvia is floating through life. She is not relationally connected to many people or groups and does not occupy many social roles. Money figures prominently into how she understands and values life and the world, so it is unsurprising that Sylvia sees her life purpose as earning money, even though she is currently unemployed. When asked about her highest life priorities, she responds, "I don't have that high of any goals, I would be happy with just having a job. Not even a very [big] income, just an income." In the meantime, she whittles away her free time, perhaps unsure of the next step or overwhelmed by her limited options, given that she has only a GED, and not much work experience. "I don't do nothing. I'm on my computer and I'm watching TV. That's all I do," she declares. "If I'm online, I'm either playing Farmville [a farming-simulation social networking game] or I'm doing a survey."

When we ask Sylvia what would count as living a good life, her answer is simple: "Just being able to be happy." And when we ask for clarification, she returns to her disdain for the neighbors. "What would make me happy? What would make me happy is if I didn't live in this neighborhood with Mexican music and dogs and chickens." We ask why she does not confront the neighbors about the noise, and she deadpans, "I don't talk Spanish." Instead of confronting reality, she preoccupies herself with the infeasible goal of moving away to a better neighborhood and bigger house. "I'm hoping we find a house soon, just me my husband and my daughter are going to probably live there. And I get a job." Over the previous year or two, Danny and Sylvia made offers on several homes, but all of their offers were declined. With a bankruptcy in their financial history, finding a suitable home is not an easy task. In the meantime, Sylvia has life on hold and is waiting to move before she looks for a job. After our interviews wrapped up on a Sunday evening, the neighbors began playing a tuba and trumpet along to a CD. "The mariachi band has started up," Danny jokes, to which Sylvia responds, "Fucking immigrants," under her breath. She is clearly unhappy and stressed out by her living situation.

Before writing Sylvia off as a noise-sensitive, mindless bigot, it is worth considering how she came to this attitude and what fuels the contempt she has for people who migrate to the United States.

> It's a lot of different things. Like I know my mother was really sick and she couldn't get any help, she couldn't get any help, but we feel like the illegal immigrants come here and they get all these benefits. They come here and they have their thirty children. The people that were born here, worked here their whole lives, can't even get any help from the government.

Sylvia is frustrated because her mother could not attain government aid in a time of need, despite the fact that Sylvia and her family play by the supposed rules: they are natural citizens and gainfully employed. It upsets her to think that the benefits she and her family deserve by virtue of paying into the programs with their tax dollars go to "illegal immigrants" instead. According to Sylvia, undeserving others are taking what her mother needs—what the government owes her. Sylvia does not comment on the perspective of immigrants, legal or illegal, who face a labor market with a propensity to treat them as chattel. Instead, she homes in on those factors that should work in her family's favor. Exasperated, she believes that "the illegal immigrants" who "get all these benefits" and "have their thirty children" are cheating and abusing the system—and the system, she believes, is a zero-sum game with scarce resources.

When we ask Sylvia how she makes *moral* decisions, her answer turns exclusively on the law. A house down the block, she says, grows and sells non-medical marijuana and she thinks this is wrong. Why? "Cause it's wrong. It's, it's wrong, come on. It's illegal, it's against the law." Is there anything else other than the law that makes it wrong? "I don't know," she becomes exasperated, "It's just, it's the law, it's against the law, right? It's doing drugs. It's bad." In this framework, people are not responsible for one another and do not need to cultivate their moral sensibilities. We as individuals simply need to play by the rules. In turn, the law takes on the burden of informing people what is and is not moral and sets the boundaries of obligations to others. Taking Sylvia's logic to its furthest extent, people are essentially absolved of non-legal responsibilities to others. No morality exists above the law.

And because, as far as Sylvia is concerned, there are no laws that draw lines on how much is too much for people to own or consume, as long as people can afford it, she sees no problem with any amount of materialism, even crass indulgence. She refuses to stipulate any self-imposed limit to spending—a five-thousand-square-foot home? Fine. Several BMWs? Also fine. However, her husband, Danny, points out, "If the quantity is there, and somebody else wasn't gonna be shorted because [of it]. . . But if somebody else wasn't gonna get the opportunity to buy one because somebody wanted to buy them all then, no, of course not, no." Sylvia and Danny also think it is fine to donate money generously, but just as people should be free to buy what they wish, people should also be free to donate what they wish, or to abstain from giving. As Sylvia succinctly puts it, "I think it's good and it is optional." Aside from the occasional change given to a panhandler, the Ramirezes do not donate anything of their $60,000 income (which although above the national median, is still a modest income in their particular location). When we ask Sylvia if she would be interested in practicing more generosity later in life, she tells us, "If I had money to give away, then I would do it." At first glance, her answer seems antithetical to her de facto operating mode of utilitarian individualism. But when she explains *why* she would give money away, her desire to give still fits her framework. "Because it would be a tax write-off credit," she says. "Most of it is. If I had the money to give away, I would." In other words, as long as it is in her own direct financial interest, she is willing to donate money. This common refrain for Sylvia, like Doug and Michelle Arnold, involves making plans of actions based on personal or family self-interest. It is stressful enough to provide for one's own family, without thinking about the needs of others.

Sylvia is socially isolated, so her motivation and desire to do what is best for herself and the family makes sense. "I'm not religious. I don't really go very many places. I don't feel like I belong to any specific group. Family, that's it," she says. So even if she did have money to give away, she does not have a specific place or cause to which she would readily donate. The same pertains with volunteering. "I have never, ever thought about volunteering. I've never read anything about volunteering, I don't even know where you would start when it comes to volunteering," she admits. She does, however, occasionally donate material goods—food and clothing—to people who are in predicaments similar to the ones she faced growing up. Sylvia's life as a child was chaotic and she moved around a lot. After her dad left the family, she and her mother moved from apartment to apartment in Southern California. Her mom worked a couple of jobs to make ends meet, and Sylvia grew up as a latchkey kid without much structure. Life was not easy, and it did not get any easier after she turned eighteen. Sylvia recalls her first apartment as roach-infested, but she had nowhere else to go. Given the difficult circumstances of her formative years, it is understandable that she looks out for herself and her family. She remains thankful for the food bank that helped her out in that first year on her own. She recalls them as being very generous, so she likes to donate canned goods every year when her postal carrier asks for donations around the holidays. Although Sylvia does not make a connection to her own childhood in this, she also enjoys giving her daughter's hand-me-downs to the neighbors.

> The little girls next door, the dad's not working and the mom's [working at a fast food restaurant] and there's four little girls and the mom's never home. So I felt bad for the little girls, they're always really dirty, and they smell like pee, and you know, they're really dirty. And they got their dad watching them and he's always, you know, it's a man, always, you know, he's a man. I feel like I'm trying to help them a little bit, and if it's just like old clothes. And my daughter's clothes that are old aren't really nasty and old, they still look brand new.

Sylvia here is giving away old clothing that her daughter has outgrown, offering aid without drawing on her own family's needed resources. These acts display Sylvia's ability to be generous, but she hesitates to offer to care for the neighbor girls every so often or purchase new clothing for them.

In general, Sylvia operates in a mode of self-reliance. This becomes especially apparent when we ask her about her possible religious experiences or beliefs. As a little girl, Sylvia saw a ghost, so she is pretty sure there is an afterlife, but she no longer practices or believes the Catholic faith she grew up with. "I believe that my thoughts about the Catholic Church have changed with all of the priests molesting children." She does not believe in God, a personal force, a heaven, or a hell, mostly because she does not find anything personally useful in religion.

> I'm sure it helps some people. I'm sure a lot of people go and they get stuff from it. It doesn't do anything for me. I just know that I've tried it in the past, I didn't get anything from it. So, I don't think about it, I don't sit here thinking about it.

Others may need religion, but Sylvia prides herself in thinking that she is self-reliant and resourceful enough to not need the extra help. Danny also left the Catholic faith, but whereas Sylvia sees faith as a crutch that she does not need, he sees it as unable to bear the weight of those who most want to use it as a crutch. Danny told us, "A friend of mine died. He committed suicide, I didn't know about it for a long time. We were real close, he was a close friend of mine, and it was sad for me when I found out." This news snapped the already brittle thread of faith Danny had been holding on to and he soon renounced his Catholic beliefs. The wound of his friend's death left a scar that disfigured Danny's view of the world. In the midst of the evil and suffering he saw, the presence of the good and loving God he had felt as a child and young man became preposterous to him. "So when I found out about it years later," Danny says, "it was hard. It was difficult, because I bear, I myself I bear, I feel like I bear guilt of responsibility for it, no matter what." He says he feels guilty because:

> The last letter I got from him, I didn't realize it at the time cause I was so caught up in my life, but I think that he was, he was having, the guy always had trouble. I always kept him out of trouble, he was always—the guy went A.W.O.L. a couple times and I used to have to go get him and bring him

back. He was a wild, crazy person. He just was. . . . I got busy, and I probably didn't keep in contact with him as best as I should've cause I got a letter from him saying he was in trouble. And I didn't, I should have answered him, I didn't. And I should've, I feel like sometimes he was asking me for help, it didn't seem so, but now that I dwell on it more, it feels like you know it's, he might have been, I don't know. It's just a question that's there.

Danny struggled to get the words out and became visibly upset at this point of the interview. The question of whether his continued presence could have made a difference for his friend haunts him. He still ruminates on the possibility of what might have happened had he not been "so caught up in my life." He seems stuck on this thought.

Danny is stuck in other ways, too. He sees a worsening of humanity and is anxious. Even though his struggling over the loss of his friend suggests a high regard for the value of other people, Danny is not so sure. "I think that the world's just going down the drain. I think we lose who we are, people in general have lost their humanity." Can anything constructive be done, or is his motivation to make a difference sapped? "No, I wouldn't say it makes me not want to do anything. It makes me wonder what the future has in store, what is the future, basically, what will happen? I feel that if it doesn't change, it's just basically over." We ask him more about this shift—when did it occur and why? He cannot explain it. He only knows that a crack in human solidarity is expanding into a chasm. "I think society in general is just going down," he says.

> It's just like what I said about people not caring enough. I mean, you can't even read the newspaper or turn on the news without seeing something. It's horrible to watch the news, if you really think about it, you sit there and watch it, it's like depressing, it's horrible. It's just death and murder, and it's the worst possible things you can imagine. And that's just the news, that's just the news, that's the things you hear about. But it just goes back to people not caring.

When housing developments for the upper-middle class expanded in the hills near Danny's house, he noticed an increase in roadkill, and wildlife fleeing the construction sites.

> It was getting bad, and I'm thinkin', and I started really thinking about it. What's causing this? It's the development, it's causing all the wildlife to run into the street and I started thinking further, deeper, and this is our physical

impact on our environment here. Our greed has caused this. Because somebody's greedy and wants this land for money, we're destroying our environment, the wildlife, because of greed. And it's not gonna change. I don't
know if by nature we're just greedy. It made me think about our impact on
the environment, and God, this is bad. So after that I started thinking more
about it, you know, and it's like wow, we're going to run our planet into the
ground if something's not done.

So Danny believes that people are changing, a process that has been
about thirty years or so in the making. People do not look out for one
another; they have no regard for the environment. Like Danny in his
own friend's time of need, they are too caught up in themselves. Danny
thinks that "people should care more about each other instead of themselves so much. It just seems like the latter seems more toward that
way, just about the individual and I think that's the problem with people
nowadays." Yet he himself does very little in his life to help others.
One recent afternoon, he witnessed a crime and no one bothered to
intervene—including Danny.

Nobody's worried about anybody else. For instance, I was coming home
from work one day, taking the bus home instead of having my wife pick
me up, because I was angry at her from an argument we had. So I was in [a
nearby city], waiting for the bus, it was about three o'clock in the afternoon,
and I see this guy with a bicycle get beat up on the street in broad daylight.
And not a soul lifted their hand to help. And that made me think like, "Wow,
is this the, what kind of society we live in these days, where this could occur
and not a person cares?"

We ask whether he thought people were afraid to help or just did
not care.

It seemed like nobody, well, combination of both. But I would say more the
latter, that people just didn't care too much. They were two bums or two
drug users, just you know, alcoholics, I don't know what they were. That's
a notorious area for drugs and prostitution, I imagine they were just drug
users. But just because of who they were, I imagine, nobody cared.

Do you think, we asked, people would have cared more if they were
wearing business suits or something? "Mmm, probably not so much.

Maybe a little bit more, maybe they would've called the police or the police would've intervened. Not so much, the basic thing about people [is] just not caring about one another thriving." Danny thinks that the victim would have been helped by others a few decades back, but now, no one can be bothered to care and help—including Danny. He not only failed to intervene and aid the victim, but he also did not feel compelled to explain his inaction to us. He simply seemed to think that no action would make a difference. He recognized that he is part of the downward trend he described, but also seems to think that his observation of the change somehow places him beyond the very demise he laments.

Danny has good intentions. He says he would step up and provide support for anyone in desperate need. And he thinks the fact that no one bothered to help the assaulted man at the bus stop is grievous. Yet he himself does little to act. His anxiety about the world appears to make him apathetic. Danny envisions the world as a place gone awry. He retreats into his own perceived busyness, by which he is overwhelmed to the point of lethargy. He does not see his refusal to aid the assaulted victim as a reason to feel guilty. He does not see the need for a possible change in himself that might require a personal action or stand. It is not particularly surprising that Danny is not interested in generosity. But, unlike Sylvia, who is pragmatic about their lack of financial giving, Danny believes the family could give more and carries around some guilt about this. He is aware that there are needy organizations, but he falls into the trap he laments of people who "don't care enough."

> I think about financial giving. Most of the time the thought is there, but usually I don't follow through. And I can't give a reason why. I believe it's just I'm so caught up in other things that I just never take the time to actually do things. And it's not just that, it's just a lot of things in general.

Similarly, Danny used to give blood, but says the donation site now is too far away and he does not have the time or gas money to make the trip. Time is especially scarce. Recall this quote of his from Chapter 2:

> Modern life is just fast-paced, everything. Everything. It's just go go go go go, everything automated, everything's supposed to be designed to make our lives easier, but I feel that it just makes it harder. We're always in a hurry to be everywhere. For me that's what it does. Everything's

designed to make it easier, but, in actuality, I think it just makes it that much more hurried. If you really think about it, you're always trying to get somewhere.

Yet Danny is not actually as busy as he describes himself to be. He has a few friends from work, "the guys," but he doesn't spend much time with them outside of the job. On an ordinary day, he goes to work in the morning, promptly returns home in the evenings, and usually stays home until it is time to go to work again the following morning. He does not see himself as having much of a purpose: "I can't say I know my own purpose. I do and I don't. I mean, yeah, it's to take care and provide and do the best I can for my family. But I don't know if I exactly know where I'm going with it." Not believing that one person can make any difference in the world does not encourage a strong sense of purpose.

Similarly, it is difficult to practice generosity when basic thresholds of comfort are unmet. Sylvia and Danny's house does not have air-conditioning, and with the temperature reaching the mid-90s in the late afternoon, it has a stifling and dank feeling that seemed to add to the difficulty of finding a motivation to do much of anything. A lot of their personal leisure time is spent independently. Danny played video games over the course of four hours while we interviewed Sylvia. She, in turn, spent much of her time on the computer when we interviewed Danny, playing Farmville and checking her Facebook page. Some technology was constantly up and running, keeping them from ever having a real conversation. During our time spent with the family on a Sunday evening, mostly ignoring their daughter's persistent attempts to find a playmate, Sylvia and Danny spent a few hours watching the Travel Channel. Even with the family together, Sylvia and Danny both seem to prefer spending time alone in the same space. While watching one episode about seven natural wonders in the world, Sylvia asked why they even bother watching it, since they will never travel anywhere like that themselves. Danny replied that that is the whole point, and began to doze, while Sylvia opened her laptop to play more Farmville. That was the last conversation of the evening.

With fading dreams of moving into the solid middle class, the Ramirez family navigates ever-tightening financial straits. Sylvia, vapid and reactionary, complains about a scarcity of public goods like healthcare for her mom and vents disgust with her entitled and annoying neighbors. Danny, ponderous and disquieted, has grown anxious about how selfish Americans no longer seem to care about others, yet he represents the very trend he bemoans. For both, their primary response is to retreat and accept apathy, a response made understandable by their limited opportunities, hardships, and lack of efficacy. In many ways, generous behavior is a form of advocacy, a cultural practice closely associated with middle- and upper-middle-class characteristics.[1] Neither Sylvia nor Danny is particularly interested in or inspired by generosity. Neither places much hope or stock in their communities. And neither is happy, oriented toward personal growth, or facing a brighter future.

Ungenerous Americans and Life Well-being

The particularities of Michelle and Doug Arnold's and Danny and Sylvia Ramirez's lives are unique to these two families. But their stories provide glimpses of the bigger picture of what an ungenerous life in America looks and sounds like. Not everyone we talked to was as overtly callous as the Arnolds. And not everyone voiced the same concerns about the demise of humanity as Danny, or the same lack of empathy for others as Sylvia. But their interviews did highlight some of the recurrent themes that came up in our discussions with other ungenerous Americans. We turn now to these other voices. Our particular task in what follows is to relate what they say about their lack of generosity to their well-being or lack thereof.

Physical Health

Like their generous counterparts, many ungenerous Americans face setbacks in health. Some have chronic conditions, like Crohn's disease or diabetes. Others are dealing with the ramifications of prior or ongoing alcohol or cigarette addictions. Many face the health burdens of obesity. When it comes to physical health, our interviews validate what we found in Chapter 1: ungenerous Americans tend to be less healthy than those who regularly practice acts of generosity. As we will show in the examples of Henry and Cynthia Fountain and Martin Cizek (Chapter 5 case studies), generous people tend not to feel so stressed or harried. Life for them often does not move at the frenetic pace perceived by many ungenerous people. Generous people make time to cook meals at home, eat well, take evening strolls, ride bikes with their kids, and run with their friends. In addition, since they are generally more social and active in their communities, few highly generous Americans live sedentary lives or find their time zapped by a full DVR queue, or surfing the Internet. Lower stress levels and more expansive social lives also seem to be linked with a lower use of alcohol, cigarettes, and other health-reducing substances. None of the generous people we interviewed currently suffers from a debilitating addiction, although two are recovered addicts. The patterns and lifestyle choices associated with practicing generosity promote bodily health, and their undermining tarnishes health.

On the whole, it is clear from our interviews that ungenerous Americans suffer greater life stress and, per Danny Ramirez and Michelle Arnold, perceive life to be moving at a more frenetic pace. Their perceptions of life as overbearing and burdensome can lead to poor eating and exercise habits. When time is seen as short, it is easier to eat fast food, takeout dinners, and frozen meals, which are usually less nutritious and more expensive than a good home-cooked meal. Preparing the latter is more time-consuming and many Americans we interviewed deem it an additional stress they want to avoid. It is also easier to spend time surfing the Internet or television cable channels to unwind than it is to exercise at the gym or take a walk at the end of the day.

Our direct observations in the inside of people's homes confirm this explanation. Whenever possible, our research team took digital photos of the kitchens, contents of refrigerators and pantries, and other rooms in their houses. We also noted the food and beverages consumed during our interviews and observations. Sometimes we accompanied people on their weekly trips to the grocery store. The results? The households of ungenerous Americans purchase and consume more processed foods and sodas than generous households. Though upper-middle-class households tend to consume fewer processed foods when compared to lower-middle-class households, generous upper-middle-class households eat healthier meals than ungenerous upper-middle-class households. In addition, although we suggested sharing a family meal as one possible activity to join in (shopping trips, errands, and any typical afternoon or evening were other suggestions), none of the ungenerous households that we interviewed invited us to share, let alone observe, a meal at home with them. This suggests the plausible possibility that ungenerous people are less comfortable practicing hospitality and less inclined to invite non-family members to join family dinner. It could also mean that meals shared as a family may not be part of the household's daily rhythm. Occasionally, we noticed people preparing and eating meals on their own. Others preferred fast food. Randall Weir, a single dad in Northern California earning a solidly middle-class $60,000 salary, but not a generous person, skips breakfast and finds it easier to order his meals from a particular fast-food restaurant's dollar menu, a habit he maintains even when his teenage son is with him for the week. The Arnolds inhaled take-home pizzas that Doug picked up in a rush on his way home with the girls in the car.

The time crunch that ungenerous Americans often feel leads not only to less healthy eating habits, but also translates into less frequent exercise and physical activity. Thinking they are already too busy and lacking time, they also believe they do not have time to exercise. In reality, however, exercise is regenerative and known to boost energy, optimize cognitive functioning, and decrease stress. Even a twenty-minute stroll has a subtle but noticeably positive impact on mood that can last throughout the day. By "stressing" our bodies physically, we ease mental stress. By contrast, over time a sedentary lifestyle can lead to chronic stress, which often complicates more serious mental conditions, such as depression or anxiety disorders. In response, some people get into unhealthy temporary fixes, like upticks in sugar consumption, alcohol use, or smoking cigarettes, all of which further impede physical health.

With all of this in mind, it is not surprising that many of the ungenerous Americans we interviewed are unhappy with the numbers they see when they step onto their bathroom scales. While all of those who are overweight would like to shave off some pounds, few are very successful. Rose Steinecker in Illinois, who is part of a church group to help members slim down, makes an effort, but reaching her target weight is a constant struggle. "I've gone to it for, probably, about three or four years," Rose tells us, "It's more like, they do try to lose weight, but they like to sit and talk. And I'd like to do more learning or try to keep myself from gaining or to lose weight." Most who struggle with their weight, however, are more like Elaine Woods, a Californian in her forties. "I wish I cared more about exercising. I really wish I could just set aside the time to do it, but I don't. So, I wish I had more self-discipline in that way," she tells us. Elaine is not alone. Many of the ungenerous Americans we interviewed are troubled by their lack of exercise, but ultimately are apathetic about it or over-whelmed to the point of apathy. "Sarah Walker" in Michigan, for instance, tells us, "I'm an obese person myself, and I'm trying to work on that, it's just something I'm struggling with." But, in his interview, her husband, "Ken," complains that she does not take real steps to become a healthier person, and Sarah herself offers no specifics about how she aims to whittle down the weight. Taking control of their bodies, they think, requires more self-discipline than they think they have, so they give up. Even though their weight or inactive lifestyles or poor diets bother them, the ungener-ous Americans we interviewed rarely act on their concerns or make con-crete plans to lead healthier lives, unlike the generous with similar health concerns. "Gabriel Ellison" of Washington, DC, for instance, knows what he needs to do to get into shape, he just does not do it: "The way you're supposed to be active, like get to the gym and do this and do that, I don't do that." "Jillian Ramos," Gabriel's fiancée, is in her second trimester of pregnancy and shares his outlook. When we ask her if there is anything she would like to change about herself, she tells us that she is unhappy with her weight, but feels helpless:

I would like to lose weight, but physically, it's just like, I don't know if I could ever do that. I try eating-wise, they always tell you don't eat big por-tions. Okay, so I don't eat big portions, and I only eat three meals a day, so they're like alright so make it three more, make it six. I always come back to three meals. And then not being active. . . [trails off].

Even though Jillian's doctor advises her to eat smaller meals through-out the day to maintain her metabolism and ward off hunger, Jillian does not follow through on that more time-consuming plan and keeps returning to larger meals. Jillian's heavy weight also adversely affects her reproductive health. After trying for a few frustrating years, Jillian and Gabriel were only able to conceive with the help of hormonal stimu-lants. Now that she is pregnant, she worries about how her diet will affect the baby:

I listened to a heartbeat like two weeks ago, sounds healthy and everything. So I'm just hoping and praying it's good. Because my diet, I'm not the type of person that eats healthy. But, I don't know, I'm trying and I don't want nothing bad or negative to happen, cause I don't think I would be able to deal with that stress, of having an abnormal baby. So, I just worry about everything.

Jillian here seems more worried about how a special-needs baby would affect her own stress levels than about the challenges her child would face. In any case, she is doing her best to eat more fresh fruits and vegetables than usual. Still, her own bodily health and potentially her child's health are compromised by her excessive weight and her not eating well.

Other ungenerous Americans, much like their generous counterparts, have chronic health conditions. Stacey Spiegel in Connecticut lives with Crohn's disease. Adam Berry of Nevada, only in his early forties, has gout. Kimberly Little has a painful ovarian cyst and her health insurance does not cover its removal. "Shelly Martinez" in Georgia has Type 2 diabetes and can no longer control her sugar level with oral medication alone. "The doctor's got me on insulin now," she says, "so I know it's for the best, but it's still kind of depressing." The connection between physical and mental health is evident here, as dealing with her illness is "kind of depressing." Depression or anger about health problems is another pattern we noticed in our interviews with ungenerous people. They tend to be more upset by the news and experience of poor health, or even just the reality of becoming older, than do more generous Americans. For example, when we ask what had made her the most sad or depressed about life in the past couple of years, "Alice Dunlap" of South Carolina talks about her general decline in health as she ages: "My health, that's deteriorating, and it happens to everyone as they get older." She also mentions that "being alone," that is, living alone, is difficult. Again, the ungenerous people we spoke with experience more loneliness, and this particularly shapes how they *perceive* their health problems. Because they more often face their health problems alone, we heard more pessimism, and even a sense of defeat, in many of them when they talked about health problems.[2] As a result, when compared with generous people who face similar chronic conditions, diseases, or complications, ungenerous Americans tend to experience a more pervasive depression or anger regarding health problems. People physically benefit not only from the nurturing, care, and support offered by loved ones when healing from routine surgery or optimizing the prognosis of a life-threatening illness, but also from a sense of encouragement that they are not facing an illness alone.[3] In our interviews, this difference was not expressed in outright admissions of loneliness, but rather, in stark contrast with the generous interviewees, an absence of support networks and mentions of how other people accommodate and support them.

"Kyle Jones" in South Carolina, for instance, has his fair share of health problems and is as a result dismayed. "I got epilepsy and my back's going out, and that overweight thing's really kicking my ass right now, so if

I could fix or work on that, it would help." A diagnosis of epilepsy would certainly unnerve anyone, but how did Kyle handle it? "When I got epilepsy I was pretty pissed off. I was pissed off for a long time about that." In fact, he is still "pissed off." He seems unable to move beyond his anger to a state of acceptance and constructive response. He did not mention it, but his wife "Ruby" told us how she helps him adjust to epilepsy by driving him to and from work, regulating his medications, and listening to his frustrations. Kyle mentions turning to drugs and alcohol at an earlier point in life for self-medication, but chain-smoking (he went through half a pack during our interview with him) seems to ease his anger presently. Similarly, "Bryan Johnson" in Washington, who is generally upset with the direction his life is headed, knocks back three beers during the two hours of our first interview with him, and later that night at dinner, he had another two beers. The second day of interviews was much the same. Drinking for Bryan seems to be a coping mechanism, although the extent of his drinking runs the risk of damaging his health.

As a whole, these examples illustrate that ungenerous Americans experience more health problems, are more frustrated by their health challenges, and are pessimistic about their ability to improve or heal. While physical health is influenced by a variety of factors, we believe that we can safely propose that a lifestyle lacking in generosity is yet another factor affecting bodily health. This is also the case for mental health, to which we turn next.

Depression and Mental Wellness

Almost all of the ungenerous people we spoke with experienced some form or another of unhappiness, but at least eleven people (slightly more than one-third of the total number of interviewees) described common symptoms of depression or anxiety disorders. Their reasons for feeling depressed, anxious, and angry are varied, but loneliness and work-related worries are common themes. In this section, we recount only a few of their struggles with mental wellness.

Kimberly Little in Oregon has recently taken the positive step to seek counseling as a way to confront her negative outlook on life:

> I'm a good mother, good wife, but there's just some things that I'm working on with my counselor right now. I don't look very good upon myself, so, it's kind of hard to list good things [about me], because I mainly focus on the negatives right now. Next Tuesday will be my third meeting with the counselor, but it's coming along. It's just a lot of stuff that, like I said, it's happened in my past and what not, my mother being the main reason why I can't deal with things as easily as I used to.

Kimberly admits that she focuses more on the negatives than the positives in life and suffers from low self-esteem. She also "can't deal with things as easily as [she] used to." Throughout our discussion, it is clear that Kimberly feels stuck in life, like she is not going anywhere. Sarah Walker in Michigan remembers being "often very bored and lonely and depressed" as a child, an outlook that has not dissipated with adulthood. She has moments when she feels "frazzled. I feel for the most part, in control, with maybe moments of out-of-control, or feel like maybe my sink is shipping, or ship is sinking, sorry." Her tongue-tied moment seems indicative of the stress she endures. "I feel very hurried. Very stressed out and busy." Kyle Jones of South Carolina, who says he is "stressed all the time. . . I'm going 90 miles an hour at work all the time," also experiences anxiety and depression related to his difficult financial standing. He tells us, "When I moved up [north] for a year, I got laid off for six months. I wasn't working, I was depressed. I got real bad, almost started drinking again." Others describe even more robust forms of depression and anxiety.

Corrine Cizek, a physician who works fifty or sixty hours a week, recalls giving a deposition for a court case. The trial was taxing and she could not sleep or eat well.

> It devastated [me]. I'd come home stressed out, worried about the court case, having to make the deposition, having to meet with the lawyers, and [my husband] said what are we going to do when you're actually sued? And I said I'm going to have to see a psychiatrist because I wasn't sleeping or eating well at the time.

Corrine acknowledges her struggles to control her anger. "My family would tell me that I have a really bad temper, that I need to control my anger and emotions." If she could get a better handle on her emotions, she told us, life would improve. "I cry easily at TV shows and movies," she explains, but the main problem is the anger pent up inside her: "I wish I could be able to control my anger and yelling." The issue of yelling comes up throughout her interview: "When I feel like I'm out of control and I don't feel like things are going my way, I start yelling and I get angry." At work, she is able to keep her patience, she reports, but at home, she lets loose. "I've [yelled at] my daughter and husband, both of them." Later she says:

> You know, it came from my dad. The thing is, I hate to blame it on the parents, but my dad, everybody would say your dad is such a nice man, he's a wonderful man. And I would say that's how people would describe me at work. People, friends, they would be shocked by me yelling at my husband

and my daughter. I told that to my aunt and she said, "yeah that's not good, but I just can't imagine you doing it, you should stop," and I said, yeah I should. That I think I got from my dad, who used to always say, "Control your emotions just focus on your studies, work hard, and control your emotion." He studied hard, but he never controlled his own emotions.

When Corrine talks about suffering postpartum depression, she mentions that it was so difficult, in part, because she did not have support from her family. "I had postpartum depression," she explains, "because I didn't have family support, but I had my husband to help me and he thinks that I had depression while I was pregnant." When she and Martin learned that they were unintentionally pregnant a second time, Corrine considered an abortion, "the idea of being pregnant again scared me," but she miscarried instead. "I sometimes let my emotions run me and, not a good thing, because then if I'm upset by something I feel like nothing gets done and I'm just feeling overwhelmed and frazzled."

Most people feel overwhelmed from time to time, but Corrine's chronic and grating anger gnaws away at her well-being. Corrine experiences a distinct sense of loneliness, which corresponds to her memories of having to rely exclusively on herself in times of duress. She talks about having had an unsupportive family during her pregnancy. And she gets upset if "nothing gets done," implying that she will end up taking on the responsibility to fix things, just as she takes on the responsibility to be her family's breadwinner even though she hates her job. Similarly, even though Corrine herself was not on trial—she was one of many doctors who handled the suing patient—she takes a great deal of personal responsibility for the wrong that was done, to the extent that it impeded her ability to sleep or eat well. Overall, she takes on inordinate personal responsibility and holds herself to impossibly high standards. As someone who, she tells us, has little desire to practice generosity, she fails not only to extend graciousness and mercy to others in times of troubles, but also to herself. Believing that people ought to take responsibility for their own lot in life, she is also loath to ask others for help, even when it is clearly in her best interest to do so.

What Corrine describes about herself—the yelling, depression, and feeling so frazzled that she cannot control her emotions—is not uncommon. Rose Steinecker in Illinois, for example, admits that she gets upset with her kids too easily and, like Corrine, also relates it back to her upbringing.

I'm a yelling type of person. My mom raised us, she yelled at us all the time. So my children, I yelled at them for years and years and years and Dale, he would get mad, like, "You don't treat your kids that way, you know?" But I've been workin' on it, so I've realized that it's the wrong thing to do, and I've been workin' on it so I don't do it quite as much with my grandkids, but if I don't watch myself, I get yelling at 'em, screaming at 'em and stuff like that. Things upset me easily.

Her anger has dissipated some since she started taking a medication for depression, but Rose continues to struggle. Like Corrine, she feels on edge. "Maria Berry" in Nevada also finds her children to be a source of frustration. She talks at length about her frustration with life as a home-maker and her inability to relax:

> Most of the time, I'm very stressed. A lot of stress is because my kids, they make you go crazy sometimes. I can't relax. Maybe in the evening, I relax sometimes with my husband. I can sit down and nobody is asking me some-thing like [my daughter] does. And the other one, he is crying and protesting all the time and he wants something or he is making something bad.

It does not help matters that Maria feels alone in her community: "I feel like I'm living alone in this neighborhood," she says, "I don't belong here." Not surprisingly, Maria also has problems controlling her anger: "I get mad easily. . . It's hard to do a lot of stuff at the same time, you know? And right now, I'm not very happy. . . so I'm not doing too good, I guess." Her outlook on life seems particularly bleak when she confides that, "This is my life here, in my home. I don't have a social life, I don't have any friends. My parents live [far away], my friends are [far away], so I talk to them through the Internet or cell phone. So that is my life." Her hus-band, Adam, struggles with his own problems and is not of much help to Maria. He describes suffering bouts of anxiety and panic. "There's times I've woken up in the morning thinking about money, like how am I going to do this, how am I going to take care of this, and things like that," Adam explains. "So there's definitely a lot of anxiety there and stuff." His anxi-ety is mostly tethered to financial worries—understandably so, given that Adam and his family are in the process of filing for bankruptcy after years of living beyond their means and burning through their lines of credit.

As with the relatively stronger physical and mental health of generous people, we cannot peg ungenerous people's lack of physical or mental health squarely on the failure to practice generosity. The causes for these matters are obviously very complex. However, we have ample evidence that ungenerous Americans tend to be more dismayed about their health and more likely to experience symptoms of depression, anxiety, or other mental ailments. Generous practices seem to act as a buffer against these ailments. Generous people are more likely to feel connected to their communities, better able to forgive and extend mercy to others and therefore to themselves, and are generally not as worried about potential setbacks in life as are ungenerous Americans. Again, we believe the causal directions run both ways here. But one of those ways, evident in our research interviews, is that failing to practice generosity leaves one more vulnerable to lower levels of physical and mental health.

Personal Growth

Clearly and overwhelmingly, unlike the generous Americans we interviewed, the ungenerous do not strive toward personal growth. Nineteen of the thirty individuals we interviewed whom we classify as ungenerous expressed some general desire for personal growth, but fourteen of that nineteen told us they had very little desire to actually pursue it. Most are simply uninterested in developing and improving. While they appreciate some kinds of growth, like learning how to be a better dancer or moving up the career ladder, these goals are not connected, for them, to more expansive life projects that aim to build character or increase virtue. Rather, they tend to think of self-growth as involving the accumulation of skills, wealth, or travel experiences. They do not seem aware that the kind of growth associated with becoming a person with a deeper reservoir of purpose or integrity exists, or is different from the kind of growth achieved by doing something like taking cooking classes or learning Spanish to advance a career. On the whole, they do not make much of character development, largely lacking a vocabulary to even think about this kind of growth. Others, however, profess to want to grow personally and embark on self-improvement projects, but they feel helpless when it comes to following through on those intentions. According to this group, the very pursuit of growth is a self-defeating venture. Most of these people who desire growth believe that they are their own worst enemies when it comes to what keeps them from growing—that is, they think they are getting in their own way. A noticeable minority, by contrast, trace the source of their apparent growth impediment to external factors that they deem far beyond their control, which only reinforces their belief that growth is impossible, adding to their perceived helplessness and belief that the world is a depressing, treacherous place that is out to get them.

Alice Dunlap exemplifies the first type: "I guess at my age I'm kind of settled, I'm not gonna do a lot of changing at this point." Even though she is a cancer survivor and a relatively young retiree who travels the world—experiences which, one might assume, would increase an interest in personal growth—she says she is content with the status quo. Elaine Woods does not directly tell us that she is not interested in personal growth, but when we ask her if there's anything about herself that she would like to change or is working on changing, she responds simply, "At a very superficial level, I really wish I could sing and dance, but I can't." Elaine has a habit of falling into things rather than choosing them, which becomes clear during her interview. She describes her jobs, friendships, and career path as serendipitous happenstances. She did not look for work as a business consultant—actually, she had hoped to become a school librarian—but several years ago, the opportunity opened and she took it. Now, it seems too difficult to get back on the original path that she thinks would lead to greater happiness.

Still others we interviewed, like Bill Kalon of Southern California, define "personal growth" as the attainment of an outlandish paycheck or celebrity status. Realizing that this kind of growth is not plausible for him, he takes on a blasé attitude. "I do kind of worry sometimes like oh, what am I doing in order to be who I want to be?" he questions, "and am I going to be thirty-five years old and still working part-time? You know, stuff like that. I don't want to have a small fear of being unaccomplished." But this possible fear is erased when he reassesses his goals and creates a new standard of accomplishment:

I feel like I'm average. Meaning, like average goals: work at a job, make money. I'm not striving to be on the big screen, I don't have like huge aspirations. I'm just kind of keeping simple in the way that that's me, and I feel comfortable. Things are just routine. I'm a very routine person.

With these sorts of aspirations, personal growth is not a necessary ingredient of a rich and rewarding life. Others, like "Howard Philips," a Maryland man in his fifties and a retiree, fill their time with pursuits that they acknowledge as aimless. These sorts of activities crowd out time that could otherwise be devoted to growth. He is not interested in a real relationship, but Howard prefers to spend most of his time flirting or hooking up with women. He jokingly tells us that, "Most of the guys call me doggy-dog cause I like the women. 'Every time I see you, you're up in some woman's ways.'" How does he spend the rest of his time? He guesses he spends "about 60 percent" of his time watching television. Given that the average American watches about three hours of television every day, it is not surprising that many of the ungenerous people we interviewed are avid TV-watchers.[4] Take another example: Truman Wright, from Indiana. He is recently retired, he never married or partnered and does not have children. He lives a life without responsibilities to others and, other than the absence of an eight-hour work day, not much has changed in the past thirty years, since he started working as a mechanic. When we ask him what a typical day looks like, he lists the following:

> Drinking. Chase women. And sometimes just talk, just bullshit. Drink and bullshit. And chase women. And look at women, stuff like that. I have girlfriends off and on. Far as relationships go, I just try to hang in there the best I can, and whatever happens, happens. That's basically my life. Wake up everyday, get on the computer, watch TV, watch the court shows, have coffee, I normally do that till maybe about three or four o'clock in the afternoon.

The monotony of Truman's daily routine, and his noncommittal attitude of "whatever happens, happens," suggest that he does not actually feel the kind of control over life that research suggests is necessary to pursue growth. Still another example: Kyle Jones from South Carolina tells us that he gave up on his dreams of becoming a professional rodeo cowboy. After overcoming a drug addiction, he settled down and has a family but does not desire much else. It is interesting that he overcame something so significant, and yet now is content just to go to work, provide for the family, and watch movies. His wife tells us that he buys a new DVD at the end of each work week. By his own description, his is a static life of television-watching, chain-smoking, work, and family. His wife Ruby also reports, "I'm just kind of living the moment, and hope for the best." Still others, like "Liz Kalon" in California, do not know how to even answer the question about whether or not she has ideas for personal growth. She is so dedicated to the pleasures of television dramas and soap operas that she schedules her entire life, and our interviews, around her favorite shows.

Many of those we interviewed who admittedly spend most of their free time alone engaged in passive activities—like watching television, playing video games, and drinking—believe that personal growth is theoretically possible but personally unattainable in their cases. Many are stressed, understandably, by the time crunch wrought by working long hours. Others feel depleted by monotonous jobs that seldom lend pleasure or meaning. And still others, again understandably, are exhausted after directing an intense focus on navigating life on a tight budget, in which survival through the end of the month is an act of brinksmanship. Gabriel Ellison in Washington, DC, is one such respondent. Overwhelmed by his long hours on the job as a security guard, he spends the rest of his time at home on his laptop, with a television kept on for background noise and a parade of images that fill his sparsely furnished apartment. When we ask him if there are any ways in which he would like to grow as a person, he memorably responds, "I try to go through the world like water, just let everything brush off of me. So I just got to keep moving, get through things, keep people happy." Like so many, including Danny Ramirez and Michelle Arnold, who spend lots of time recovering from the stress and busyness of life with television, computer games, and shallow novels, Gabriel uses these as therapeutic distractions to shore up some semblance of leisure in life. He turns to these activities for restoration and a sense of peace, yet we know that these kinds of activities ultimately do not refresh people or function as an effective stress reliever, so the vicious cycle only continues.

As another example, Brandon Tribble in New York City spends most of his free time watching television and daydreaming about furthering his education and changing careers. Like many emerging adults hit hard by the Great Recession, he is in a long life transition, but also does not believe actual growth is possible until he can embark on something other than the bachelor's degree in computer science that he has been working toward over the previous six years. As he explains, "Well, I'm shifting. I would think the most important things in life are actually, I would say, having the will to do new things. I mean, being in control, self-control." After deciding that the field is not a good fit for him he maintains a vague aspiration of becoming a translator, but for the time being he feels a sense of aimlessness and lack of control.

Other ungenerous Americans we interviewed compare themselves with people who do achieve growth and then become frustrated with their own lack of ambition. One such person, Rose Steinecker from Illinois, is a homemaker in her late fifties mentioned earlier. After she completes her chores for the day and while her husband is still at work, she reports, "I just sit for four or five hours and watch TV." She would like to be more productive with her time. Specifically, she wants to become a person of greater religious faith and increase her knowledge about her beliefs:

> I would like to spend more time with the Lord. I'd like to take more time reading. I do every day a little bit, but I'd like to really cut out watching

TV as much. My husband, Dale, puts me to shame. He studies all the time. He reads, he's in communication with the Lord all the time, and I'm not anything like that.

While some people scale the steep inclines of personal growth, others, like Rose, feel like they're still at the base camp, unable to even reach the trailhead—or worse, still at home dreaming about a climb someday but too frustrated or uninterested to take the first steps. Rather than being inspired by Dale's pursuit of a faithful life, Rose simply feels put "to shame."

Finally, as noted above, some of the ungenerous people we interviewed believe that external circumstances prevent them growing or achieving their goals. Sarah Walker in Michigan, a homemaker and mother of eight children, would like to return to school or start a job outside the home. "I feel like I'm the old lady in the shoe," she complains, acknowledging that it will be quite some time before her children are out of the house and she can venture onto a different path. Meanwhile, she feels stuck with who and where she is. Stacey Spiegel, a white-collar worker from Connecticut looking for a new job, exemplifies this type when she cites the poor job market as robbing her of the control she needs to reach her goals. "These days with the job market, I wish I had better control," she reports, "but it's frustrating, because in that aspect I feel like someone else is controlling what I wanna accomplish." Certainly, it is easy to appreciate the additional barriers to personal growth that a bad job market and serving as the primary caregiver to eight children can pose. But Sarah and Stacey are unable to look past their current circumstances and are unwilling to work within their current parameters to pursue change or assert control. Yet in Chapter 5, we see examples of generous people, like Tina on permanent disability or Denise whose husband is in prison, who keep pursuing growth and development in spite of unpromising circumstances.

In sum, ungenerous Americans we interviewed are much more likely than generous Americans to see themselves as having quite limited control when it comes to personal growth and their capacity to address personal and social problems. Their attitude often is, essentially, "If I can't solve the problem completely, why even bother trying? It's better to be distracted and try to find some personal happiness." This stands in stark contrast to the generous people we interviewed. The more Americans practice generosity, we observe, the more likely they are to learn to navigate life with a "good enough" principle, as they contribute their time and money to personal and social problems. Generous Americans tend to give their very best efforts—some even work doggedly—but they are also realistic and realize that there are rarely easy solutions, and even their best efforts may still fall short. Still, *they would rather do something than nothing*. And generous people use this same "good enough" principle in their personal lives. More often than not, they aim to stretch themselves. But rarely do they seek perfection—their personal goals, while ambitious, are also usually attainable. And, in their minds, the means, the effort that they put into their personal growth, matter just as much as the ends. The orientation is quite different and, our interviews suggest, is clearly connected to what is learned and gained in part by practicing generosity.

Purpose and the Good Life

Ungenerous Americans generally wade in murky waters when it comes to distilling their vision for life, especially as compared to generous Americans. We find four common, sometimes overlapping, ways in which ungenerous people express such a lack of purpose and varying degrees of feeling stuck or bored with life. Beginning with the most common, these are: 1) they have not thought much about the possibility of a purpose and do not know if they have one or what it might be; 2) they think that no one really has a purpose in life other than to live pleasurably and not screw things up too badly; 3) they only want to fulfill family obligations or achieve the standard markers of adulthood; and 4) they believe they do have a life purpose, but they also think they are failing to fulfill it.

Of those who have not given much thought to whether their life has any purpose, most respond with a long pause, some nervous laughter, or both. They seem uncomfortable with the question and cannot gather many words for an answer. Kimberly Little's response is typical: "Purpose of my life. . . . That's a good one," she says, laughing. Not only is life purpose not something on Kimberly's radar, her laughter suggests that purpose is not something one needs to ponder. Sarah Walker in Michigan simply says: "I don't know that I see my life as having a purpose." Or, consider Kyle Jones of South Carolina's thoughts: "[Long pause] I'm not really sure. That's not something I've thought about. I usually just go day-by-day." He says he has no criterion by which he could judge the life he has lived and, laughing, "absolutely" no idea about what life's purpose is. How, then, does he chart a path in life or make decisions? "I guess I'm just kind of living in the moment, and hope for the best," he says. This idea that we live in the moment, let the cards fall where they may, and hope for the best is not uncommon among many Americans. Later in his interview, Kyle repeats that his life is mostly a reaction to circumstances: "Everything that's happened, it's kind of been a forced-on-me kinda deal." As far as Kyle is concerned, he can carry life's challenges on his own shoulders, handling things all on his own:

> Well, there's an old saying, "you don't work to live, you live to work." And right now I'm working to live, so, you just gotta keep on keepin' on. You just gotta do what you gotta do. Ain't nobody gonna take care of you, you gotta take care of yourself.

Kyle maintains a lonely form of self-reliance. He has or makes no time to think about life's purpose or what the good life might look like because he is too caught up in reacting to all that is "forced-on-me," which crowds out the possibility that the search for a meaningful life is possible or worthwhile.

Others who are not generous Americans have given their purpose in life more thought, however. Many of them also do not believe their life has a purpose—not for a lack of interest in such questions, but rather because they doubt whether any purpose exists for humanity at all. Bryan Johnson from Washington is clear on this point. He sees very little purpose in life other than to exist and live by a karma-infused Golden Rule in which it is in people's best interests to treat others as they would like to be treated. That, he tells us, is the reason he does not cheat on his wife, for instance: "So, I don't want my wife to cheat on me, then I shouldn't cheat on my wife, you know?" According to Bryan, what goes around comes around, so it's best to treat others well enough in order to avoid or minimize pain in the future.

> The ultimate meaning of all life is just to exist. I don't hold up some exalted Ten Commandments or anything like that, but it's mainly to exist. Because we're all organisms in a web of life. We can have all the religion and everything we want, but that's all we are. We're cogs in some greater piece of machinery. So to me, the value is just to live as you feel is good, the Golden Rule, I always believe in doing to others as you have had done unto you.

The liberty Bryan takes with the Golden Rule ("as you have had done" rather than "as you *would*, or *want to*, have done") is revealing because in this way he seems to envision relationships of direct exchange. Rather than a pay-it-forward system of proactive generosity, Bryan appears to suggest an impartial pay-it-back system. If life itself is so intrinsically meaningless that the best we can do is "mainly to exist," and if when all is said and done humans are only "cogs in some greater piece of machinery," then what is left but to simply survive, exist, and "feel good"? And where, with such a view of the human person, would any seriously normative vision of a life purpose fit? Later in his interview, Bryan explains how he came to devalue humanity, and to see the point of living as simply maximizing personal happiness:

> Being [on tour with the military] and seeing exactly how cheap and dispos-able human life is, I mean, people die all the time. There's nothing magical and spiritual about it. It happens in some very ugly ways. And I've seen it and I've done it, so to me, it's pretty straightforward. If there was a God or some higher being, he wouldn't have let me do that, because that's just nasty.

Bryan's perspective here is a more extreme example of what some others express in subtler terms. Elaine Woods of California similarly expresses her thoughts about her life purpose this way:

> I don't believe there's an external purpose. I don't know why we're put on the planet to be perfectly honest. But I think it's gonna have to be whatever I make of it. 'Cause I don't think I've been put here for a purpose, I think I just have to find something that I can do.

Elaine, who does not understand the value of giving money away and wishes that her husband would stop his voluntary financial giving, is, how-ever, a compulsive volunteer. She dedicates large amounts of time to her son's school and other local organizations that request her help. Elaine's ruminations on life purpose shed some light on what motivates her to vol-unteer so much, even though her giving does not extend beyond volun-teered time. Volunteering, she says, gives her "something that I can do." Like Kyle, though, she takes an individualistic tack, believing that it is entirely up to her to direct her life. Some life purpose is not out there, waiting to be learned; rather, it is an internal creation invented by each individual for her or himself. Brandon Tribble of New York City similarly says: "You're just here because of electronic particles, just for random purposes. It's what you kind of make of it."

Still others of a different sort, like Truman Wright from Indiana, offer a laundry list of personal accomplishments in place of a life purpose: "Work, make money, retire, do the things that life has granted for you to do." He continues, "Not being locked up, not living a dismal life, in other words, not doing things that are gonna get you hurt or killed. Just doing things that lift you up, that make you a better person than a dirty low-down dog." Ultimately, Truman cannot put into words how this kind of life purpose unfolds into a good life well lived without roping off the parameters with such negative statements. In the end, it is actually avoiding a bad life and not screwing things up irreparably that count as fulfilling a life purpose. Other ungenerous Americans similarly embrace the traditional social-achievement markers of adulthood—marriage, children, and home ownership—as interchangeable with fulfilling a life purpose. According to Bill Kalon:

> Before marriage and having a child, I didn't even really have expectations. I was in a place where, living at home with my parents just partying, doing stuff like that. Didn't really have goals, I was kind of doing whatever, like that, but I would say the path I'm on now, I'm satisfied.

Family is now Bill's main purpose in life and there is no longer a need to grow or find purpose as a person. Bill's wife, Liz, also finds purpose in her role as a mother, wife, and homeowner. "The purpose of life? I don't know," she says, "I just feel like I finally have a purpose with Dylan [my son]. So I guess just living that idea you are taught when you're young, to have a house and marriage and kids and that kind of stuff." Both Bill and Liz, now in their thirties, describe a sense of aimlessness in life prior to their settling down with a marriage, son, and home. But now the Kalons believe that by attaining a conventional life, they fulfill their purpose—and there is not much left to search for or strive toward in life, it seems. The risk of stagnation is evident.

In sum, our interviews reveal that most ungenerous Americans do not think much about life's purpose. And if they do, they tend to deny the possibility that a purpose may involve anything more than following a standard life-course script, or deciding to enjoy pleasures and otherwise not screw life up. However, some other ungenerous Americans with whom we spoke do believe that they have a purpose in life that exceeds epicurean visions. Their problem is that they are unsure whether they have actually discovered theirs. Unlike most generous Americans, they experience much doubt, uncertainty, and anxiety on the matter. Kimberly Little in Oregon, for instance, assumes that caring for her family is her life's purpose, but she finds this unsatisfying. "I would like to say that there is more to my life than just my kids," she tells us, "I honestly just have no idea what it is." She is awake to the fact that there may be more to her life, but she cannot locate the pulse animating her hunch.

One subset of this last group believes that they have found their purpose, but they simply cannot seem to execute or accomplish it well. Since many ungenerous people tend not to feel in control of their lives, it is not surprising that those among them who believe they have found their purpose in life also express concern about their inability to realize or achieve it. As a wife, mother of a teenage daughter, and physician, Corrine tells us "I think I'm living my purpose of life." But she adds:

> I've told myself that I think I wish I could have had more kids, but I feel like God put us in this position to only have one child, because when I look at myself and the way that I raise and yell at my daughter, how impatient I am and how sometimes I feel like I do spoil her, I feel like I'm not as good as a parent as I could be to her. And I don't know if [I'm not a good parent because] I'm working long hours, but I know it's because I do yell and I can be very impatient.

Corrine believes part of her purpose in life is to be a good parent, but she also sees herself failing in that role in various ways. Corrine lacks patience and has a short fuse, she yells and can be impatient with her daughter. She expresses guilt over spoiling her daughter and working long hours. As a result, she holds herself in low regard when it comes to fulfilling her life's purpose. This sense of failure impinges on her happiness, but she hedges against this failure insofar as she is the family breadwinner and financial security, in her mind, is of utmost importance. Even so, she finds the salary-earning role unfulfilling as well—she would rather not work the long hours, but asserts that she is locked into it for the sake of her family's upper-middle-class lifestyle.

> What I would like to do is have the lifestyle I have now, [but] where I can stay home all the time, and go shopping when I want to, get things that I need, feel like I can get the things I need, even though I'm not out there buying all the time, just that whole idea, that [my need for financial] security of it is what makes me feel helpless [to change my job situation].

Corrine makes a Faustian bargain of sorts. As much as she would like to cut back on her time at work and thus reduce her levels of stress, both of which she thinks would improve her relationship with her daughter, she is also unwilling to forgo her comfortable standard of living. Corrine selects financial security over what she actually considers to be her highest purpose in life.

Similarly, "Bethany Harris," a stay-at-home mother in Texas, pauses and mutters a bit after we ask her if she thinks her life has real purpose, or if she is more or less just living. Then she laughs and admits: "I never really thought that over, I guess I'm just living. So you know, is it my purpose just to be here as a housewife and everything? [pause] I don't. . . ." Her answer trails off, then, after a few moments, we ask how she came to this sensibility. "Probably by not even thinking about it [laughs]. Just taking it one day at a time," she responds. Like others who have not given much thought to the idea of a purpose in life, Bethany struggles to answer the question, and her nervous laughter and mumbling betray an uneasiness or perhaps even embarrassment about the possibility that her purpose might be "just to be here as a housewife," indicating that she believes she may be falling short of her potential, that being a housewife is not enough. Yet as her answer trails off, she does not seem comfortable entertaining that possibility. She feels like she is "just living" in part because she is "not even thinking about" her purpose. After we wrapped up all of our interviews with Bethany, she confided that she cried for several hours the night after her first interview, which brought to the fore many questions about whether or not she was really happy with the decisions she's made, especially about giving up her career as a schoolteacher to stay at home and raise her children. As the week went along and she had time to reflect on her life, she said she began to feel better about the path she has charted. But the interview clearly elicited an emotional response when she realized just how little thought she had given to whether she was living with a purpose or was just swept up in the daily currents of life.

Howard Philips in New York offers a different perspective worth considering. He thinks of his purpose as being part of the overarching purpose of humanity, one that we humans as a whole are failing to live out:

> I believe that everybody was put here for a purpose. They're just, you know, come here, be nice to people. Take care of people, repopulate the earth, 'cause you know one day that you're gonna pass on. And just bring your children up. You know, for each generation be better than the last. But it's not going to be that way, it don't seem to be going that way.

Like most, Howard does not articulate a well-defined meaning of life. We should be kind to others, he thinks, continue the species, and aim for improvement over time. Howard has one son with whom he has mostly fallen out of contact, and this may color his pessimism that "it's not going to be that way," that is, that each generation improves upon the one before. The fact that he also does not contemplate a life purpose that is personal is also telling—it is as though Howard refuses to believe that such a thing is possible, given the declining state of the world. Regardless, he is not alone in his doubt about the state and future of the world and the prospects people have to create meaningful lives. Many ungenerous Americans struggle, too, with the whole idea of having a real purpose in life.

Happiness

As we show in the next chapter, generous Americans experience happiness in a different way—their lives are far from perfect, but a genuine contentedness is present. They also trust that the world is an abundant place full of blessings, a world in which they can rest easy. In contrast, by the lights of ungenerous Americans, there are many ways to be unhappy, to live an unfulfilled life. The possibilities for how unhappiness can manifest itself in the lives of the ungenerous people whom we interviewed seem endless. Charting the course for a good life—one that is happy, vibrant, and fulfilling—is, in fact, difficult. This is especially true when the farthest sight on the horizon is an acquisitive American dream of picket fences, shiny new cars, and white-sand vacations. Of course, these are some of the comforts and privileges that most of the people we interviewed want out of life, including those who are generous. But we observe a crucial difference between people who practice generosity and those who do not. Generous Americans have many desires that are not materialistic and actively seek non-materialistic means to their happiness in relationships and communities. Their lives are about much more than accumulating token middle-class belongings. Generous Americans cannot always articulate it, but the pattern of their approach to life, as evidenced in our interviews, suggests that their pursuit of a good life involves much more than the enjoyment of earthly pleasures. By contrast, ungenerous Americans *do* articulate the flipside of this difference well, albeit indirectly. On this point, Tocqueville's observations are as timely as ever:

> I have seen the freest and best educated of men in circumstances the happiest to be found in the world; yet it seemed to me that a cloud habitually hung on their brow, and they seemed serious and almost sad in their pleasures because they never stop thinking of the good things they have not got.[5]

Sarah Walker of Michigan exemplifies this perspective, saying, "I just wish there was a money tree in the backyard!" Shane Little from Oregon told us, "I can never get ahead and I absolutely hate that." He continues, "I feel I've gotten screwed over by somebody else. There are people that are self-made millionaires by, say, 25, and yet here I am struggling in an apartment at almost 29, with no real job and no real future at the moment." Maria Berry from Nevada offers yet another example of the unhappiness focused on not having enough. "I would like to have more money too, buy a bigger house in a nice neighborhood here." She adds, "The situation of the money that makes me feel sad, and it's hard for me because that was a problem for a lot of years in our life." The situation she refers to is her family's inability to keep up with their credit card payments after years of spending beyond their means. Truman Wright in Indiana continues the theme:

> I like toys. I like toys. I like items, nice items and stuff. Everything I got is good, is up-to-date, and high performance. Yeah, I like good toys, too. I like things up to date too, things that are, you know, high quality. I don't believe in cheap. If you gonna get something, get something nice, get something good, get something that's gonna last.

But is he made happy by his new "toys"? Not necessarily. As we learn below, Truman has a lot of fears, especially the fear of not having enough.

According to Tocqueville, and reiterated by Robert Bellah and collaborators in their landmark study of American life *Habits of the Heart,* this pursuit of what one does not have makes it difficult for people to form bonds with one another. Their minds "are more anxious and on edge." Because "they clutch everything," they can "hold nothing fast."[6] Yet there is more to the unhappiness ungenerous Americans experience than an expansive and self-defeating pursuit of material goods. The banal melancholy that results from wanting more and refusing to be satisfied with what one already has is only part of the problem. We find two other interrelated themes that affect well-being. The first is a sense of insecurity in a perceived world of scarce resources. The second is a loneliness that unanchored individual autonomy often produces. When tethered to ungenerous mindsets and lifestyles, these two are particularly apt to corrupt people's sense of security, happiness, and belonging, which they actually desire.

The highly educated and "granola" "Levi" family in upstate New York gives plenty of their time to volunteer activities, but gives away less than 1 percent of their $120,000 earnings ($200 to charity and $750 to their synagogue), which they do not consider an act of financial generosity. With the help of her overflowing day planner, "Annette Levi" holds down several different jobs and wears many hats in the community: teaching at two local universities, a consulting gig, work for a national weight loss program, and she says with laughter, "I run the house."

> I juggle everything all the time and everything bleeds into everything else so, for example, I teach one night a week. In the spring I often have to teach one night and one day, or one night and Saturday, plus I teach two days and so I try to volunteer at school. I try to get to all their plays. But I draw the line at class trips. Sixty screaming kids on buses is just my limit.

Despite all of her activities and involvement in her community, Annette is lonely. At the end of our interviews, she admits that she has not had a similar in-depth discussion with anyone, including her husband, in years. When we ask her about her friends, she admits, "I don't have any friends. I don't know why. I guess I'm difficult to be with." This has not always been the case. "I had some dear friends in all other stages of my life, and then we moved to [another city] and I had a good friend there, it was only ten months, but I had one friend [laughing]. I don't even know where she is anymore and now I moved here and it just, I got nobody."

In addition to loneliness, Annette is fearful of not having enough money. But holding onto resources as tightly as she does is stressful and a drag on her happiness. Although she says "I would like to give more money," she cannot bring herself to be more financially generous, and feels guilty as a result. "I often feel that I'm far too selfish." It is not that she is ungrateful. "I feel very blessed," she says, "Gosh, I've been given every advantage in the world." She is simply too worried about what will happen if she needs the resources that she gives away. Sometimes, she even stresses and debates over whether or not she should give her sons' used and outgrown clothing away—perhaps someday she will need it. Her anxiety becomes palpable when she talks about wanting to give away an expensive device that her son no longer needs to an institute that helped her son's hearing problems, but ultimately being unable to act generously.

> He used to have a hearing impediment and we went to [a specialist institute] and it always bothered me that I didn't give money when I was there. I don't know. I worried over the $75 I was paying for his checkup. That was even after insurance, $75 to have this hearing test. And then the equipment was $1,400 and I felt worried about that, so I couldn't seem to make a donation.

Here is a place that helps everybody, whether they have money or not. I can afford, well I borrowed money from the bank for the $1,400 hearing aid, but I can do that because I have a house. If I didn't have a house, I couldn't borrow the money and he wouldn't have had it. It's kids. How will they possibly get a $1,400 hearing aid? And he's not the only kid with a hearing loss at the third grade, so it bothered me and I still have the device. I still have the hearing tool, and when he took the test and he cleared, he passed the test, my first thought was well I should donate this to the [institute] so they can give it to a needy child. But I couldn't let it go. I brought it home. It's in my drawer, just in case. Just in case he should lose hearing, you know. It bothers me that I can't just hand it over.

Annette clearly desires to be a generous person beyond just volunteering, but a fear that she might someday need the hearing aid, even though this is an unlikely scenario, nags at her and squelches her desire to give the expensive device to a child whose parents cannot afford one. Her discussion suggests that she is troubled by her split desires. It is as though she is verbally processing her simultaneous compassion and fear about a possible act of generosity. This is a recurrent pattern in Annette's life. At the end of his life, for instance, her grandfather needed a kidney transplant, but died without one. Knowing how much of a difference she could make to someone else on dialysis, Annette would like to give one of her kidneys as a memorial to her grandfather. But her fear about the worst-case scenario again overwhelms her and blocks her desire to give:

I thought of donating a kidney and I just feel like I'm an extraordinarily healthy person, except I have these weird injuries that keep popping up. So there's this, I have this fear that if I give away a kidney, God, you know, I'll probably get kidney cancer in the other one and [laughing] then what will I be? But I wish I could give away a kidney and not worry about that, because living on dialysis is the worst way to live.

Annette demonstrates a great deal of potential compassion here, more than most people ever even imagine—donating a kidney to a stranger is no small thing. But her bigheartedness is finally trumped by her pessimistic realism. She does not operate in a world of perceived abundance, but of scarcity. Her mind easily conjures up worst-case scenarios, which kill her generous impulses. She and her husband, "Benjamin," have not always been tight-fisted. When Annette was previously in a more lucrative line of work, she gave more money away:

I mean, when I was working before, I had plenty of money. First time in my life I ever had money. It was an incredible feeling and I was perfectly happy to write a check to whoever needed or asked. I did the thing where on your electric bill you give an extra dollar to help pay somebody else's electric bill, like that. Why not?

But now with two teenage children, the Levis say they are strapped for cash, even though they realize this deprivation is highly relative. Annette admits, "It's really pathetic. Yeah, it's really embarrassing. I know how rich we are and yet I also always feel afraid that we don't have enough." She laughs while saying this, revealing her uneasiness. This kind of fear and embarrassment of never having enough can weigh heavily on people, as we theorized in Chapter 2. Living with a perspective of scarcity rather than abundance—that is, from a place of fear—is stressful and inevitably diminishes people's well-being.

Annette is not the only American who hoards her resources for her family, with worst-case scenarios constantly looming in mind. Many we interviewed shared the same concerns. As Stacey Spiegel from Connecticut succinctly puts it: "I worry about what's gonna come down the pipe." Truman Wright, retired on a cushy severance package, rattles off a litany of his dreads: "Fear of dying, fear of your loved ones dying, and fear of your finances being taken from you, the fear of being out there on the streets, the fear of just having nothing man, hitting rock bottom, that's my fear." When we ask him if anything may limit his desire to donate money, he laughs and responds as if the answer is obvious: "Yeah, the feeling of being broke. The feeling of not having enough. Like I said, I gotta put it all in a nutshell [i.e., squirreled away]." Kyle Jones is another example of someone who worries a lot. "I'm scared all the time," he says. Like Truman, he rattles off a list of fears: "I'm scared that I'm gonna go into work tomorrow and not have a job, cause the way the economy is. I'm scared I'm gonna frickin' have a seizure and hit my head and be frickin' paralyzed. I'm scared my frickin' kids are gonna walk outside and frickin' get hit by a car." Kyle's fears stem from his previous experience with unemployment and his ongoing struggle with epilepsy, and rest at the forefront of his mind. This kind of consuming fear not only short-circuits generosity, it also erodes happiness.

Still other Americans suffer a scarcity of time, and their chronic busyness is stressful. Kyle's wife, Ruby, for example, never feels like she has enough time. "I feel like it's pretty busy. I'm constantly on the run, trying to make sure things get done, just, I feel like I'm constantly going." Consider Corrine Cizek too, who finds volunteering to be just another source of stress: "I just don't feel like I have the time. I just feel stressed and I feel like it's too much responsibility to add to my stuff that I do already." Corrine hates the long workweeks required of her job, but she is trapped. As much as she would like to transition into a less time-consuming career, she does not want to give up her upper-middle-class standard of living. "I don't know, I always thought I would be working part time as a physician and when I see other physicians who go in early and then leave early, while I'm still there, that's sort of like, that's very irritating to me." She has looked into other occupations, especially teaching.

> But then I know, I think just any kind of job would make me unhappy. If I could work maybe just four days a week, I could be happy. If I could have one extra day off, and I would like to live in a small house and not have to have a maid come every week. If I could cut my hours down, I could take care of my own house. And I feel like I wish I didn't have all this stuff [belongings], with just the three of us in this house.

Corrine is hardly the only slave to money we interviewed. Many Americans who would like to "downshift" from lucrative but stressful careers are unable to stomach the loss of a high-end lifestyle to which they have grown accustomed. The cycle of consumerism and the search for ultimate security in material well-being is a seemingly endless and ever-widening chore, one that people like Corrine in the end find stifling.

The second drag on happiness and well-being that came out clearly in our interviews with ungenerous Americans is a loneliness stemming from unanchored individual autonomy, which is directly associated with their lack of generosity.[7] "I'm an asshole," Bryan Johnson admits with some laughter, as he slogs his way through his three beers the afternoon we first interviewed him. "I'm not Mother Teresa." The previous year, Bryan's wife, Shannon, wanted to give the money that they had set aside for their Christmas gifts to a charity in their home state, but, "I was like 'Eh, I don't like that idea.'" Why not, we asked? "I wanted something for myself for Christmas. I'm selfish." Even though Bryan himself does not practice generosity, he says he does think it is important for people to be generous, "because we're all living in a community with social values and people as a greater whole look down upon you if you are an asshole." Social pressure thus is a problem. So why does he not give away more money, other than the hundred dollars or so each year he gives to public radio and a hiking trail he frequents? "Because I've got a lot of my own problems on my plate, and self-interest, selfishness, I got it, but, I've got a budget," he jokes. "It's just not a priority. Just daily life. I don't spend a lot of time worrying about starving children. It sucks, but. . . " After pausing, he continues: "I've got a life that's pretty wrapped up in myself right now. Between spending a lot of money on a house and trying to achieve my own dream of running my own business and all." Life is wrapped up in his own personal needs and desire for success. Bryan thinks of himself as being very busy, which makes him cranky and anxious. "Busy at work, certainly. After working all day, and I've got two, three hours before I gotta go to bed and go to work the next day. So I sorta feel like a slave to work." Bryan even feels busy on the weekends, as he attempts to scale the economic ladder to nicer homeownership: "I feel busy when I get to my weekend, because I end up [spending it] house-hunting."

In addition to being busy, Bryan is also lonely. Though he is married and has friends in the military in Europe and on the East Coast, he likes maintaining his independence in the marriage, and does not talk to his friends much. "I don't really have any close friends in this area or anything like that," he explains. He is also uncertain about what the future holds, a topic that stokes his anxiety. "I got out of [the military] a year ago, and there's very many positive things to that, but there's the negative turmoil of income, and there's more of ambiguity as to what's in the future." He wants to grow and change, he says, but that has not happened yet. Rather than feeling hopeful about his future, he is worried. "There's aspects of my life right now, which comes about with the stress of the living situation and then, you know, looking to do something more and better with my life." Yet he doesn't have much motivation to follow through: "I think I tend to be a little lazy. I need to feel more motivated. I always wanted to learn a couple musical instruments, kinda half tried in the past and not followed completely through on. I tend to do things for a little while and then stop doing them."

Recall that earlier, Bryan said that humans are mere organisms among other animals whose purpose is just to exist and enjoy pleasure. Perhaps this low conception of humanity helps explain his limited ambition. If humans are of such little significance, what is the point of making an effort to change beyond a simple search for personal pleasure? He jokes about this and its relation to generosity:

I'm a monkey. I got my little nuts, and my squirrel, and the things—my fruits. I squirrel it all away and this is mine. So giving something away doesn't intrinsically make me feel awesome and beautiful about myself like it does for some people. And that's just the flat honest truth.

According to Bryan, people should do whatever makes them "feel awesome and beautiful" about themselves, and only act altruistically and benevolently insofar as some benefit comes to the self as a result. Like Doug and Michelle Arnold, he relies on a self-interested arithmetic to make decisions and take actions. Not surprisingly, he solves the equation for happiness with a tabulation of itemized material goods: "Job . . . House . . . Oh, you know, the usual, make a whole lot of money and retire and travel. Not really have to work!" We ask Bryan if there are any specific items he would really like to be able to buy or own or consume or experience, or whether what he has now is enough.

> I'm an American! How much time you got? [laughs] I can think of things all day long if you want. Well, an actual castle. That would be a cool thing to buy. Living in Europe, I always liked castles. A yacht. I would like to have, you know, lots of land, private jet, so I could fly around to places and travel. If I had a summer home or if I could live in different parts of Europe or something like that, different times in the year, definitely.

Bryan is not the only one whose larger unhappiness is connected to a self-imposed atomistic understanding of human life. The years following Randall Weir's recent divorce have presented him with some significant challenges, the biggest of which he thinks is "Probably just keeping the business running." Life has not always been so difficult:

> It was going very well. When I had a complete family, I was able to go and focus on work, and then come away from work, that was useful. I'm just needed in too many different places and so the business was starting to deteriorate partially because of my performance, partially because of the industry. So, holding that all together has been a struggle.

Randall had done everything right, or so his story goes. His twenty-five-year-old son no longer speaks to him, but that, he argues, is not his fault.

> My older son probably hasn't talked to me in a couple of years. I did everything right. I couldn't have done any better as a parent for him, but he won't talk to me. I'm that bad in his eyes. I guess it's good that my son doesn't talk to me, although it would be nice to hear how well he's doing. I'm sure he won't talk to me until he's doing well enough to admit it and I think that's

part of the problem. If he's struggling with life too and he can't bear to say, "Oh, hey, guess what, Dad? My life sucks." Because all the while he was telling me how great it was going to be when he didn't have to deal with me anymore. Well, hey, come back and tell me how great it is, I want to hear.

The story is much the same with Randall's wife. She was the one to drive all of his friends away, "a real Bates-Motel spouse" he recalls, alluding to the Alfred Hitchcock movie *Psycho*. She was never right, never logical, and she wrongfully claimed that he was controlling. He has no idea why she would think that. That he has a conflict-ridden relationship with his ex-wife has nothing to do with him. Randall would like an amicable relationship post-divorce, but she does not. Thankfully, Randall's fourteen-year-old son provides some vindication. He is smart and thoughtful and adores his dad. He is the proof that Randall did not sabotage his relationships.

Randall prides himself on being independent, free-wheeling, conservative, logical, solitary, and a perfectionist whose work is never finished. He repeatedly mentions that he is a thinker, not a feeler. "See, you're trained to empathize with people," he tells us, commenting on his interviewer's interest in his life, "Not me." Randall's tragic flaw seems to be his esteem for a particular kind of logic. As noted above, he lacks empathy for people who cannot get their act together. The earthquake in Haiti was tragic, and those people should be helped, but, "Why can't people who are starving just move to the water source? That's what I would do." As long as he tells himself that his failed marriage and estranged son are not at all his fault, he can continue telling himself that everyone else ought to get it together and make it work for themselves. Inner-city youth, for example, should be given a plot of land and told to work it: that, he thinks, would solve the problem of urban crime. Randall keeps to himself and likes to keep his friends separate from each other—he does not want his friends to know one another. It seems likely that the perfectionist in him is terrified that his friends, if they could put their observations and heads together, would see his real flaws. By keeping his relationships fractured, others may never pick up on that inevitable reality, and Randall will never need to confront his losses or take responsibility for them. It seems that he cannot stand to let others fully see who he is, so he keeps himself available only in pieces, and those who know him separate from each other. This may relate to why his house is cluttered and in shambles. His living room contains three old computer monitors, piles of folded towels, pictures that have yet to be hung, and stacks of paper. Perhaps Randall is afraid of letting anything go or come to any closure, whether it is his failed marriage, his oldest son's hatred, or the piles of junk that make his house (or "sty" as he refers to it) nearly unlivable. Life seems very difficult for Randall, who does not trust any other people. "I'm a surreptitious thinker," he told us over the phone on our third and finally successful attempt to schedule an interview with him. He is, however, moderately troubled by how his life has turned out.

> Yeah, I've had a few missed opportunities. Life's turned out to be a struggle, it's been difficult. In comparison to some other people's struggles, that you become aware of as you read things, I think I'm doing well. I think I've had less of the disaster and destruction and disappointments that some people's lives turn to be.

Bryan and Randall are of course not the only Americans who struggle with loneliness. Nearly all of the ungenerous people we spoke with have acquaintances, but remarkably few have many close friends. Some are simply too busy, like Sarah Walker, who says, "I would like to go out and do things and be with my friends and stuff. And we just don't have time for that." She is too busy and stressed: "I feel very hurried. Very stressed out and busy, but I realize it could be so much worse." Others, like "Ursula King," a single Bostonian in her forties, prefer to keep friends at a distance. "I try to stay in my little bubble," she reports. Like Michelle Arnold, Ursula expects other people to take care of themselves and becomes perturbed when her friends try to rely on her for too much. She offers an example of a relational lack of generosity when a friend beset with a family crisis overstayed her welcome:

> I didn't know it was going to be three weeks, I thought it was going to be a couple of days and then it grew and grew and grew, but I wasn't going to kick her out. So she was pretty much living here. But the part that I resented was that she did have a place to stay if her mother would have made room for her. So here I had to make room for their family because their family wasn't willing to adjust their lives for her. And she stayed over here a few other times and finally I said no. I was just like, you know, what it's coming out of me, it's coming out of my day, my schedule.

When Ursula notes that "it's coming out of my day, my schedule," she is making the point that she should be free to do as she wishes without being infringed upon by others, including friends. She also assumes that immediate families should provide for their own, absolving Ursula of a responsibility to care for her friends—which, even if true in theory, does not always work out in the real world, hence the importance of real friendships.[8] By staying "in [her] own little bubble," however, Ursula avoids developing the kinds of rewarding friendships based on mutual care and generosity she might otherwise enjoy. But most of the friends she made in young adulthood have since moved away to the suburbs, and it is not surprising that she maintains little contact with them and finds her social life thin and lonely.

Similarly, Elaine Woods of California traces her self-disclosed inability to form close ties with other people back to her family of origin. "I think that I and everyone in my family, we have a very narrow range of emotional-attachment capability," she says, "which means we don't hate each other or fight, but we don't love each other." Elaine discloses that she has difficulty establishing friendships. "I've never really been good with friends. I'm one of those. I mean I have people that I'm more, my friends are the people I do things with because I see them anyways," she says. Activity-based or work-based friendships that do not exceed the limits of those contexts are common for ungenerous Americans. Gabriel Ellison remarks that he is a "try-to-keep-to-myself guy. So all my friends are my co-workers at work and I deal with them at work," otherwise, "it's just me and [my fiancée]." Gabriel expresses another common theme we picked upon in our conversations with ungenerous people. They tend to isolate themselves within their marriages and nuclear families, even though (and probably as a consequence) relying on these relationships alone typically proves dissatisfying, even difficult. Adam Berry of Nevada, on the other hand, simply does not prioritize his friendships: "We're not very social people. And I don't really have a lot of friends. There might be times I don't talk to my friends for a month and then maybe a text or email and that's about it." When we ask him about what he most hopes to achieve in life, he tells us that he wants to be faithful to his wife, raise a family with her, and be as close as possible. Yet this relationship involves strife, as Adam and Maria argue frequently over money. By focusing on their marriages and families, at the expense of nearly all other relationships, many ungenerous Americans believe that they will be able to satisfy their desires for fulfillment and intimacy. Often, however, this approach backfires, and instead of intimacy, they find themselves with together-but-alone evenings, like the ones we witnessed in the Ramirez and Arnold households.

Like Adam, Bill Kalon of California does not make much effort to stay connected with his friends.

My wife and I met and then, as our relationship got deeper, and marriage and a son and all that, I kind of grew apart from my older friends that I used to hang out with on a daily basis. I don't really talk to those guys anymore, just like changed phone numbers. I changed my number and never really put effort to try to really reconnect.

But again, Bill and his wife Liz have problems that make it unlikely for their relationship to be able to meet all of their relational needs. When we ask Liz what has made her the most sad or depressed in the past couple of years, she divulges that they had arguments over money when they first moved into their new home. "I have had rough times with Bill, but we have gotten through it. That would be it. He is my problem." So, although many people neglect friendships and rely on their spouses for most of their relational support, they are not necessarily happier for it. Oftentimes, isolated marriages cannot bear the weight of expectations and demands placed on them, and that itself can lead to lonesomeness.

Loneliness and isolation are not the only outcomes of an atomistic vision of individualistic life that sap happiness. Sometimes people—like Bryan, who called himself an asshole several times throughout the interview—realize that their autonomous inclinations are not desirable and they feel vaguely ashamed or embarrassed. Brandon Tribble similarly says: "I'm probably going to sound like a monster, but other people, probably in Africa, I'm not really thinking about. Or someone in Texas, poor person, I'm not necessarily thinking about." While he would likely not accept the label of monster, he is aware that his approach to life makes him socially undesirable. Still others do not necessarily think of themselves as poorly, or at least are unwilling to admit as much in an interview, but they do observe, along with Danny Ramirez, that many other people are too wrapped up in themselves to establish a vibrant caring society. Rose in Illinois told us, "I feel like people are getting eviler. And you know, that our government is getting more and more away from what it started out to be, you know?" Elaine in California said, "I think people are becoming far too insular and disconnected from other people. I think they're becoming far too selfish in a traditional sense of the word." Alice in South Carolina observed, "I think at this point, this country's just in deep trouble. Because people are going around murdering each other and the kids are out of control, and just tons of things that are just not right." And Annette in New York agreed: "We all want it cheap, and the moral implications of that are people in China who are used like chattel and who are destroying the environment producing stuff for us." Stacey in Connecticut related, "It would be nice if we all just looked after each

BUDDHIST WISDOM ON GENEROSITY

If you knew what I know about the power of giving, you would not let a single meal pass without sharing it in some way.

—The Buddha

Giving brings happiness in every state of its expression. We experience joy in forming the intention to be generous; we experience joy in the actual act of giving something; and we experience joy in remembering the fact that we have given.

—The Buddha

Teach this triple truth to all: A generous heart, kind speech, and a life of service and compassion are the things which renew humanity.

—The Buddha

Thousands of candles can be lit from a single candle, and the life of the candle will not be shortened. Happiness never decreases by being shared.

—The Buddha

"If I give this to others, what shall I have to enjoy?" Such self-cherishing is the mind of a hungry spirit. "If I enjoy this, what shall I have to give to others?" Such cherishing of others is the mind of the enlightened ones.

—Buddhist poem

other, but I don't think this society is like that. I think we're all pretty much out for ourselves in our own little individual unit, whether it be yourself or family." And if this is the kind of world envisioned by many, the practice of generosity is nonsensical; it is better to hold tightly to what one has rather than share it, only to be punished by a cold and cruel society. This logic particularly resonates with our working-class and working-poor respondents who have plummeted to the bottom without a safety to catch them on the way, or those are grasping at the edges of an eroding middle class. A practice of generosity is understandably difficult to achieve when memories of scarcity loom large in one's thinking.

Among all of the ungenerous respondents, Kyle Jones, someone well-versed with times of need and inadequate aid, is most adamant about this social decline and connects it with the need to put one's self and family first. "I think we're fucked as a society," he reports. "You gotta take care of yourself first. If you're not taking care of yourself, ain't nobody else gonna take care of you. . . you take care of you and yours, and let everybody else worry about them and theirs." When we ask him what he thinks about a series of political and global issues, AIDS in particular, he fires back, "AIDS in Africa don't bother me. I'm not getting AIDS." So if it does not impact him personally, Kyle refuses to care about it. He cares only about his immediate family, to whom he points: "Those three, four people in there? That's my world right there. That's all I'm worried about. As long

The greatest achievement is selflessness. The greatest worth is self-mastery. The greatest quality is seeking to serve others.

> —Atisha (tenth-century Buddhist teacher)

With gentleness, overcome anger. With generosity, overcome meanness. With truth, overcome delusion.

> —The Dhammapada

Giving, a Dharma life, caring for relatives, and blameless deeds: this is the greatest fortune.

> —Sutta Nipata 263, Buddhist Sutras

A vast shower of merit will pour down on a giver. . . . By giving one unites friends.

> —Samyutta Nikaya I.101, I.215, Buddhist Sutras

Directing one's mind to the states of faith, learning, generosity, and wisdom, one has a comfortable abiding.

> —Majjhima Nikaya 68.10, Buddhist Sutras

If beings knew, as the Great Sage has said, how the result of sharing has such great fruit, then subduing the stain of selfishness with brightened awareness, they'd give in season to the noble one, where a gift bears great fruit.

> —Itivuttaka 26, Buddhist Sutras

as they're taken care of, a roof over their heads, food in their bellies, that's all I'm worried about." No one, not even the wealthiest person, has any responsibility for others, he says: "It's their money, that's their money. Do what you wanna do with it. If you wanna frickin' light it on fire, light it on fire. I'm not gonna give large amounts of money to anybody. I don't care who you are." Freedom is king among Kyle's values, so when asked if people should be generous in volunteering their time, he said, "It's your choice. I mean if you wanna volunteer, volunteer. If you don't, don't. I mean, nobody's putting a gun to your head saying 'You need to do this.' I got better things to do with my time." But where does all of this individual freedom get Kyle? He clearly feels the heavy weight of solely caring for his family, he is "stressed all the time" as we learned earlier, he feels alone in his struggle with epilepsy, and he is very worried about a general national decline. By holding on so tightly to what he has and neglecting the concerns of all but immediate family, he creates an isolated, private world that he alone must sustain without help or support. Such a task, it turns out, makes for a grueling and tiring way to live.

Conclusion

Like generous people, Americans who do not practice generosity have the capacity to care for and love the people in their lives. They try to be good spouses, parents, and friends. Many are concerned about problems in the world, and most feel compassion when they see a television commercial for starving children in Africa, or hear news of a devastating natural disaster. They do not mind volunteering a couple of hours here or there to a daughter's soccer team or community event. Many even wish they could be more generous with their time and money. For the most part, they are doing what they think is their best to be a reasonably decent person.

Nevertheless, we find consistent evidence that ungenerous lifestyles associate with an apathy riddled by anxiety. Our interviews with Americans who do not practice generosity reveal that they are deeply unsettled by individual and social problems. Yet they do not think they have any obligation to respond, and even if they do, they feel inadequate to make a difference without sacrificing their ability to care for their own needs. Feeling vulnerable to broader societal problems, the instability of the marketplace, material scarcity, and the challenges that come with relational intimacy, they respond by hunkering down, either alone or with immediate family members, to simply try to weather the storm. They imagine other people as restrictions on their autonomy. Self-preservation and financial security are the main standards by which ungenerous Americans assess their lives. This approach thus stokes an anxiety that at worst is soothed by apathy and a withdrawal from concerns beyond one's own individual concerns, and at best results in some intermittent caring, volunteering, and financial generosity. This framework also encourages a hoarding mentality. When it comes to safety and security, it is necessary to err on the side of saving up too much. Again, some seem to have learned this response after experiencing food insecurity, inadequate mental or physical health care, or financial vulnerability while trying to make it on an unlivable minimum wage. The Great Recession and mortgage crisis likely strengthened the resolve of some of those we interviewed in the middle class who prefer to protect rather than share some of their assets. Fear is a powerful motivator and the fear of having too little, sometimes rooted in reality and sometimes fabricated or expanded, powerfully motivates them to protect their resources. As an analogy, airline patrons are, in the event of an emergency, admonished to secure their own oxygen mask before attempting to help others. The logic of most ungenerous people takes this a step further. Each person only needs to get his own mask on and not worry about anyone else until after he has safely exited the aircraft, but by then it is probably too late, so why bother to return with aid?

At the same time, ungenerous Americans recoil from impositions of all kinds, not only those of needy people. They prefer to live without

TAOIST WISDOM ON GENEROSITY

The wise man does not lay up his own treasures. The more he gives to others, the more he has for his own.

—Lao Tzu

If you would take, you must first give, this is the beginning of intelligence.

—Lao Tzu

The sage does not hoard. The more he helps others, the more he benefits himself. The more he gives to others, the more he gets himself.

—Lao Tzu

Kindness in words creates confidence. Kindness in thinking creates profoundness. Kindness in giving creates love.

—Lao Tzu

authoritative moral codes, religious traditions, or even close, non-familial friendships that might ask them to act in ways that cut against their self-interest. They do not see and cannot accept that it actually *is* in their own best interest to reach beyond a materialistic neoliberal concept of self-interest. Fear of not having enough and a desire for greater security loom large in their thinking, and ultimately prevent them from acting on whatever generous impulses they may have. Their pursuit of happiness is often derailed by their desires for materially comfortable lives. They do not search for genuine contentment in the way generous people do, beyond the superficialities of accumulating material possessions. In their minds, being a good person is not so much about what one does, as about what one does not do. So it is fine to spend all of one's money and time on what seemingly leads to happiness—a bigger house or weekends spent watching television—so long as one does not *directly* hurt others in the process. The only responsibility anyone has toward others is to not do them direct harm. As Elaine Woods of California put it plainly, "Do I feel an obligation to do things that are not going to harm other people? Yes, I do. Do I feel an obligation to care for other people? No." To state it differently, the ungenerous Americans we talked with fail to grasp the fact that their actions do not take place in a social, political, economic, and environmental vacuum. They do not see that *everyone's* life, however lived, sends out ripples of influence, positive and negative, toward untold numbers of other people. We cannot help but be responsible to some extent to and for others. But the notion that it is possible to give more generously of one's resources to others rarely, if ever, crosses the minds of the ungenerous.

In the end, however, the fear of not having enough, coupled with an autonomously individualistic lifestyle, nearly always proves to be deeply unfulfilling. Attaining the sort of happiness found in material well-being and security, which the majority of ungenerous Americans pursue without regard for others, comes at a great personal cost. The battle is won, but the war is lost. The means people use to achieve this version of happiness leads to a self-defeated end. And that frustrated end obscures the deeper, richer, more complex kinds of happiness humans want, sending them on misguided searches for more of what already does not satisfy.

CHAPTER 5

The Lived Experiences of Generous
Americans

IN OUR INTERVIEWS WITH forty families, seventeen households with
twenty-six household members appeared, to us, to practice generosity
regularly. We also interviewed five other people who are generous but
married to people who are clearly *un*generous (these are the generous
spouses of some ungenerous people featured in Chapter 4).[1] Altogether,
we interviewed thirty-one notably generous Americans. Beyond the four
or five hours of interviews, we also typically spent two or three hours in
the homes of each family sharing dinners, and tagging along for trips to
malls, grocery stores, and local parks. Sometimes we joined them for their
religious worship services. What do our interviews and time spent observing these households reveal about how generous Americans think about
generosity? In what ways are they generous? And how does their generosity seem to influence their lives?

In this chapter, we introduce our discussion with a few general charac-
terizations of generous Americans. We then engage in an in-depth discussion of one case that exemplifies the larger themes in our study, a generous
man we interviewed whom we call "Martin Cizec." We do not present his
case as representative of all generous households, but we find it illuminat-
ing of many general processes. Moving forward, we then draw on many
interviews with various generous Americans to explore the links between
giving and well-being in the forms of bodily health, mental wellness, personal growth, having a sense of one's life purpose, and overall happiness.

Enjoying Giving

To begin to understand generous Americans, it is necessary to understand that the practice of giving is a core part of their personal identities.

They tell us things like, "My giving is related to my bigger values and my bigger sense also of living intentionally," and "I think that giving is part of my spirituality, is who I am as a person, who I am as a Christian, that's all part of, that has to be part of my life, so I will set it as part of my life." Generosity is an essential part of such people's lives, a non-negotiable practice that naturally flows from their values, the meaning they make of life, and their sense of spirituality. The generous lifestyle is thus for them a fulfilling one—it fills out and expresses who they *are*. So the more they practice generosity, the more they want to be generous. "Susan Traber" in South Carolina elucidates this point: "I think more now about how others can benefit more, now that I'm older. Before I used to just write one check to the church and think, oh, I've done my duty." Recently, she expanded the reach of her generosity beyond her church, to include giving money to other causes and volunteering.

The generous people we interviewed *enjoy* practicing generosity. Giving is not a burden; rather, generous people typically light up with a warm glow when helping others. Alan Bradshaw, for example, finds pleasure in assisting people who are unable to pay their utility bills or rent in full. "It's really fun to just be able to go, 'Hm, let me cover that.' And not have to worry about where it's coming from and that people even have any idea where it came from," he says. Or, take Dale Steinecker as an example. Like many Americans, Dale would like a more impressive financial portfolio—but not for his own sake per se. "Well, I would actually like to be quite wealthy 'cause I would probably give most of it away," he explains, " 'cause there are a lot of people, especially in today's society right now, there are so many people hurting so bad." As it stands, Dale already gives away about 10 percent of his $50,000 annual income.

While practicing generosity is often gratifying, it is not necessarily easy to part with the comforts that the missing money could provide, or the leisure that might be enjoyed instead of spending time as a volunteer. Matthew Duhamel, a chemistry student in Indiana, gave up his daily trips to Starbucks to scrounge up enough money to sponsor a second child in a program alleviating poverty overseas, about which he reports:

I think sometimes it can be hard to do, but I think with most of my giving I am genuinely excited about it. To see, especially with my World Vision giving, they periodically send back pictures or little reports about how the children you are sponsoring are doing, and I just think that's really exciting because you get a tangible feedback on what your money is doing and you can see that it is actually really helping somebody else's life.

Knowing that he reduces some of the struggles that impoverished children face provides Matthew the kind of joy that a café mocha never could. Our interviews show that generous Americans typically seek and experience this richer and more lasting sense of happiness.

Although monitoring the use of money and time and looking for opportunities to share resources with others is part of practicing generosity, a generous lifestyle usually calls for more than simply cutting back on takeout coffee. How do generous people make the decision to give away more substantial resources? Factors like real and disposable income, family responsibilities, and health enable or constrain financial generosity. But, rather than pursuing the most their money can buy and then some, generous people tend to simplify their lifestyles and live modestly within, or even substantially below, their means. Because they desire to live generously, they are aware of their resources and handle them carefully. Several of the generous people we interviewed are environmentally conscious, and not only give some of their resources away, but also seek to conserve natural resources for future generations. To quote one, Oregonian Mary Ann Birch:

We have a smaller home than we can afford. We have one car and it's 12 years old. My husband bikes to work. We tend to not use it very much. We have solar panels on our roof, which were costly. We turn off lights, the little things. If you consider how much electricity we use, it is less than half of what an [average] American household uses. We use about half of what an American household uses in terms of water. . . . We try to have a small footprint and think about those kinds of things.

While their actions in part derive from knowledge—"we've been aware of climate change issues for a long time"—the Birch family's stewardship and awareness of mass consumerism's environmental harms also frees them up to give away about $4,000 each year. Similarly, "Shannon McCracken" of Washington says, "I already feel like we have too much, and we don't even have near what I think a lot of Americans own. We make a point to reuse and keep anything that's useable." Others want the cushioning that a modest lifestyle provides in the event of a financial crisis, like the one in 2008. In Texas, "Gerald Harris" explains how his family weathered a year-long spell of unemployment.

> We always try to live our life conservatively, as far as financially, you know. Smaller house. Paid for our home. Both vehicles are paid for. Everything's paid for. So it's not a pleasant situation, if you're facing mortgage, vehicle, credit card bills, all those things, I mean I can see where people just nearly have a breakdown.

Some of the generous people we interviewed are so enthusiastic about their lifestyles and management of resources that they like to share their knowledge and habits with others. "Tammy Philpot" also lives below her means and balances the family budget with finesse, as discussed in Chapter 2. As a former accountant, she is also passionate about sharing her knowledge with others as they navigate financial quagmires: "I helped an uncle earlier this week with a financial issue, and then my girlfriend was having financial issues and trying to figure out how to do her budget and how to balance the checkbook. I spend a lot of time helping people." Mindfulness about finances is common among the generous people we interviewed. It gives them greater control and knowledge of their finances, and they tend to have more peace of mind, even amid rockier bouts of unemployment or a down market. If they live above the poverty threshold (not all generous people we spoke with do—two subsist on welfare or disability insurance), they give at least 3 or 4 percent of their income away. A sizeable minority report giving away 10 percent or more.

The simple act of giving money away is neither necessary nor sufficient for practicing a generous lifestyle. Financial generosity is, however, often a harbinger of a generous disposition and practices that give rise to a distinctly generous way of life. Money is a precious, even sacred, commodity in American life, a source of much-prized security and stability. Many Americans also believe that having more money will lead to a proportionate boost in happiness, although empirical studies show this to be false.[2] So, because money is thought to bring greater security or happiness, releasing that "good" for the sake of others, for the "greater good" even in modest or moderate amounts, is an act of trust and generosity that belies a deeper belief in contentment with one's present abundance—however abundant it actually is.

Some of those we interviewed are selective about the organizations they give to, and prefer to give one or two large gifts. Others, like Mary Ann and Markus Birch in Oregon, give one large gift to a humanitarian

A bit of fragrance always clings to the hand that gives roses.
If you are generous, you will gain everything.

—*Confucius*

He who wishes to secure the good of others has already secured his own.

—*Confucius*

If you want happiness for an hour—take a nap.
If you want happiness for a day—go fishing.
If you want happiness for a month—get married.
If you want happiness for a year—inherit a fortune.

If you want happiness for a lifetime—help someone else.

—*Confucius*

organization each year and supplement their generosity with ten smaller donations to alma maters and various organizations that serve the public good. The majority of generous people we spoke with (twenty-five out of thirty-one) also give of their time through volunteering. Five others have done so in the past, and only one has never volunteered. For example, in her spare time, Susan Traber knits baby blankets and hats for needy families. During all local charity-run fundraisers, Shannon Johnson registers participants and hands out water. Matthew Duhamel tutors people learning English as a new language. Tina Kennedy in California works as a community liaison for her sons' schools. Simon Philpot plays the viola on Sunday mornings at church and, with his son in tow, occasionally volunteers to help build a Habitat for Humanity home.

Beyond formal volunteering, the generous people we met also give of their time relationally and regularly practice acts of kindness. Most were hospitable during our interviews, offering snacks, meals, or beverages, adjusting their thermostats to more comfortable summer temperatures, and making sure we had adequate directions to our next locations. Examples of this type of generosity pepper our interviews with generous people. Dale Steinecker, for instance, shovels snow for his neighbors during the cold winter months in Illinois: "I enjoy helping the neighbors out. I'll help in the winter, shovel driveways and stuff, and the same way with the neighbor over there." "Rodrigo Martinez" rattles off a list of the family members he helps regularly, sometimes driving across his home state of Georgia to paint a niece's new apartment, mow the lawn once a week or more for his sister, or run errands with his autistic brother. These activities eat up a large portion of Rodrigo's time, but he values his generosity, telling us, "I feel good doing that, I guess that's one of the reasons or purposes [of life]." In addition, most who meet the Red Cross requirements donate blood, and only a few of those who are eligible do not wish to donate their organs upon death. Again, generosity is a way of life for these people. Generally, if they give money, they also give time. If they give their time, they also provide relational care and support. And if they are medically able, they donate blood. Of course, there are many ways to be generous, and countless combinations of practices can cohere into a generous lifestyle. And those kinds of lifestyles lead in paths to flourishing.

Martin Cizec: A Case Study

"I get that everybody likes nice stuff, but if that's all there is . . . " Martin Cizec lives on the bustling outskirts of a city in Michigan, with his wife, Corrine, and their daughter, Olivia. Their corner of an upper-middle-class suburb has a fair amount of racial diversity. Martin is the grandson of Polish migrants and Corrine the daughter of Filipino migrants. They and their neighbors were shaken by the Great Recession of 2008, but no one in their social circles actually went bankrupt. The Cizecs live in a tidy world of new money, granite countertops, and paint-your-own-pottery studios. As a suburb long developed to its outer limits, there is little room left for new housing developments. It is not uncommon for new buyers here to purchase a modest home, bulldoze it, and then construct an oversized Victorian-style home too big for the plot size. Luxury SUVs cart children to school, piano lessons, soccer, and Spanish classes. "This whole suburban thing is kinda not me," Martin admits, "but the way we got jobs and figured out where they were on the map and kinda put in [the halfway point]."

Between their two careers—Martin is a professor of political science at a research university and Corrine a radiologist—the Cizecs are financially comfortable. Even as they prepare to send their daughter to college soon and continue saving for retirement, they also give away about 4 percent of their family income to their own alma maters and a handful of other charities. Both Martin and Corrine are grateful for their financial stability, even though as noted in Chapter 4, Corrine is somewhat unhappy with the long hours she puts in at work to maintain the family's lifestyle. Martin, who wants to prioritize Corrine's happiness, would not mind downsizing. "I think [suburbia] can be nice," he says, but then tethers his optimism with this:

There's an emptiness about suburban life, a little something not diverse. I have a nice lawn, I go out there and pot around, but I actually don't like grass, I would rather it be weeds. But I just couldn't live around here if I let it do that. So there are times when it's satisfying and nice, but from the bigger sense, I wouldn't stay here forever.

Martin resists believing that the privileges of the better off provide contentedness. Instead, he believes that relying on material goods and status for fulfillment are apt to dead-end in spiritual emptiness.

I'm concerned that Americans are sort of shallow. People can be incredibly materialistic and empty. And it bothers me, living in an upper-middle-end suburb like this. I don't think it's good for people's souls to be so materialistic. I've been to gatherings and parties with neighbors, and if they could quit talking about their granite countertops or new SUV they want to buy, it's like, I get that everybody likes nice stuff, but if that's all there is, it's a very unsettling way to be.

Martin yearns for more meaning even as he himself enjoys "an upper-middle-end" lifestyle. In his twenties, existential questions filled him with dread. While he has gained more peace about such matters, when we ask whether he believes his life has a purpose, he supposes it does, but wavers. "I think it's all quite circumstantial," he explains, and the existential questions are "endlessly ponderable." Then pragmatism kicks in. He reminds himself that, "This is the way things are in my life now and I'll do my best to do my best," so he strives "to be good to people, the best that I can, I think that's [my] purpose." He does not need "a very, very deep, big, profound answer to that question [of meaning]"—even if he had one, he doubts he would be able to make it actionable. Instead, he prefers to think realistically about how he can be "good to people."

I have to direct my efforts towards things that are actually profoundly obvious. To be honest with you, I've read and thought about these things [the purpose of life] more than you might think, or than I'd want to admit. It actually can create a great deal of anxiety, where you just feel better when you stop thinking about it. So I think I try to keep it focused on the immediate, tangible circumstances of my life now. Those questions are endlessly fascinating to me, but the thought of nothingness, a cold universe, is not real settling.

Instead, other people are central to Martin's understanding of what a meaningful life looks like. He expresses this most clearly when we ask him to describe what life would look like if he did not live up to his own purpose.

> If I felt I had alienated a lot of people, I don't think that would be a nice feeling. Or being an unusually big burden to people would bother me. I hope that what I do now on a daily basis, through people I know outside of work or people at work and anybody else that ends up in my family in the future, that I am not a burden or didn't offer them something [valuable]. I would hate to come to the end of my life and have people think, "Well, he took so much and never gave back."

Martin senses that something sacred about humanity is profaned by attempting to satiate a hunger for meaning and identity with bigger and better products and social-status markers. Even so, he too sometimes gets caught up in wanting more—"I think it's an unfortunate human thing to always want something, and once it's realized to feel that it's not quite what we want." When he thinks about his own life, Martin is content, but "sometimes [the desire for more] can take the best of me. I'll feel like I got all this, and I'm just so happy, [but then] I want something else." Still, at the end of the day, Martin operates by a kind of pragmatism—he has more than enough, so why shouldn't he share some of his resources with others? In this way, he withstands the pull of materialism. Unlike Doug Arnold's version of pragmatism, dictated by providing as much security to his immediate family as possible and operating in a framework of perceived scarcity, Martin's pragmatism, oriented by a belief that the world is basically a place of abundance, if we could only properly allocate its resources, is expressed in routine practices of generosity. By regularly donating money, giving blood, showing care for his family and friends, demonstrating compassion to the needy, altering his lifestyle to minimize ecological damage, and planning an estate gift in his will, Martin locates himself in a moral framework in which "the good life" depends on contributing to the flourishing of other people.

Though he no longer practices the Catholicism of his childhood, it still informs Martin's vision of a life well lived. "You can go on vacation two different ways. You can take the package deal and get on the bus and have somebody show you all the sites, or you can go with a backpack on your own. I've become more of the second." Though he forgoes the "package deal" the Catholic Church offers, and veers toward independence and individualism, he lives by a moral compass attuned to the Church's teachings about the dignity of all human persons. It is important to Martin also that he provides his thirteen-year-old daughter with a similar moral guide. When he thinks about the qualities he most wants to cultivate in her, he says he wants her to have "a sense of humanity, and giving is part of that."

Furthermore, the self-made man is a farce in Martin's account. Some people, he insists, simply do not have the bootstraps (or "panties," as Michelle Arnold phrases it) to pull themselves up on their own. At the same time, as a social scientist, Martin thinks carefully about the structural implications of charity, but again reverts to his pragmatic attitude.

> I mean, Marxists will tell you that charity makes you feel good and assuages your bad feelings, but that it never meets the needs of those to whom you give money. They think everybody should be cared for by the state. I understand that perspective. But my attitude is, yeah well, unless that's going to happen somebody needs to write a check.

Martin thus believes that giving some of one's money away is a moral obligation. He donates about one-twentieth of his family's income annually. That level of giving, he tells us, requires planning: "There's not a lot of spontaneous [giving]. I'm not a wild and crazy guy like that, I won't throw money around without thinking about it ahead of time." At the same time, he remains open to giving smaller, more episodic gifts:

> My wife and I both went to small, private colleges as undergraduates. We give to them, that's our biggest gifts each year. And then the rest tends to be more episodic, like if somebody is raising funds at work or something, we'll give in small amounts. I have given to political campaigns before but I don't consider that charity. So we have two long-standing things we give most of our money to annually, and the money increases when we can. Then there's routine things that pop up. Somebody wants to do a cancer walk, we'll support that, sometimes even walk ourselves.

A small donation preceded our second day of interviewing Martin: he and Corrine purchased a benefit table at a luncheon raising funds for a local halfway house. The mainstay of their financial generosity, however, is reserved for their alma maters. Martin tells us that he wants to make life easier for hardworking college students. In terms of planning his estate, he is less interested in leaving his daughter a family nest egg than in establishing a large charitable gift. In addition, he regularly donates blood and is registered as an organ donor.

> It's super easy. They have blood drives where I work. It's something that can be done during the lunch hour. Corrine is a doctor, so I see that people need blood, that it's important. And it seems almost every year a student will ask for money for the Kappa Gammas or some campus club, like, "we're having a competition," so I'll go do that, just to be a part of it.

Martin considers himself an introvert and sometimes hesitates to volunteer his time. But, as a scuba diver and environmentalist, he says that the BP oil spill in 2009 "just horrified me." So he offered to travel to the Gulf to participate in the cleanup effort. "I have some skills that not a lot of people have, and I think if we all, people like me, crowded in down there and helped out, we could [make a difference]." In general, Martin says he prefers his generosity "to be sort of behind the scenes, quiet generosity, I don't like to be seen giving, but I think I'm generous with my time if people have concerns." He reserves the most affection and relational generosity for his family members, however: "I show my daughter I love her, I give her hugs all the time and kiss her, and I like to, for sure, it's important. I think doing that for people you don't know well is a little vulgar, I'm kind of a private person. But this is my home and these are my family members, so I give them kisses and hugs, sure." Martin especially finds great happiness being a father. "I'm thrilled to be a dad," he tells us, "I very much identify with that role, even though pushing her down the street teaching her how to ride a bike or kissing her skinned knee, that's all done." He somewhat laments the passing of the childhood stage of fatherhood, but also wants to give his daughter the space and independence she needs as a teenager.

Martin also recalls showing generosity to his graduate-school roommate, a quadriplegic. "I helped him in the morning to get dressed, bathed him when he needed it, helped him shave and fix his hair, and he went off to work in a wheelchair and then I made his meals and put him to bed at night. I have very fond memories, he's a friend of mine." When we expressed admiration at this, he admits, "sometimes it was a little tedious," but adds that he "never felt put upon." Martin also mentions caring for an elderly grandfather: "My grandpa lived two and a half hours away, with my uncle and his daughters. And [in] his frail years they cared for him. But when he was sick and they wanted to go out I would go over there and sit with him, he needed somebody around and I didn't feel put upon to do that. But that was increasing in frequency leading up to his death, and not a big deal." He notes that his caring for family members who had sacrificed much for their children and grandchildren by emigrating to the US from Poland was a small token of gratitude. That pattern holds true across Martin's relationships—giving and receiving, generosity and gratitude.

Martin's life is not perfect. He is unhappy that Corrine is dissatisfied in life. A few years ago his mother had cancer, and whenever she has a routine appointment with her doctor, he finds himself feeling anxious. After the economy took a hit in 2008, much of his research money dried up. "There were some changes at work upsetting to me, [but] not big things." He also admits to occasional bouts of mild depression. "I think I tend to have slight depression. Nothing super-clinical, but I can get myself funked up. Sometimes there's an event that triggers it, but sometimes I just cycle into it." Like nearly all people, including generous people, Martin's life is messy and complicated. He does not sugarcoat his answers. But for him to live a generally content and satisfied life requires promoting the well-being of his students as they take on intellectual challenges:

> I like my job, I teach, I have two courses this term. I have my big kids, my graduate students, and my little kids are undergrads. I like my job, it's not a big social-event type of job. I actually like it quiet and I'm quite happy working on abstract things. But I do like interacting with my students. I like it when they stop by.

When Martin retires, he hopes to volunteer as an ESL teacher: "I might sit down at a junior college and learn how to do English as a second language, and work in literacy." He is constantly scanning his environment for ways to be useful and care for others. He maintains a posture of hopeful pragmatism and acceptance, and this leads to basic life satisfaction.

"I'm content," he says, "I find a little softness and peace," and "that isn't just that I'm happy because it was perfect all along." Martin's happiness has been formed in part by generous life practices.

Generous Practices and Positive Life Outcomes

Next we explore various life outcomes described in Chapter 1, showing with interview data how many of the processes described in Chapter 2 operate in generous people's lives.

Physical Health

Many generous people, like their ungenerous counterparts, face health setbacks. As noted earlier, some have chronic conditions like recurrent migraines, fibromyalgia, or diabetes. Others deal with the effects of a prior alcohol or cigarette addiction. Several are overweight, but they are, for the most part, making an effort to shed the pounds through diet and exercise. Yet, when it comes to bodily health and optimism about health-related outcomes, generous people surpass the ungenerous. For the generous people in our study, life moves at a more manageable pace, with time for exercise and eating well, all of which promote bodily health. They eat healthier meals, usually home-cooked and almost always with others, and they spend more time informally exercising by taking walks with loved ones, going on bike rides with their kids, or playing with their grandchildren. In addition, since they tend to be more social and active in their communities, they spend less time sitting in front of computer and television screens. Generous people are generally busy, but they are less stressed-out about their commitments and obligations than the ungenerous people we studied. And because they are less stressed, coping mechanisms like heavy drinking, smoking cigarettes, and other substance use carry less appeal. None of the generous people we interviewed suffered from a debilitating addiction, though two are recovered alcoholics. Such lifestyle choices and patterns promote bodily health.

This desire to maintain a healthy diet can transcend social class and income levels. By accompanying people on their trips to grocery stores and peering inside pantries and refrigerators when possible, we learn that generous people, like "Henry and Cynthia Fountain," keep their kitchens stocked with healthier food options and fewer ready-made products. A handful, like Simon and Tammy Philpot in the warm climate of South

Carolina, are even growing some of their own fruits and vegetables and trying to reduce their carbon footprint. "I'm into this new green thing. We're dabbling in gardening and trying to eat some things local," Tammy explains. On a tighter budget, the Harris family shops with all the coupons they can use, but are resolved to eat home-cooked meals, with only the occasional pizza delivered to the house. Almost all of the generous married households invited us to share a meal with them at their own expense, sometimes more than once. Mandy Jackson and Stan Guthrie would not let us leave without taking home some leftovers handed over in Tupperware. This kind of hospitality, which seems to be a regular part of life for the generous people in our study, may also indirectly aid bodily health, given that the meals are homemade and lengthened by conversations, allowing the family members to eat more slowly and so enabling them to be mindful of when they are full.

In addition to eating better, generous people typically build physical activities into their schedules. Often, the time they spend exercising is also time spent socializing with friends or family. "Alan and Miranda Bradshaw," for example, take their two children on bike rides through their neighborhood when the weather is pleasant. Shannon McCracken, highlighted in Chapter 2 for her volunteer work as a soccer coach, makes new friends and cultivates older friendships through a running group. "Most of the people I know in the area, I've met through running," she says, "So my closest friend I see several times a week." Ken Walker solidified his bonds with some work colleagues by participating in his company's track team for fourteen years: "I was very intense and competitive," he recalls, noting these as qualities that help his career in technology. He also keeps in shape by coaching a son's soccer team and playing basketball—"It's Sunday nights, an hour and a half. Open gym. January through April, I'll play Sunday nights and another weeknight in the men's league." Others enjoy more solitary activities. Markus Birch in Oregon similarly prioritizes staying in shape, moonlighting as a mountaineer—"I've climbed Mt. Rainier"—and regularly accompanying his son's scouting troop on camping trips. To keep fit for his adventures, he commutes to work every day on a bike, noting, "I've done month-long solo bicycle trips." His wife, Mary Ann, admits, "I fluctuate in how physically fit I am," but by all outward measures she is still a picture of health. Most recently, she speedily recovered from a hysterectomy, allowing her to participate in her family's hiking outings.

I have been working out and feeling pretty good about it and here we were at elevation. We did quite a number of hikes that were 12 miles and gained a huge amount of elevation. That was beautiful and fun and we got along and it worked. Very nice. Those kinds of events definitely make me happy.

Others, like "Rachel and Rob Siegfried" in Texas, also take pleasure in their physical well-being and tout the common refrain sung by most generous households: "We're in really good health," Rachel says. They leverage their wellness to donate blood. "We don't take any prescription medicine or do any drugs or anything. So our blood is really good, that's why we feel like we should donate." Donating blood is a routine joint activity for the couple: "We give blood together, we give on a regular basis, like every 8 weeks. We were almost up to 5 gallons in [the state we lived in last year], and here my next [visit] should be a gallon. Rob just met his gallon because they called him." Ken Walker takes a different approach to donating blood. He explains how giving blood stokes his excitement for competition and enhances his athletic performance.

> I'm extremely competitive. I started giving blood at work, I think they came in 3 or 4 times a year at work, and I would give blood. I was also training hard and very fit at the time, and they would give the instruction about the pint and it should take about 4 minutes and everybody's blood typically comes out that brown sludge, chocolate syrup color, mine was eraser pink, and I'm just cranking out a pint in like 2 minutes and 47 seconds. They're like, "What are you doing?" I say, "I'm winning!"

Why, we asked, did he get into donating blood in the first place?

> Not as generous as it may seem. I had read some stuff that giving blood, having your body regenerate the donated blood, boosts the oxygen content of all the blood cells and makes your blood transport more efficient. So I began giving at work, the blood drives, trying to get participation from as many people as possible. I also conveniently scheduled it before some of my regional and national competitions, three weeks in advance, so I could have my artificial oxygen transport.

He does not mention here how other people benefit from his donation, but medical researchers and people in need of transfusions are "winning," too, thanks to Ken's generosity (self-serving though it may be). While most generous people, including Ken, give blood in part because they are healthy, Ken has the incentive of boosting his own overall health and increasing the chances of securing a title for his company track team, having already apparently won the office award for speediest pint delivery. Most of the blood donors we interviewed are not as self-seeking as Ken, but his story offers yet another account of how generosity helps induce bodily health in an upwardly moving spiral.

Not all of the generous people we spoke with, however, are in good health. Some manage difficult chronic health conditions, yet their relatively poor health often does little more than put a wrinkle in their overall sense of well-being. "Susan Traber" regularly experiences "terrible headaches and fatigue." When we ask about what has saddened her the most in recent memory, she recalls:

> My dad, he passed away, and my mom had an episode like a week after he died we had to put her in the hospital because of blood pressure, and I was under a lot of stress, so I had a heart attack [laughs]. And so for the last three years it's been lots of physical things for me.

Susan admits that, "it's been stressful for that part" of life. Losing a parent, watching another face a serious health issue, and then having a heart attack could unravel anyone. It is a strong demonstration of resilience when Susan also tells us, "I'm pretty content." She spends more time recounting the good things in life when we talk with her, such as, "I was happy when we had grandchildren, excited about that. Just happy when we get a nice order and we're making the bills and everything's running smoothly and we're able to take a week of vacation and just relax, all that makes me happy." Her husband Philip agrees, "Health issues, that sort of thing are always a concern, but we deal with it." In Arizona, fifty-something "George Shyer" muses over what he is most proud of accomplishing in life, and settles on a story about surviving a serious brain injury as a young adult.

> What am I most proud of, well [laughs], just being able to survive and do what I do. This accident, it happened to me when I was twenty-five. I was normal back then, and then I had head damage from an accident. So I use crutches now for balance and to get around and stuff, and I've just kind of strived to make it this far.

George is mostly homebound, relies on crutches, and during our discussion with him he frequently had trouble finding the right words to explain himself. George could focus on how the accident left him with an unhappy life. Instead, he is grateful and takes pride in his ability to help others in his apartment community who have suffered similar setbacks and are adjusting to a new way of life.

Another interviewee, "Rhonda Guthrie," has fibromyalgia but still strives to lead a satisfying life. When we called Stan and Rhonda to set up their interviews, Rhonda was at a hospital for a heart catheterization test. She said:

> I had a heart cath Thursday because the fibromyalgia can, it actually affects the chest wall. My chest makes me feel like I'm having a heart attack, and I've been to the ER several times with it and everything always checks out. It's scary. I get real short of breath and my chest hurts.

She describes fibromyalgia as "the greatest, biggest stressor" in her life. "It's a chronic pain condition that I have," she explains. Yet somehow she is thankful.

> Stan is gonna try to retire after this year. I'm really looking forward to that because when I'm feeling well we like to travel and go places together. We have lots of fun. So, that's kinda my life. I enjoy sewing. I sit and I sew and that kind of stuff.

Despite her health problem, Rhonda quickly transitions to focusing on the positives in her life. This is part of her intentional self-soothing process: when her condition flares up, she tells us that she does "self-talk" to relax and put her life into perspective, and that she is thus better able to cope with her condition. "I'm relaxed, I'm comfortable, I'm happy, I'm content with my life," she says. Life is objectively troubled, but Rhonda refuses to let her fibromyalgia ravage her spirit. Like George, she could easily wallow in her limited capabilities. That would be an understandable human response to a difficult health condition. Instead, George, Rhonda, Susan, and other generous people we interviewed who cope with less than ideal health choose to focus on all the good they do have: grandchildren, close friends, and supportive spouses. They choose gratitude. They *cultivate* loving relationships of care and trust that boost their ability to cope with poor health. The negative impact of disease or degeneration on their lives, therefore, is reduced. Generosity does not inoculate people against illness or damage to human bodies. But practicing generosity even in that context does boost an immunity to negative and harmful dispositions that tend to further compromise well-being.

Mental Health and Generosity

We also find that generous practices are linked with better mental health. Few of the generous people we interviewed exhibit symptoms of depression or anxiety. Instead, they tend to be content. Some are very happy, even peaceful. Though many can recall times in life when they were sad, perhaps even depressed and overwhelmed, only five of the thirty-one generous people we interviewed talked about or display symptoms of depression or anxiety. And those who do experience bouts of darkness or panic are also more likely to see brighter times ahead. They believe their conditions are not permanent or unchangeable, so they are not as likely to sink down into more permanent forms of depression.

When life gets tough, generous people do not glide by without heaviness or burden. They experience and acknowledge the rough patches and, after some struggle, work through the problems. They work to get perspective, accept reality, and live within its parameters, instead of caving into loathing, gloom, or a fixation on how their lives could have and should have turned out differently. Matthew Duhamel, for example, the twenty-something PhD student described above who cut back on his daily takeout coffee habit to sponsor another needy child, recalls one such time, when he broke up with his then-girlfriend at the start of his graduate studies.

> Definitely one thing that has been challenging for me was coming down here to go to grad school. I had a fairly long-term relationship that ended, so that was really a difficult time in my life. It was a dark, difficult, chaotic time, because that relationship had been very important to me, so to see it end was not good. But at the same time I was at a new place, figuring out my way through a new place.

Matthew admits that this "dark time" in life "probably slowed down my progress in grad school." But he also notes that that time allowed him to sort out questions about his ultimate values and the kind of person he wants to be. It was painful, but Matthew also remembers personal growth accomplished during those difficult months. "It was a time of reflecting on who I was and what was really important to me," he recalls, "It forced me to reach out to other people more, try to make more friends, do that sorta thing, so I do think that had a big [positive] impact." At the time of our interview, two years into graduate school, Matthew was happy with his work and excited about his future, including the prospect of marrying his new girlfriend and starting a family with her.

Like Matthew, Simon Philpot of South Carolina, who donates about 10 percent of his salary to his congregation and a variety of local charity organizations, also faced his troubles head-on, although he was still dealing with them when we interviewed him. He spoke openly about struggling with insecurity and social fears: "I'm not content at all with the anxiety I have with people. I would like to change that. I just started seriously working on that lately." He regularly sees a therapist to work through his hurt and gain self-understanding. Simon's low self-evaluation peppers our discussion—he frequently doubts his answers and asks if his response is what we were looking for or makes sense. "I think part of my problem with people may have something to do with pain that I have inside about things that happened much earlier in my life. I am trying to get that worked on or fixed or understand what I need to do, and I guess that's probably the biggest challenge confronting me." Though Simon does not enjoy a sense of mental happiness in the present, he at least is able to admit his lack of happiness and take tangible steps toward improvement. Given what we know about the link between generosity and efficacy, we have good reason to believe that Simon's generosity may be playing an indirect but crucial role in his improvement.

Naturally ruminative, Markus Birch also suffers from occasional bouts of anxiety and tends to brood over his existence. "I'm introspective, I think a lot about myself, about things, about the world," he explains. "Sometimes that's good, leading me to new insights." But he acknowledges certain perils in his habits of thought: "Sometimes it's bad, spending a lot of time obsessing over things. I can tend towards being a bit depressed or anxious about things. I worry a bunch." Even so, as an avid photographer, Markus also recognizes the insights his struggles provide, noting, for instance, that "I can be pretty creative." That is not to say that his anxiety is consistently well-managed and benign: "The biggest challenge I went through recently was a period of maybe a year when I had some pretty bad insomnia and accompanying, I wouldn't call it anxiety attacks, but you know, I was really unhappy, and I ended up seeing various people and trying various things. And now I'm on an antidepressant, and that has helped enormously. So, as far as my personal life goes, that was definitely the hardest." Like the others highlighted in this section, Markus is not flippant about this darker time in his life. Nor has he made a 360-degree turn in his outlook on life. But, compared with many of the ungenerous people we interviewed who also have experienced depression or anxiety, Markus is making more progress. When we compare the generous and ungenerous Americans who struggle with mental health issues, it is clear that the generous are quicker to seek help and to experience their afflictions as episodic and not chronic. This observation holds true across the lines of social class.

Many factors are involved in people's soundness of mind and flourishing of spirit. Our evidence shows that generosity is one of these factors. It is not a magic pill—in fact, in some cases, people start volunteering as a response to their depression. Some kinds of generosity may also be motivated by guilt, which likely does not produce the same benefits as a desire to give for others' good. Evidence in our interviews, however, suggests that generosity can serve as a buffer against hard circumstances that normally stoke depression and anxiety. Markus's wife, Mary Ann, lives with chronic minor depression, but, given her difficult childhood, she is doing well. "I grew up in a pretty chaotic family when you could not predict what was going to happen and you couldn't trust other people," she says. She explains, "my father was an alcoholic, using alcohol to self-medicate serious depression. He committed suicide a couple weeks before he turned fifty, when I was twelve." Her mother also "had some significant mental health issues, also abusing alcohol, probably for similar reasons of self-medication. The first time she had been hospitalized with a nervous breakdown I was six years old." When Mary Ann was sixteen, her mother was finally diagnosed as bipolar. However, despite this tumultuous childhood, Mary Ann is not only fairly well-adjusted, she is also faring well as a highly educated and capable leader in her community, a loving wife and mother, and an avid outdoorswoman. She wears many hats as a volunteer, tutor, museum docent, and community organizer, which gives her a sense of purpose beyond taking care of herself and family. Her dogged dedication to the needs of others seems to draw her attention away from self-absorption and other problems. This frees her to be grateful and to focus on what she can do, rather than what she cannot, which is empowering and seems to guard against serious depression.

Matthew, Simon, Markus, and Mary Ann are outliers among the generous people we interviewed, however. Most of the latter are more similar to Philip Traber, a fifty-something from South Carolina, who declares, "I don't generally get depressed." Like many people, Philip finds himself "sad and depressed" on occasion. This most often happens when he thinks about growing older. "You think about, 'Well, I squandered this opportunity' or 'I let myself get into this kind of shape,'" he explains. "If you really dwell on it, that can be a major downer, obviously," which is why Philip, like almost all of our generous respondents, focuses instead on what he can be grateful for, which brightens his outlook. Again, generosity offers neither an ironclad protection nor pure respite from mental illness or disrupted wellness. Generosity by itself can in no way produce optimal mental health. Still, our evidence suggests that when people recurrently step outside of themselves to see life's bigger picture, as part of their practice of generosity, it is beneficial to mental well-being. Cultivating generous practices and attitudes helps people avoid self-absorption and downward mental and emotional spirals.

Personal Growth and Generosity

"Happiness," wrote W. B. Yeats, "is neither virtue nor pleasure, nor this thing nor that, it is simply growth. We are happy when we are growing." Although this may be overstated, personal growth does play an important role in fostering human well-being. Embracing and mastering challenges gives us newfound pride in and awareness of our capabilities and strengths. And the recognition of our own endurance and fortitude can strengthen us further. Denise Powell in Oregon, a typical generous respondent, believes that she possesses a reasonable amount of control over her projects, such as bringing her home up to code for her husband's pending release from prison, as well as her relationships with her now-adult foster children, which can be unpredictable at times. Even though she does not expect to bring about widespread change as one individual, she has the gumption to follow through on her endeavors, which increases the chances of her success, and thus allows her to experience the positive rewards of conquering a challenge.

> If I set on something, if something means a whole lot, I will work really hard to get it changed. It may or may not happen. And I think, in the scheme of things, I have very little control of change in anything. I have one voice amongst millions, but if I can sway other people to my outlook, then I will.

Denise gives us insight on personal growth. As we noted in Chapter 4, ungenerous people are less likely to pursue projects of personal growth because they do not believe they have an ability to effect change, either personally or socially. By contrast, a realistic and hopeful attitude like Denise's helps people take on the challenges of growing in the first place. Tammy Philpot exhibits a similar belief in her own limited efficacy: "I think everybody's got the ability to control a little sphere of influence, whether it's talking to other people about things or engaging that kind of thing." She lists her own experiences of being generous—volunteering in the library, at schools, as a "lunch buddy" in the cafeteria, and tutoring at her children's school—as activities that have strengthened her personal resolve and motivation to try something new in life, now that her children are older. "I'm beginning to think, I was looking into it the other day, that I'd like to get involved in some adult-literacy work, to do some of that at the community college." Later in our interview, she mentioned that she would like to "be more involved in some of the human-rights issues worldwide. I would like to know, other than just giving money, how I could be involved in that. I haven't figured that out yet, but I do have an interest in that." From what we know of Tammy, she will likely see that interest through. Most recently, as noted earlier, she started gardening after becoming interested in the "slow-food movement."

Susan Traber in South Carolina is another woman who works on personal growth by pursuing new activities. "I am pretty content with the kind of person that I am," she tells us, but "there are some [new] things I would like to try." In particular, she wants to try her hand at writing. Susan recently ventured to expand her generous reach from simply writing checks to making baby blankets to give away. She is generally the kind of person who constantly seeks self-expansion. Similarly, Markus Birch offers a good example of this outlook. As a young adult, he held to the mantra "Everyday in every way I'm getting better and better." Although he no longer feels "this sense of kind of progress in my life," he still maintains a vision for working to better humankind. And now, as he is "feeling mid-life-y," he seeks to redirect his efforts: "I want whatever it is I am accomplishing to be benefitting the world a bit more than some of the stuff I've [already] worked on [as a scientist]."

Yet others we interviewed are perceptive of their own flaws and shortcomings, which only motivates them to pursue personal projects that build character. Most generous people talked about their shortcomings in their relationships with family and friends. Matthew Duhamel, for example, worries that he does not spend enough time talking with friends when they reach out to him. With a heavy graduate-school load or work, he sometimes fails to be the kind of friend he would like to be.

> I think sometimes I have been too busy with work. Maybe a friend calls and they really want to have a long conversation about something meaningful, but I'm just too busy. So I'm wanting to get the conversation over as quickly as I can, so I can get back to what I'm doing. I think you can miss opportunities if you are so focused on what you are doing. You lose sight of what is ultimately important.

As a result, Matthew reports that he is working on taking the time to be more present to his friends and attentive to their needs. Stan Guthrie from Georgia also wants to improve the way he treats his friends. "If there's one [thing I'd like to change about myself], sometimes just think a little bit before I speak." He enjoys making other people laugh, but sometimes his humor comes at the cost of possibly offending others: "Since they know that I'm joking a lot [it's not that hurtful], but I shouldn't point out something about them or make a joke about them [about] the way they look, just to make other people laugh. Because I'm degrading them by trying to get a laugh, so I'm really conscious of that and trying to improve on thinking before I speak."

Others, like Shannon Johnson in Washington, shared stories of personal growth more dramatic than incremental character improvements to character or the development of new activities and skills. When asked whether there is anything she would like to change about herself, she told us about her work at "overcoming an eating disorder." In counseling, which, she says, "steered me into learning more about myself," she began to realize that her eating disorder was triggered in part by her desire to "fit in" and meet certain cultural standards of beauty. Moving beyond her poor body image required her to embrace her personal uniqueness. "I learned that why I fit in a group has to do with something different [about me], and that gave me a little bit more confidence." While "it's something I'll probably always work at," Shannon believes that she became a better person through the experience of confronting a personal demon: "it ended up being beneficial." Still others we spoke with have turned their whole lives around for the better. This kind of growth requires real effort, grit, and (self-)forgiveness.

After hitting what seemed to be rock bottom, Tina Kennedy, Rodrigo Martinez, and Troy Musser each engaged deeply with the necessary, and difficult, restorative and regenerative work. Their growth did not directly result from giving money or time away, but the self-efficacy skills and characteristics they had all cultivated as generous people, which they were able to draw on, propelled them toward flourishing. Seventeen years previously, with her eldest son, then a newborn, Tina fled what she described as an abusive relationship. With no money, little work experience, and an infant to care for, she moved into a women's shelter. "I was at the bottom when I lived there," she recounted. Her description of that time is gut-wrenching, but she also recalls it as a time of positive personal transformation. As she sees it, when people are hurt, they generally respond in one of two ways: they become bitter or they "do the opposite." Tina took the latter, more constructive approach. She embraced the care offered to her. "They. Took. Care. Of. Us," she said, locking eyes with us, deliberately enunciating every word. "Sometimes the shoe has to go on the other foot," she said, meaning that no one is self-sufficient, and we all have needs that we cannot meet on our own. "And I was down on the bottom one time, and I had to be like I have to [receive] now." That experience and insight expanded in Tina into a desire to also care for others whenever possible. That care is now evident in her dogged work to improve conditions in her sons' ailing schools, her willingness to feed and provide shelter for friends in need, and her ability to forgive and empathize.

> I've seen a lot of things and people with, you know, different backgrounds and people who went through different stuff there. To go through all that and still stand, that's big, right there. So I grew from that and I have much admiration and respect for that, definitely. You never can say what a person is going through, why a person is like that. You never know a person's background until you get to know them.

Tina could have responded to the harm done to her with bitterness, but instead she took advantage of the care offered at the shelter, earned her license as a cosmetologist, and now cares for others. The depth of her compassion for others is remarkable.

Similarly, Rodrigo Martinez recently began turning his life around. A near-death experience while driving drunk served as the catalyst for him to confront his problems.

> If I would have kept going the way I was going, like I told you before, drinking, all that, I had a bad, some bad accidents, I almost died. It was a pretty serious accident. I would say that I was going to quit drinking, and I got over an accident and just started up again and again. If I would have kept doing that, I guess I wouldn't be here right now then.

When Rodrigo's cousin invited him to church, "things changed from then. It just changed something, I just snapped or something." According to Rodrigo, Christian faith played a large role in his ability to change, "I don't know. Maybe it was God, I mean I think it was Him, that just said, 'You know what? You're going the wrong way, you've got to change your life, take care of your family, something better than what you're doing.'" Rodrigo is now on a trajectory to a healthier, happier life. Perhaps Rodrigo's transformation is bound up with his generosity—he regularly cares for family members and gives money to his church when he can. He also notes a change in his perspective as to what really matters in life: "Well, I thought that when I was young, well, I wanted to have maybe all this money and all this stuff, and this, and materialistic stuff, and I think all that is just material stuff. It's better to have a family, health, and all that." Now, he derives much of his life purpose, which we will discuss in the next section, from caring for others, particularly his autistic brother. "I'm helping out my brother right now, because he's kind of disabled and all that stuff," Rodrigo tells us, "So I got to help him with, taking him to the store and bringing him back, because he can't read. So I feel good doing that, I guess that's one of the reasons or purposes."

Likewise, Troy stared down his alcoholism after confronting the ravaging hold it had on his life. "I couldn't remember driving home, numerous times. My driving record wasn't too awful bad. Should've been," he tells us. Troy made big changes and quit drinking eight years prior to our interview. "I finally decided to give the kids a better life, I didn't want them seein' me drinkin' all the time. That would just lead them to drinkin'. So it was easier for me to quit and I'm so happy I did. Things have gone a lot better." Troy's life is still far from perfect. "I've been slackin' for so many years, and there are elements in my life that I know need improvement. And that's just a daily thing I know I need to work on." But he has friends and a roommate as sounding boards to help him work on become a better father and friend. As with these cases, most of the generous people we spoke with are striving toward growth, toward becoming better, more loving, more fulfilled people. In our interviews, they do not typically make a direct connection between their generosity and growth, but their personal growth tends to reflect the sorts of existential adjustments needed to become generous. Troy confronted his demons, but he did so primarily because he realized how his alcoholism had negatively impacted his children and his previous marriage. For the most part, his self-growth is other-oriented, much like generous practices that seek good for the other. Although the majority of our generous interviewees have stories of growth less dramatic than those of Tina, Rodrigo, or Troy, nearly all set their sights on actively improving and growing in life.

Generosity and Life Purpose

Unlike most of the ungenerous people we interviewed, Americans who practice generosity believe they have a real purpose in life. They find life to be intrinsically valuable and meaningful, a vision that motivates them to pursue goals and adhere to moral codes involving more than mere self-satisfaction. By finding a substantial life purpose in which to believe, generous people set on a directed life quest with a helpful accompanying roadmap. Naming a purpose, even a somewhat vague one, tends to provide people with plans of action. By organizing their lives around some life purpose, generous people avoid aimlessness, and so are more likely to find satisfaction and happiness. Most generous people relate their life's purpose to a call to reach out and care for others. George Shyer in Texas is typical in this respect. When we asked if he knows what his life purpose might be, without skipping a beat he answers, "Other than trying to help people, no." About two-thirds of the generous people we interviewed deem helping and caring for other people to be the mainstay of their life purpose. Sometimes, their answers are somewhat vague, such as "To make an impact and help people, to make sure I am not just being selfish." More often than not, generous people talk about wanting to be happy. "Pamela Choi," for example, a teacher in her mid-thirties, believes that "life is all about being happy." But generous people are also clear that what it takes to be happy is giving to those around them. As Pamela explains, "At the same time, happiness depends on what [you are] giving to your community and other people." Promoting the flourishing of others, she explains, promotes her own.

> How are you helping, giving most of yourself and things that you feel passionate about? Trying to make change in the world. Doing things that make things better, make the world a better place. It's all about evolving to a higher plane, like enlightenment, and just helping other people get there.

Pamela's view may seem glib, but she actually organizes her life and relationships in ways that promote the kind of generosity she talks about. Her generosity, the happiness she gleans from her practices, and her personal knowledge of the paradox of generosity are most evident when she talks about being an adoptive mother. Realizing that she had the resources to raise a child who requires more time and attention than most, she decided specifically to adopt a daughter with special needs. As a single parent, motherhood is seldom easy for Pamela—she talked at length about the trials of her daughter's recent ear infection, for instance—yet it is consistently rewarding. Pamela beamed when talking about her adopted child.

Similarly, "Cynthia Fountain," who believes that, "We're all here to help each other. And we're all God's children. That's just the way I see. And we should be helping each other. Helping our neighbor, loving our neighbor," articulates finding her purpose in both motherhood and her work as a pediatrician by "influencing and helping children who are physically disabled, acutely or chronic or whatever, and helping them. I think my purpose is to help them. And to be an influence to my kids. They see me living one way, then hopefully, they will turn their lives in and they will live a certain way and love other people, and live honestly, and justly." Her husband, "Henry," a social worker, also locates purpose in his devotion to others:

> I think the purpose is really learning how to free yourself from a lot of stuff, and learn compassion for others. I, yeah. I would say the purpose is really about doing service, and learning how to do that well. Kinda sounds so damn Pollyanna. I should listen to myself.

Christina Heffner, an unmarried corporate accountant in Boston, thinks about purpose in terms of remaining positive and maintaining what she calls "a little bubble of goodness" in spite of "all this nasty negativity in this world." Convinced that she can make a difference by counteracting the darker contours of the world, she talks about her life purpose in terms of being positive and trying "to do good things." She has not entirely worked out what "goodness" means, but she knows it must involve more than promoting her career. "I work for someone who's got it all planned out, you know? Next step up the corporate ladder and a house and all that stuff, and I don't necessarily want that. I hate to think that my job is my purpose in life." By eschewing "the corporate ladder," Christina makes the tacit decision to find a life purpose beyond the narrow confines of her job. Seeking a life purpose beyond financial security is significant for Christina. Growing up, after her parents divorced, her mother filed for bankruptcy. "There were times when we didn't have hot water and electricity for a few days," she explains. While it would certainly be understandable if Christina opted to establish an entirely secure financial future, she reflects on her ability to help others and thinks it is a personal moral obligation to give some of her income away: "I'm happy to [donate]. Yeah but I also think that I do have the moral obligation. I feel like I should do it." Earlier in the interview, we asked Christina what she believed to be most important in life. Her answer ties together her disdain for her previous employer's desire to climb the corporate ladder and her own desire to give back to others:

> I had this when I worked with a very, very manipulative, horrible, I-can't-stand-him guy. And it's just people like that seek to make their lives better

by cutting other people down. I think that's horrible. I just think life is all about helping other people and doing what's right for you and doing the best things for yourself and being as happy as you can be.

Others, realizing that their responses may sound trite, sprinkle their thoughts about life purpose with humor. Their jokes and banter demonstrate a measure of self-deprecating self-awareness, yet they always return to a serious tone regarding their life's purpose, showing that they do take the issue seriously. Denise Powell told us, "As you age, you find purposes in life. What is my value to the community? What is my value to my family? How can I be of value? And I guess that's the purpose, trying to be of value to someone other than just myself—myself and my pets." Her words come across as both true and clichéd simultaneously, so she cracks a joke about her two cats and pet bird: "My purpose is to keep all these animals alive! Make sure the bird gets fed, the cats, the water, yeah." But she then returns to her original and more serious tone: "I think it's how you can be of value or of aid to the community around you or the world around you. You have something beyond yourself." Or take what Alan Bradshaw of Indiana told us: "I think we are here to help other people. I think most of my answers up to this point have been along those lines and for sure that common family. I guess that's one way to describe it." Others see their purpose in life to be happy and whole persons, but, again, they cannot separate their happiness from the happiness of others. "I think everyone has a purpose to be involved in other people's lives. We all touch other people in some way or another for the most part and I think that for most of us, that's our purpose," Markus Birch of Oregon said. Consistently and without prompting, generous people externalize their purposes, meaning that their ultimate goals in life do not exclusively revolve around their own well-being.

Other respondents offer more distilled versions of such externalized purposes. They focus on how their careers complement their life's purpose of helping others. Stan Guthrie, for example, finds meaning in his vocation: "Teaching children is the calling of my life." Rob Siegfried, now nearing retirement, also expresses this theme: "The last five years, anyway, it's not about me anymore, it's about trying to help other younger people be successful. You know, all of that early on was to prove to yourself that you're capable of operating at a high level, and now it's trying to get others to be able to realize their potential, and to me that's the important thing." Not all of the generous people we interviewed believe unequivocally that they have a purpose in life. Even so, the handful of those who are unsure of what their purpose might be are still in search mode, looking for a key to unlock an overarching sense of meaning. But these are exceptions. Most generous people are likely to express a rich, robust, and externally focused life purpose, which contributes to their general personal well-being.

Happiness and Generosity

The more people practice generosity, the more likely they are to express happiness. Many reach for words like "content" and "satisfied," and phrases like "so much better than I thought possible" to describe their lives. They are not happy because life is perfect, but rather because they enjoy life for whatever it happens to be. When we ask Alan Bradshaw if he likes where his life has been headed in the past couple of years, he answers this way: "I feel like the opportunities for what I'm doing now and where I'd like to be are coming together, and I definitely am enjoying that. And at home, too, the kids are growing and busy." When we turn the conversation toward whether or not he is satisfied with life, he continues to speak positively. "I tend to be a content person, a half-full person versus a half-empty person. When I look at what I have, I'm very thankful for it, versus always wanting more." Would he like to make any changes in the way that he and his family are living? "No, we are living the life we would like. I enjoy things where they are and I guess I see more positive things in the future. Nothing happens quickly. We have some bigger goals and we can see that we are heading in the right direction to them." Alan sets his sights on the long-term, avoiding the trap(ping)s of instant gratification. He is insightful on this, since "always wanting more" tends to leave people with less. Gerald Harris from Texas is also quietly content. What specifically is he happy about? "Our children, very well behaved, they do quite well in school. I'm happily married." He does note that he would not mind having more money. "Can always make more money," he quips, "but you can always make less." But lack of money does not impede his satisfaction. "I mean, I'm healthy, my children are healthy, and my wife's healthy, so yeah." Like many others, Gerald recognizes that life could be better, that he could make more money, but he also believes that he has enough. This recognition of having enough, we find, is a common characteristic of people who are both generous and happy. In addition, our generous respondents are more likely than the ungenerous to have deep and meaningful friendships, to be able to maintain a sense of peace amid trouble or suffering, and to see the world in terms of abundance rather than scarcity.

One of the common themes to emerge from our interviews with generous Americans is that they have close and meaningful relationships, friendships, and community ties. Henry Fountain, for example, is a social worker and the kind of person who sees the best in others as they face challenging circumstances. "I love life. I love people," he tells us, "And in my work, I just really believe in the capacity of people to do good things. And to overcome things. I wouldn't say I'm Pollyanna, but I do have, I do trust a lot. Yeah, I really do trust a lot of people. I love life." Later in our interview he explains that, "the neat thing about my job is I get to do that and get paid. So I can earn a living, being able to help others. So I think that that's part of a responsibility within your home, family, and then to extend that through learning to help and love others." In loving others he finds a great deal of happiness and satisfaction. When we asked Stan Guthrie of Georgia, for example, what makes him so happy (he gives himself a self-rating of nine on his happiness scale of ten), he said that quality time with his family makes the biggest difference. He enjoys cheering for a basketball-playing grandson and takes annual weekend getaway trips with his wife, Rhonda. Similarly, Shannon McCracken of Washington partially chalks up her happiness to her close-knit family and friendships: "I'm grateful for a very loving and supportive family, I'm thankful for my husband, I'm thankful for the wonderful friends I've had, and I think I'm grateful that I haven't had a particularly difficult life. You know, I've had a lot of good opportunities and parents that helped us; things could've been a lot worse." Denise Powell of Oregon concurs: "I have some good friends, several of which are long distance, lifelong, been a long, long time." She continues in an upbeat voice:

> I've got one in Alabama who's a very, very dear friend. We got together recently. She moved there, I moved here, but the Internet and cell-phone freebie phone calls make for continuing relationships, it's great. Got a very dear friend who was my prayer partner when I first adopted my son. She adopted his sister. And so we formed a very close relationship that has lasted many, many years. And here I've got a coworker that has become a friend. And then I've got church friends that we have a Bible study we do together once a week and form some fairly close, two or three really close relationships, that if you have a problem you can call up and talk to them. You know, close friends that are willing to, "Ok Denise, you need a drywall hoist, I've got one in my hangar, here!" You know, what can we do to help you? I've got some decent relationships like that.

Denise's friends not only provide emotional support, they also help to make her life easier with their willingness to offer a practical helping hand. Similarly, Rhonda Guthrie in Georgia enjoys the time she spends with her friends in town and enjoys being part of a regular "ladies night out," reporting, "We'll go do something, and go to high school ball-games, or Stan's, since he coaches, we'll go to whatever sport he's in at the moment. So, it's really community things that we do, that kind of stuff." When we ask her husband, Stan, about his friendships, he spends more than seven minutes gushing about them. He feels as though they know him well. "Most people think I'm just a happy go lucky, just a funny guy, not a serious bone in my body. But the ones who know me, they know me pretty well." Those kinds of relationships are crucial for happiness in life, since enjoying friends with whom one can be oneself makes people better able to weather stressful times and minor mental afflictions. Marlene Davis in Nevada also gains a sense of peace from her friendships and provides that same security in return, saying that, "if I need somebody, I know they're there. I know that, and if they need me, they know I'm there." Rob Siegfried in Texas provides yet another example of the quality of friendships that the generous people we spoke with usually enjoy:

> We have block parties, so we use our house and its size to help entertain. We've got good neighbors that we can call on for different things, you know, our next door neighbor looks after the cats and we know all the neighbors right here in the cul de sac. We've had couples come visit us who were close friends, and we say "we love you," and that sort of thing, because they would do anything for us, we would do anything for them. And we have in the past had people we go on vacation together, so yes, strong emotional ties with them, personal long-term friendships with several couples like that.

According to his wife Rachel, their hospitable generosity facilitates these relationships and friendships, which they find so fulfilling: "Because we go, 'want to go out to eat?' or 'Want to come over to our house?' We're just like that, we're social. We got this house so we could have people over."

Troy Musser in Illinois lives with "Gary", whom he calls his "husband-in-law." He and Troy divorced the same woman, and now he helps raise Troy's children.

> I have a roommate, my ex-wife's next husband. She's divorced him also, and she's with her third husband. Her former husband [Gary] rents a room

from me. I know it sounds kind of weird, but he was stepdad to my kids for twelve years. And when he and their mother were separating, she thought he would just disappear, the way she thought I would when she divorced me—but with the three kids that wasn't going to happen. My daughter came to me and said, "Dad, I won't have him out on the street." He was not going to be homeless, since he was working. But the attitude and caring I heard in her voice, I thought, "Well, I'd never really thought about it that way." He had been in their lives since the two youngest ones were three and five.

It is a complicated situation, but Troy prioritizes his children's relationship with their stepfather over enjoying a less complicated living arrangement. Troy wants to help Gary and his kids, so he provides a way for them to maintain the relational ties they have cultivated over the years. Troy also expresses similar compassion for himself as he reflects on the mistakes he made earlier in his life: the drunk-driving incidents, and a lot of hostility and anger. Troy is not chasing an elusive ideal life; rather, he is creating a better life through learned forgiveness, compassion, and care for others. Troy's general satisfaction in life derives from his efforts to make other people happy.

Thus, not only do generous people have more friends, but enjoying more friendships and other important relational ties affords generous people a reprieve from themselves. They want others to be happy, and it is often easier to be happy and content when not actively examining or chasing after one's own individual happiness. A self-centered happiness that is not contingent upon the happiness of others is an insecure, shallow happiness. And, on the whole, the generous people we spoke with derive a lot of their happiness from their close friendships and familial relationships.

Generous people are also generally happier because they are better equipped to take life in stride and maintain peace and perspective when circumstances are tough. Recall Tina Kennedy, the Northern Californian single mother of three boys, from Chapter 2. Shortly after giving birth to her youngest son and recovering from a botched epidural, she learned that her partner was cheating on her with her best friend. "I was in pain, and my mind was just like, woah, and then to get that news. So I had to take that all in consideration, put everything [together]. I don't have that same anger that I did back then." Tina's life has not been easy. After the birth of her first son, she moved into a women's shelter to escape an abusive relationship. She noticed that many of the women with whom she interacted held onto their pain and became bitter. Convinced that she did not want that for herself or her son, she consciously made an effort to take advantage of the shelter's career-training programs. Tina takes a great deal of pride in her resilience and believes that people can sometimes overcome adversity, and that they should be supported in those endeavors. But she also feels somewhat alone in this approach:

> I feel like this world has become me me me me. People's not takin' the time to really look out for the next person. As they used to say, "We're each other's brothers keepers." That shit's scary, 'cause it's [like], "I don't wanna care for no one else, can care less." Person walking down the street just gonna keep walking, you can see a person getting beat up and just stop, would you stop and just say something? I know I would, you know, things like that.

Tina believes that abundance for everyone is possible, if resources are properly distributed and people treat one another with kindness. This view motivates her all the more to support others in whatever ways she can, whether using her cosmetology skills to prepare women for job interviews, pampering them with photo shoots to boost their self-esteem, or letting friends stay with her after being evicted from their own homes. She says:

> I've been the one who always gives and gives and gives. I was down on the bottom one time, and I had to [receive]. I considered it my weakness when I had to ask. But when you're on top, it's always good, you always feel good, you know? But sometimes the shoe has to go on the other foot. So now my life has changed. But I learned how to still give what I'm able to.

Tina pays the rent and buys food and clothes for her family on a meager public assistance check and a small stipend for her work as community liaison at one of her sons' schools. She does not have money to give away. "I mean if I had even more what I've had, like I'm poor. If I got that type of money, I would try to do something. Yeah, definitely, I wouldn't have a problem with giving." Instead she is mindful of the resources that she can offer people: "Back when I was able to do hair [before the bungled epidural], I always had people, not just homeless, that would say they need a job. They may need a job, but they don't have no clothes, no nice hair. I would be the one to do their hair and makeup and make them feel good, and then they can go out and get a job."

Tina cannot change the social structures underlying poverty, so instead she works to change the self-perceptions and self-presentations of the poor. Doing their hair and makeup for free is an act of generosity, one that is fulfilling and further supports her own sense of efficacy and belief that people can overcome adversities. Tina, more than most, understands that people can benefit from revised understandings of themselves. And what she seeks to nurture in others, she also supports in her own life. "I feel like my person's worth has a lot of weight," she tells us. "I have seen changes. I have seen changes, you know, they're slow changes at times, but yeah. One little person can make a change." Tina's ability to enact change, to take some control over situations, and to reach out to others increases her own well-being and sense of peace. None of this is to ignore or justify the multiple injustices shaping Tina's experience, but rather simply to show what unjustly treated people can do to at least prevent victimhood from becoming the dominant theme of their lives.

Other generous people we interviewed also tell stories of learning how to maintain peace and calm in spite of serious problems. Elsewhere in this chapter we mentioned Rhonda Guthrie's struggle with fibromyalgia. Stan, her husband, reports, "It's very emotionally draining, from going to the ER again with chest pains to the stress test, going to the cardiologist, scheduling the heart catheter, the unknown." An athletic coordinator at the local high school and the sole income provider in the family, Stan admits that the financial burden of these health problems is stressful, even with "pretty good insurance." Given these difficulties, when we ask Rhonda if she likes "where [her] life has been headed in the last couple of years or not," she focuses on how much she values and enjoys her husband and the activities she does with him. Rhonda is realistic about the limits that fibromyalgia places on her life. She reckons with the difficulties, but situates them in the larger context of her life and relationship with Stan. She does not let her physical troubles define or color her entire life. "I'm relaxed, I'm comfortable, I'm happy," she says. "I'm content with my life." Again, Stan and Rhonda are remarkably generous—they give a portion of their income to their local church, help pay other people's bills, and provide food and school supplies to students that Stan notices are in need. Rhonda also regularly babysits her grandchildren and picks them up from school, as an act of relational generosity. Rhonda's significant relationships and focus on others' needs help her cope as well as she does with her health problems.

Marlene Davis of Nevada demonstrates yet another example of a generous person who takes life in stride, and finds contentment even amid financial difficulties. Marlene is retired, but continues to work as a nanny to make ends meet. "It's rough with never having enough money," she explains. "Sometimes with the bills and things keep going up the way they do, but other than that, I'm fine. My health is not, I don't have insurance, but my health is in pretty good shape." Ken Walker in Michigan is not in the same sort of difficult situation as Tina, Rhonda, or Marlene, but he is the father of nine children, which presents its own set of complications. Still, he takes a positive approach:

To me, everything will work out fine, everything's always okay, and it'll be all right, something will turn up, and what's supposed to be will be. I always see things to a positive. There's always a bright side to everything. We're extremely fortunate to live in this day and age, we're fortunate to live in the United States, we're very blessed. So I'm appreciative. I don't get too stressed or rattled by hardly anything.

He continues:

Our schedule is hectic, but I don't really feel stressed over that. Sometimes, sometimes it's a little hairy just as far as okay, we've got to get this one here, and pick this one up by this and get this one here, and we rotate through it, but I don't really feel stressed by it. I enjoy watching their practices and sitting there. I think stress is what you make of it.

Ken practices astute financial planning and thrifty household budgeting. For example, "We're trying to save, you know, we've got the accounts, the [college savings] accounts for the kids and IRAs and we've got a 401(k) and we try to plow as much into that as possible, so we shouldn't get caught off guard." This also allows Ken to give money to his alma mater and his church. It is likely that those same factors—planning and perspective—help put Ken at ease, despite his life's stresses.

As simple as it may sound, the generous people we interviewed face problems and setbacks with greater aplomb, humor, and ease than their ungenerous counterparts. They are more flexible in their expectations of life and are better able to appreciate life as it is without focusing on all that it is not. Pamela Choi, described above, says that she is "stressed, but not in a bad way." She explains:

When I was twenty-four, I thought I would have [by now] gotten married, had two kids and a dog. But I am happy where I am now. My life is good. It is not what I expected. My expectations have changed now. My expectations in life now are to be a good mother and daughter and sister and friend.

When the plant where he worked as a mid-level manager for over thirty years shut down at the start of the Great Recession of 2008, Gerald Harris in Texas did not wallow in misery or become self-absorbed. Instead, he helped the men and women who worked for him find new jobs. He also expressed gratitude for his modest lifestyle, which allowed his family to weather the long months ahead without income. It took sixty days for the plant to cease operations, and Gerald stayed on for another two weeks to transfer equipment. Thankfully, he found new work within three months.

> The people are what really got to me. They announced the shutdown like that. Nobody knows it's coming, and our organization, the plant manager and HR manager and that are sworn to absolute silence. And then you call in people, everybody in their plant, about one hundred people, last shift. The shift ends and management has a box of Kleenexes. We've already been told the plant is shutting down, but the hourly workers have not been told. And you bring that [news], with people crying and really going through emotionally hard times. That's a bad, bad feeling. A lot of people were very, very upset, a lot of tears were shed that day.

So Gerald stepped in to help people update their resumes: "You try to jump in, try to help people as far as, I wrote quite a few resumes for people. I had people actually come in and go, 'What do you think I ought to do?' You're trying to counsel people career-wise when you yourself you're not sure what you're gonna do." Acting generously toward others helped Gerald himself make his way through that difficult time. By responding with action when he and many others were feeling helpless, Gerald gained a sense of efficacy. More importantly, his reaction to the shutdown suggests that Gerald operates out of a framework of abundance and security, rather than scarcity and fear. Even when facing unemployment, he maintained a sense of calm and remained focused on others. He did not feel the need to push his own needs to the top of the pile when looking for a new job. On a more practical level, his family's purposefully modest lifestyle also proved helpful, as we noted above. Recalling the stories of fright that Doug and Michelle shared in the previous chapter about the restructuring of their companies, Gerald's tone clearly deviates from such a narrative of insecurity and personal fortress-building. Whereas Doug and Michelle express fear about keeping their house and standard of living, Gerald expresses security. Whereas the Arnolds search for an elusive happiness with their possessions, Gerald seems to find greater happiness and comfort by limiting his possessions and helping other people first.

In other words, by focusing on others and by taking the practical step of setting aside resources for the betterment of others, generous people limit their search for the elusive happiness that ungenerous people crave. By asserting that their own wants are not the end-all and be-all, generous people do not fall into the same trap of wanting better, wanting more. What they want most is the flourishing of people, their loved ones, the needy, the neglected, the environment, and so on. Most generous people agree with Rhonda when she tells us, "Well, I believe we're responsible for everybody, not just my family. My neighbor is not just the person that lives next-door to me, it's anybody that I come in contact with." She confides:

> I'm only saying this because I know it is confidential, but Stan and I help a lot of people anonymously, with monetary gifts and if they need clothing or food. We believe that if you see somebody in need and you don't help them, it's a sin. We've helped a lot of people, and it's fun for us to do that. We don't do it so we can be blessed or for anybody to see us. But we feel really strongly about that, about helping others. When you work in the school system, you see needs a lot.

Similarly, Rodrigo in Georgia makes a go of life on a meager income, explaining with contentment:

> It's okay, I mean I have a house, a car, and not rich or nothing, but at least we make it. I'm happy, I mean, I think a person who would have what I have would be happy. Other people want more stuff, material stuff, so they go to school and they want more and more and more, but I'm happy, satisfied with what I have. I thought when I was young that I wanted to have maybe all this money and all this materialistic stuff. But I think all that is just material stuff. It's better to have a family, health, and all that. So I think it turned out good, I'm okay.

Some, like Troy Musser, even see money as potentially problematic. "It's not meant for us to hoard," he argues. "We can't take it with us, and you can only enjoy so much of it before it starts getting in the way." Troy earns an income of only $30,000, which he uses to support himself and pay alimony, and it is not always easy for him to make ends meet. Even so, he is happy: "Oh yeah, definitely. I decided years ago I'll never be rich and I don't care. The money doesn't matter to me." Admittedly, Troy is an optimist, explaining that some people "see a deer and all they think about is that that's the one that might run in front of their car." Troy sees the beauty

When a sparrow sips in the river, the water doesn't recede. Giving charity does not deplete wealth.

—*Punjabi proverb*

Every man goes down to his death bearing in his hands only that which he has given away.

—*Persian proverb*

He who lends to the poor gets his interest from God.

—*German proverb*

No one became poor by giving alms.

—*French proverb*

The charitable give out the door and God puts it back through the window.

—*Traditional proverb, unknown origin*

That which a man willingly shares, he keeps. That which he selfishly keeps, he loses.

—*Traditional proverb, unknown origin*

instead: "I mean, there's just so much beauty all around us, and I think a lot of things that we take for granted, all the blessings that we have. There's a lot of beauty in this world, in this country."

The Crucial Exception of "Pathological Altruism"

Like all good things in life, some moderation is crucial in practicing generosity well. When taken to extremes, generosity does not benefit the givers or even, in many cases, recipients. Yet some people are unfortunately determined to help others regardless (or perhaps because) of a high cost of personal self-neglect. This type of generosity—the recently coined term for it is "pathological altruism"—is unhealthy and harmful.[3] This pathology aptly describes two of the sixty-two people we interviewed in this study. They do not experience the normal benefits of a life shaped by generous practices. Instead, their level of happiness, orientation to personal growth, and lower sense of life purpose better match the patterns we see in ungenerous people. Again, as with those who volunteer significant amounts of time but refuse to give away much of their money, despite being well off, this finding shows not only that the behavioral practice of generosity matters, but also that the personal interest and orientation to generosity matters, too. In other words, extreme generosity may be pathological, rather than fulfilling. Both of the people in our study whom we classify as pathological altruists are women burdened by debilitating mental and physical health conditions. These factors bear heavily on their lower quality of life, regardless of their generous behaviors. Nevertheless, the evidence suggests to us that their selflessness toward others has gone awry. Their generous actions stem from self-loathing, likely triggered by mental illness, rather than a more positive place.

Our first case of pathological altruism is "Diane Krieger" of Connecticut. She reports being hospitalized fourteen times during the winter prior to our interviews, for a combination of lung problems and agoraphobic attacks. A long-time chain smoker, she says, "my lungs have taken a nosedive." In addition to agoraphobia, neuropathy, spinal arthritis, and fibromyalgia, she also suffers from post-traumatic stress disorder. "My health is going down the toilet," she tells us. Her poor health is the most significant challenge she faces in life and the reason she left her modest job in the service sector without any savings or assets. Now on welfare, she struggles to pay her own bills, but is still adamant about paying her niece's college tuition. She cannot afford it, of course, and often finds herself without enough money, but she feels compelled to support her niece anyway. Diane admits to us that she does this in part to reinforce her own perceived self-identity of absolute selflessness, an aspect of her personality that even her closest friend recognizes. "My friend Barbara used to say to me, 'It's because you have such a big heart, you know, that people walk all over you. Stop being so good to people and things will get better.' " But Diane does not believe that things can get better. When we ask her about what the purpose of her own life might be, she replies without skipping a beat, "To be abused. Seriously. I really think I was put on this earth to be abused." The abuse of which she speaks goes back to a painful childhood: "I had everything a child could want, except for love and compassion. Everything looked wonderful, you know, you come into the house and we had the best of everything, but it was far from wonderful. It was a war zone." However, it is not clear how accurate her recollections of her childhood were. At the time of our interview, she was quite certain she would die of lung failure within weeks—"I'm basically waiting to die," she said—but she was still alive two years later, as of this writing. At times during our interview, Diane psychologizes her behavior and experiences—a likely outcome of many hours spent in therapy. She also recounts to us seemingly fantastical stories of being a dancer and taking on lovers who ultimately abandon her or are unable to meet her most basic emotional needs. But the accuracy of her own life account is of little importance for our present purposes; what matters is how her narrative seems to affect her generous behavior now. Diane's accounts of pain and struggle—whether real, imagined, or some of both—shape her low sense of personal worth. This perception in turn fuels her determination to somehow "matter" and to "make a difference," often by depleting her own resources, supposedly for the good of others.

The second case of a pathological altruist we observed in our interviews is "Beverly Hastings," a woman in her fifties who lives on a small Social Security check. When we met Beverly at her apartment, the left side of her hair was uncombed and sticking straight up. The right side was cut unevenly, and covered much of her face, including some of the bruises and scars around her cheeks and eyes that we learned more about on our second day of interviewing her. Beverly led us through her kitchen and into the living room, where all of the shades were drawn, in an attempt to keep the house cool despite the summer heat. Throughout the interview, her demeanor shifted several times. Sometimes, Beverly slouched into her chair, faced away from us, and spoke toward the wall, as if she was performing a monologue to an unseen audience. Her eyes drooped and she closed them for long periods of time while talking; even after she opened them, her gaze remained heavy and unfocused. At other points, she picked up the pace of her speech, speaking so quickly that it was difficult to understand her. She would suddenly turn back toward us, opening her eyes wide, often pointing her finger at us. Beverly regularly sees a therapist who prescribes antidepressants and a medication for schizophrenia. But she adamantly refuses to take the pills—she knows that she is unwell, but believes the problem to be spiritual, completely beyond the scope of medicinal healing.

Like Diane, Beverly seems to have had a difficult life, although it does not matter for our analysis just how much of what she tells us is factually true. She told us that at the age of twelve, she was violently raped after being kidnapped. Her mother, whom Beverly hates, claims that it was her father, whom Beverly loves, who raped her. Beverly rebukes this as nonsense and says that her mother is crazy. While she does not blame those who molested and raped her, leaving "revenge" up to God, she harbors resentment against her mother. This is an important detail in Beverly's life—she thinks of her problems and sufferings, including her mental health problems, as religiously rooted and solvable. So she refuses to accept help from anyone, including her therapist and her mother. For Beverly, it is important to love the unlovable and deal with personal demons using the resources she already has; she believes that to ask for more for herself would be unthinkable. After all, two months prior to our discussion with Beverly, she tells us, "My mother tried to hurt my father again and I guess he just had enough and ripped a thing out of her hand, and she called the police and said that it was him, but my father's never been abusive, it's always been my mom. She shot him when I was twelve years old." When we ask Beverly what has made her the most sad or depressed in recent memory, she responds: "Not having a mother to love me. Why do she hate me so? Why do my mother hate me, what's different about me?" She seems perfectly capable of forgiving others who have wronged her, but not the woman who claims that she has been victimized and who "de-spiritualizes" the sexual assaults Beverly has suffered. Instead, this is a woman who apparently "hates her so."

Yet, this is not the only difficult relationship in Beverly's life. She has an ex-boyfriend who lived with her until, "He slapped me on this floor once, well, he tried to kill me if you ask me. He was crazy, violent," she confides, "I had to let him go." In addition, several years ago, Beverly began collecting disability income when her car was hit by a truck. Before that, a workplace grease fire in a kitchen caused second- and third-degree burns from which she never completely healed. "My face looked like it was burnt," she describes. "You can't tell," she says, but the scarring is still visible. "I was burnt all in my face, all in my head." Pointing out some of the marks, she says, "some of the grease splattered over here, so the third degree burns and by me being a diabetic caused other problems later on." Even after the violent encounters with her boyfriend, the grease fire, and the car accident, Beverly resists asking for help. Instead, she insists on helping others, regardless of the personal cost. It is as though by martyring herself and giving away the few resources she has, she can establish her own value and worth. Talking with Beverly, we got the sense that she perhaps welcomes these hardships as a way of showcasing her ability to rise above the suffering. Generosity is a form of self-immolating self-validation for Beverly. She continually says things like, "I like helping people. Sometimes I help people with just the little money that I have, sometimes and give blessings." And:

> I'm a giver. I got some new neighbors but the neighbors I had before I used to help them all the time. Loan them money, whatever they came down here and needed I would give it to them because I pretty much got a medicine cabinet sitting right there, anything you need, antibiotic ointment, something for pain, pretty much everything you need.

"If I got, you have it. I don't care who you are, black, white, Chinese, Japanese. I help all colors." Her most dramatic statement of her unwavering generosity, however, involves taking in a young woman who needed shelter.

> I just took a white girl in. She was downtown on the street. Twenty-three years old and I helped, she was on the back of her shoes. It was a strange

thing because it was my day off, Monday. Usually Monday I go to Indiana to visit my boys, see my sons and stuff. As I'm walking, I see this young lady sitting ahead, then when I got there I looked and I started taking out money before I even got there, $5 to put in her cup. I looked at her, just this young girl, you know, she young enough to be my child, so I ask, "How old are you?" "Twenty-three years old." I said, "You twenty-three, you don't have no family? Why are you out here like this?" She had blisters on her feet.

Beverly thought of this encounter as divinely ordained, because she had not planned on being in the city that day, so she was compelled to take action. Her thinking that the girl was young enough to be her daughter seemed to intensify her connection with her.

Do you know I made her get up and come with me. She didn't know me from Adam and Eve. I was like "Come on, hun." So then I took her into a lawyer office to get a yellow page so I can find a shelter or something for her. I got to calling around and do you know they got shelters for people at nighttime, so what they do all day? You have to reconstruct them to get back into society and living, you can't just throw them back into the street homeless. They need something, so you can help them get a job. Not just food and warm bed but they need to get back in society.

Beverly wants to help other people by showing how vital her aid is when institutions fail. It is not enough to provide someone with only twelve hours of shelter. Beverly decided to take helping the girl upon herself—even though her parked car had overstayed its metered welcome, leading to a hefty fine, yet another bill that she cannot pay. But practical factors and considerations were no match for Beverly's desire to help this young woman.

I end up taking her with me, being with me all day, me trying to find her a shelter. And I took her shopping, took her to Target, spent 300-something dollars on her, new panties, new bra, socks, shoes, pants, outfit to go look for a job and everything. I told her "I will help you. I will help you." I gave her blankets, radios, I got her food, she came here, she took a shower, she cleaned up. I say "Just throw all that stuff you just took off, throw it away, that ain't you no more, the only thing I want you to do is go to school, I will help you get a job, I will give you a job." Because my old man owned a club, so she could have worked waiting tables or whatever. She said she was twenty-three, but she ain't have no ID, so I said "I gotta get your ID."

In some ways, Beverly's radical generosity is impressive. She will drop everything to turn a young woman's life around. Even so, her generosity caused a great deal of pain. She was unprepared for the possibility that the young woman she had known for only a few hours might flee, which is what happened.

I don't know what happened to that girl. She had my telephone number. When I went to see about her, she was gone. All the clothes I gave her was gone. Somebody said, "Well, Beverly, maybe that was a scam and maybe she felt that she didn't want to 'take' you because she realized you was a good person." But I wonder, you know, I say "Lord, did I do the right thing?" Or did somebody kidnap this girl or harm her? It really bothered me for a long time. I say, "Lord, wherever she is I hope she's okay," because I really felt sorry for her and nobody wanted to help her. I took her and I gave her money, too. I shopped for her, I gave her money, I gave her food, and cleaning stuff, cleaning supplies, but she just disappeared and I ain't understand that. I still don't. I don't know whatever happened to her. She never called. I hope nobody kidnap her or she went out, but it is what it is. But I did what I could do. I didn't walk past her. Even though I had people saying, "Well, Beverly, you better stop doing that, they could be [bad or] whatever," and I was like, well, you know, that's just who Jesus made me to be. Because, see, that could have been my daughter, I would want somebody to help her.

Beverly views herself as a martyr willing to reach out to others without acknowledging the costs or questioning people's motives. But she is pained when the object of her generosity runs out on her. Her mind races to the worst-case scenario of kidnapping. She maintains the innocence of the young woman she helped. Let others believe that the homeless woman took advantage of Beverly—her concern remains with the young woman, just as it did with her likely rapist. She loves those who take from her and hates those who seem to try to protect her from herself.

Beverly's generosity seems bottomless, but it hollows her out in a sometimes-tortuous manner. This extreme version of generosity, in which its practitioners fail to care for themselves, corrodes personal well-being. The motivations and aims of people who practice this kind of "pathological altruism" are different from those who practice more modest forms of generosity. Beverly and Diane thus illustrate an important caveat to the general truth of the paradox of generosity. But it is equally important to remember that generosity taken to an unhealthy extreme, according to our study, is quite rare. Only a minority of Americans are seriously generous in the first place, as we saw in Chapter 2, and only a small percentage of them are pathologically altruistic, as we define it here. Although they do exist, cases like Beverly and Diane do nothing to undermine the larger point of this chapter—that practicing genuine, non-pathological generosity exerts strong causal tendencies which improve the life experiences of generous people.

Conclusion

Generous people, we show, tend to be happier and more fulfilled than their ungenerous counterparts. This is true in spite of the fact that many generous people we interviewed face significant life problems and setbacks, often similar to those experienced by the less generous. Practicing generosity does not guarantee a life free of troubles or crises. Given their adversities, one might expect generous people to throw in the towel and become less generous. But that usually does not happen. We often find instead that they exude greater tranquility, joy, and gratitude. The happiness that generous people tend to enjoy is not delivered by random luck. Generosity is not the result of people living charmed lives. Generous people know the hard reality of what it means to be human—to make mistakes, to hurt and be hurt, to suffer. Generosity itself does not protect people from misfortune. Instead of keeping all of their resources to protect their own families and lifestyles, generous people give away some for the well-being of others. Rather than using all that they have to build a bigger nest egg or finance a more secure lifestyle, they help to build others up and protect those who are more vulnerable. And they are noticeably happier—even though they do not have the perfect families, dream homes, or jobs, let alone the full bank accounts that their less generous counterparts point to as the alleged key to happiness. Security and happiness for the generous are not elusive goods always on the horizon; generous people do not try to find happiness by outpacing the curvature of the earth. Both generous and ungenerous people live lives that are less than ideal. But the generous possess an insight usually missing among the less generous. They know that they already have enough, and that clinging to what they have or clamoring for more will not bring about greater happiness. So they share some of their time, money, and care with others. They tend to see the beauty of life, the value of solidarity, and their connection to humanity. Their perspective tells them that the world, properly viewed, is a place of abundance. They take their hardships in stride, believing that life is good and still worth living, beautiful, and meaningful. Their problems in life do not set the dominant tone of life. So they enjoy something like what Wendell Berry describes: "There are moments when the heart is generous, and then it knows that for better or worse our lives are woven together here, one with one another and with the place and all living things."[4] And, in the end, they are much more likely to enjoy better lives.

Conclusion

THE MESSAGE OF THIS book is simple, but we think also profound and important. Generosity is paradoxical. Those who give their resources away, receive back in turn. In offering our time, money, and energy in service of others' well-being, we enhance our own well-being as well. In letting go of some of what we own for the good of others, we better secure our own lives, too. This paradox of generosity is a sociological fact, confirmed by evidence drawn from quantitative surveys and qualitative interviews. We have good reason to accept this conclusion, and no good reason to ignore it. We can also state the paradox negatively. By clinging to what we have, we lose out on higher goods we might gain. By holding onto what we possess, we diminish its long-term value to us. In protecting only ourselves against future uncertainties and misfortunes, we become more anxious about uncertainties and vulnerable to future misfortunes. In short, by failing to care well for others, we actually do not properly take care of ourselves.

Understanding the paradox of generosity is the relatively easy part; more difficult is learning how we can actually become more generous. Generosity is not an easy, one-step way of life that is easily learned. Practicing generosity requires confronting some deep existential questions about our lives, making what can seem like hard decisions, and learning new routines, attitudes, and behaviors. The good news, again, is that living generously is genuinely good for us. The harder news is that becoming truly generous often requires overcoming some mental, emotional, and perhaps financial obstacles that get in the way of practicing what is good.

We wrote this book, in part, as an attempt to help less generous readers find their way to more generous life practices, and to help more generous readers understand the facts and processes about the goods of generosity that they experience. Digging deeper into understanding the specific kinds of factors and dynamics that promote new generosity in people, according to our research findings, will require another, different book. But before closing here, we offer some final thoughts about the value of focused attention on the questions this book raises. The main point is that personal and family change often starts with honest conversations about big life issues. It is easy to be vaguely optimistic about becoming hopefully generous persons. It is harder to realistically confront just how generous we actually are, and then to make real changes toward becoming more generous. But confronting what is hard is precisely what people must do if they are to experience the paradox of generosity.

Our interviews often provoked strong feelings and reactions from those with whom we talked, mostly because we asked about topics that many people do not often consciously think about. At the completion of the interviews, some told us that they did not understand why we wanted to know so much about their generosity or lack of it. One couple said that they found our questions about giving money, time, and care to be boring. Others acknowledged that talking about purpose or morality was a challenge, and that they were a bit lost and tongue-tied in their answers. This makes sense. In our culture, few people have the opportunity to sit down for four to seven hours with a stranger who promises not to judge them, but who invites them to think about and express their vision of life's purpose and the good life, and to verbalize their deepest hopes and fears. Furthermore, the topic of one's personal use of money is generally off limits in American culture. Americans spend a great deal of time worrying about, monitoring, and delighting in their paychecks, bank balances, and maybe mutual-fund accounts. But few talk about the details of their financial, spending, and consumer lives with anyone else, other than perhaps a spouse or partner. For too many Americans, taking the time to step back and reflect on the grand scheme of things, to ask what life is really about, and what we think about the ways we are living, seems to be a luxury.

Yet soul searching about the big picture in life does not need to detract from the goods of life, or compete with the everyday demands on our time and mental resources. By doing so, we can better map out our place in the scheme of things, and think more clearly about how we are related to and responsible for other people. By sharing our stories and listening to those of others, we can learn to better embrace both the beauty and brokenness of the world. And we can rekindle memories of moments that perhaps once reoriented us to something greater than our everyday routines and private lives. The kind of honest soul searching that our research interviews ask of our respondents can pull any of us out of the bustle of daily life, and invite us to see more clearly and evaluate what we often thoughtlessly assume about our lives and take for granted as we live them. Pondering some difficult, probing questions can prod us to consider whether we are really content with the way we are living, and whether we want and need to make real changes for the better.

Generosity—the esteem that people hold it in and extent to which we practice it—may also serve as a bellwether for the moral and spiritual state of American life. After all, the practice of generosity becomes a habit in the Aristotelian and Toquevillean sense—a way of life, an orienting map. Generosity emerges from and engenders a culturally sustaining way of life in which people live out of scarcity or abundance, apathy or action, anxiety or peace. Are we willing to make sacrifices for the common good? Or do we find such a pursuit to be unnecessary and believe instead, perhaps tacitly, that individualism and freedom, particularly from the constraints that others may place on us, trump virtues of generosity and solidarity? To pursue the common good, many voices in our culture proclaim, we must pursue our own individual good and let others take care of their own needs. But such a view has ramifications far beyond individual-level well-being. One of the contributions of our book is to show how generosity is not only a healthy form of constraint in a culture that consistently celebrates the pursuit of freedom for the individual, but that the "constraint" of generosity actually turns out to be not much of a constraint at all. Rather, when generosity is embraced as a way of life, people increasingly live into the reality of what it means to be human, a fuller and truer sense of who human beings are and what we are capable of. As we have seen in the lives of generous Americans, it is more than possible to go against the dominant narrative—but it is not always easy.

Truman Wright of Michigan said in his interviews that he takes material and physical pleasure to be the highest human goods, and his statements of apathy pepper our examination of the more ungenerous of Americans. Yet his final words offer an example of the potential impact that simply talking about one's life's purpose, the good life, and generosity can have on some people. After our interviews, we invited all of our respondents to tell us what their experiences of our conversations were like. Truman said this: "I never had anybody ask me all the questions that you've asked. You asked me some questions that I never really, sometimes never even thought about." He continued:

Now I'm kinda enlightening on things. Because I never really thought about not volunteering, giving money, helping out, and stuff like that. I never really [gave] it a lot of thought. Now I kinda feel bad that I haven't done a little bit more. This interview, you kinda woke me up on a few things. I guess I just gotta take a better look at myself, the way I live my life. 'Cause I noticed in it that I kept telling you, "I never been locked up, I never been in trouble." But I guess in a sense that still don't mean I'm okay. You know what I'm saying? Maybe I should make some changes, maybe I should do a little bit more volunteer work, or maybe give a little bit more.

We think Truman Wright is a fascinating example of potential personal change arising from a focused, in-depth consideration of fundamental life questions. One of the goals in our conducting this research project, the Science of Generosity Initiative, and writing this book about the paradox of generosity has been to foster precisely these kinds of conversations and to explore the potential life changes they might produce. As sociologists, we of course also want to simply better understand the causal social mechanisms that operate to make personal and social life work the way it characteristically does. But we are interested in more than pure, abstract, social-scientific knowledge. In our view, all scientific knowledge must always serve the human good. In our case, the scientific evidence tells us quite clearly that, except in the most pathological cases, practicing generosity is good for people, both for the givers and those who receive. Generosity has the causal power to change people and at least parts of the world—not absolute power, but significant power. We hope that, as part of a larger project of inquiry and learning, this book contributes significantly to that change, and to the good it promises to promote.

| Additional Evidence on Generosity, Depression, and Personal Growth

C HAPTER I REVIEWED THE STATISTICAL evidence for the association between generous practices, better physical health, greater happiness, and greater purpose in life.
We saw there that the pattern of associations was consistent and often strong. The same is
true for the relationship between generous practices and two other important well-being
factors we measured in the Science of Generosity Survey: avoidance of depression and
interest in personal growth. In order to avoid overwhelming readers with too much
quantitative evidence in the first chapter, we limited the statistics we presented there
to health, happiness, and purpose in life. We present here the latter two measures of
well-being: avoidance of depression and interest in personal growth. The relationships
between generosity and these two forms of well-being are the same as those observed in

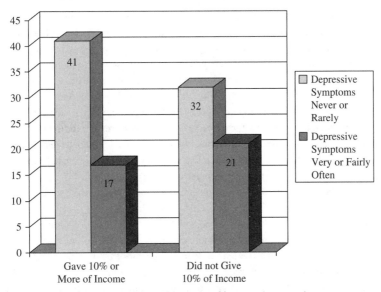

FIGURE A.1 Depression and giving 10 percent of income (percents)

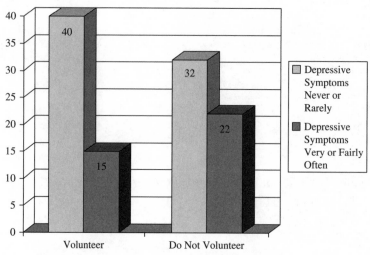

FIGURE A.2 Depression and volunteering (percents)

Chapter 1. (All of the differences are statistically significant at the p < .05 level after controlling for ten possibly confounding demographic and life-course variables, with three exceptions: Figures A.1, A.6, and A.9 are all significant at the p = .10 level.).

As Figures A.1 and A.2 show, Americans who give away at least 10 percent of their income and who volunteer are less likely to exhibit depressive symptoms than those who do not. Those who rarely or never show depressive symptoms volunteer more hours per month than those who show them more often (Figure A.3). A similar story holds when it comes to depression and relational generosity: The most relationally generous Americans are far less likely to experience depressive symptoms often than the least relationally generous, as Figure A.4 illustrates. The relationship between depression and neighborly generosity is slightly less straightforward; Figure A.5 shows a similar correlation between levels of neighborly generosity and symptoms of depression, with the exception of those who practice neighborly generosity on a weekly basis. When it comes to respondents' self-evaluations of their generosity, again, greater generosity is associated with less depression: Americans who rate their financial generosity (Figure A.6) and volunteering generosity (Figure A.7) highly are less apt to display depressive symptoms often. The numbers for depression and self-evaluated relational generosity in Figure A.8 are less consistent, but generally those who evaluate themselves as relationally generous to some degree are depressed less often than those who consider themselves ungenerous. Finally, those who disagree with the statement "It is very important to me to be a generous person" are more likely to experience depressive symptoms often.

All in all, the more generous Americans are, the less frequently they suffer symptoms of depression.

Moving on to Americans' interest in personal growth, the same relationship between generosity and interest in growth is once more evident. Those who volunteer (Figure A.11) and especially those who give away more than 10 percent of their income (Figure A.10) are more likely to express great interest in personal growth than those who do not, and those who are interested in personal growth volunteer more hours per month than those

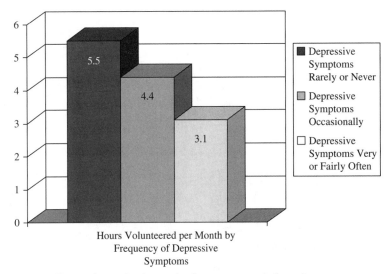

FIGURE A.3 Depression and volunteering hours per month (hours)

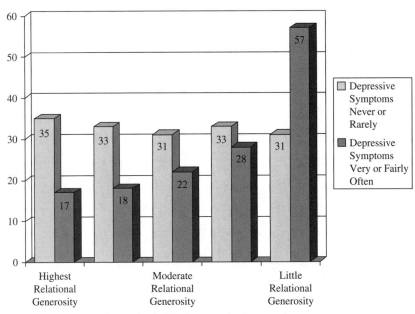

FIGURE A.4 Depression and relational generosity (percents)

who are uninterested (Figure A.12). The same positive correlation between generosity and interest in personal growth holds particularly strongly for relational generosity, as Figure A.13 illustrates, and is present as well for neighborly generosity in Figure A.14. With some exceptions, the more highly Americans rate their levels of financial generosity (A.15), volunteering generosity (A.16), and relational generosity (A.17), the more likely they are

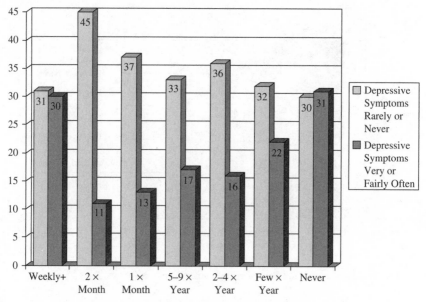

FIGURE A.5 Depression and neighborly generosity (percents)

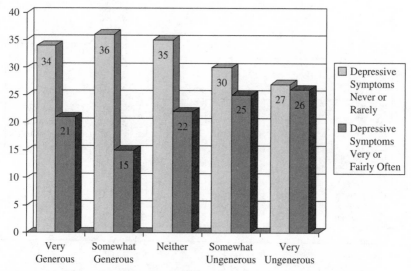

FIGURE A.6 Depression and self-evaluations of financial generosity (percents)

to be very interested in personal growth and the less likely they are to be uninterested in it. Finally, as Figure A.18 displays, the more strongly Americans agree that it's important to them to be generous, the more interested they are in pursuing personal growth. These findings, like those for depression and generosity, provide yet more evidence of the clear relationship between generous practices and mental and emotional well-being.

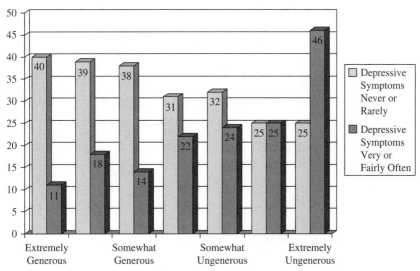

FIGURE A.7 Depression and self-evaluations of volunteering generosity (percents)

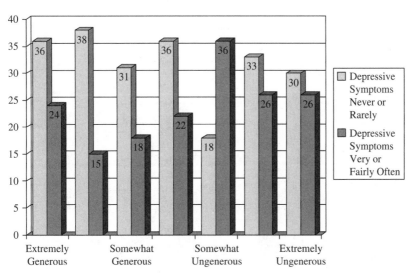

FIGURE A.8 Depression and self-evaluations of relational generosity (percents)

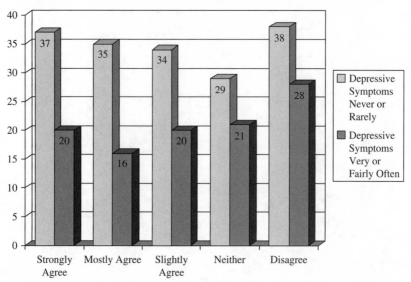

FIGURE A.9 Depression and "It is very important to me to be a generous person" (percents) (p = .13)

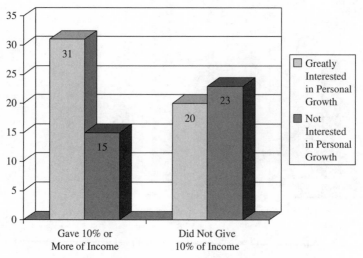

FIGURE A.10 Personal growth and giving 10 percent of income (percents)

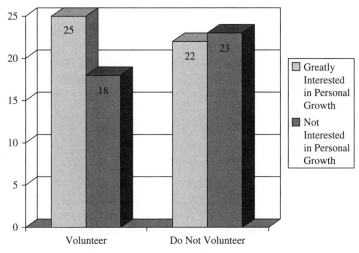

FIGURE A.11 Personal growth and volunteering (percents)

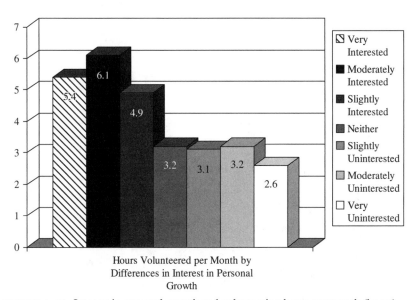

FIGURE A.12 Interest in personal growth and volunteering hours per month (hours)

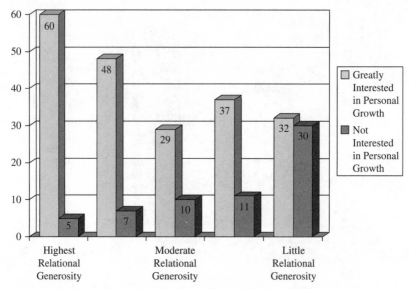

FIGURE A.13 Personal growth and relational generosity (percents)

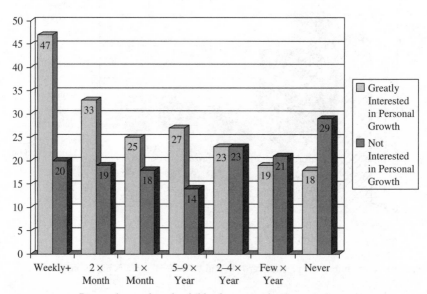

FIGURE A.14 Personal growth and neighborly generosity (percents)

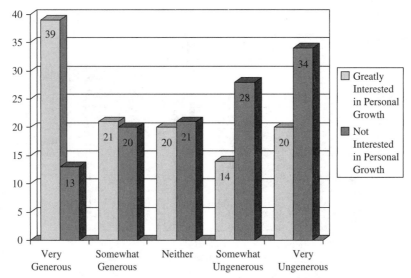

FIGURE A.15 Personal growth and self-evaluations of financial generosity (percents)

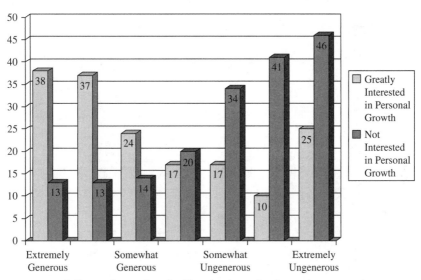

FIGURE A.16 Personal growth and self-evaluations of volunteering generosity (percents)

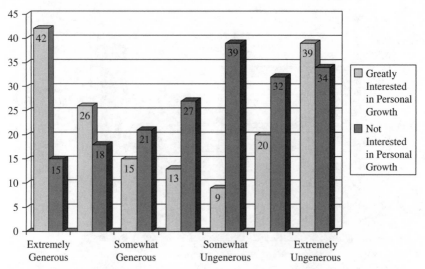

FIGURE A.17 Personal growth and self-evaluations of relational generosity (percents)

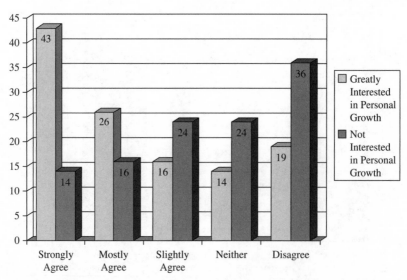

FIGURE A.18 Personal growth and "It is very important to me to be a generous person" (percents)

NOTES

Introduction

1. Both coming to English through French from the Latin word *miserabilis*, meaning "pitiable" or "wretched."

2. "Generosity," in the *Oxford English Dictionary*, 2d ed. (New York: Oxford University Press, 2004); "Generosity" in *A Concise Etymological Dictionary of the English Language*, ed. Walter Skeat (New York: Perigree Books, 1980). We rely in the following paragraphs on the OED's account.

3. For detailed information on the Science of Generosity Survey, see Christian Smith, Kraig Beyerlein, and Patricia Snell-Herzog, "Methodological Report on the Science of Generosity Project," unpublished paper, University of Notre Dame, 2012.

4. In-person interviews were conducted with sampled Science of Generosity survey respondents and, if applicable, their spouses or live-in partners. A total of 525 survey respondents were based in the twelve states selected for interviews. This geographical sample base was then used as the pool from which to select potential interviewees based on various survey and contextual measures, in order to ensure a stratified quota sample across different characteristics of interest to us. A total of fifty-one survey respondents were selected from this broader sample to complete in-person interviews, of which forty agreed, for a response rate of 78 percent. Of the forty survey respondents, twenty-two had a spouse or live-in partner who was also interviewed, making the overall interview sample consist of sixty-two interviewees in forty households. Because the interview respondents were selected from the broader pool of survey respondents, we possessed demographic information and survey responses for all those selected for interviews who were not able to complete them. For those who did complete interviews, interviewers met with them in their households to complete two separate halves of the full interview for an average of two hours per half, or an average of four hours of interviewing total per participating household respondent. All interviews were recorded and later transcribed. The interview transcripts total to well over one thousand pages of qualitative data. The sampling process for selecting potential interviewees consisted of selecting on: (1) desired general geographic locations; (2) household and family characteristics; (3) variation in participation in generous activities, such as involvement in the community; and (4) variation in

neighborhood contextual characteristics. Interview respondents were selected from different locations around the US to generally represent the major geographical areas of the Northeast/East Coast, Midwest, South/Southeast, Southwest, and West/West Coast. The states selected were Massachusetts, Maryland, Washington, DC, Illinois, Michigan, and Indiana, Georgia, North Carolina, Texas, Arizona, California, Washington, and Oregon.

5. The Science of Generosity Initiative collected fieldnote observations on all interviewee neighborhoods and households. When conducting the interviews with household respondents, interviewers also completed a number of participant observations, including detailed observations of the neighborhood in which the respondent lived, and, when applicable (if they had moved in the year prior to the interviews), an observation of the neighborhood they recently moved from. Observations were also collected on the household during each of the interview visits and during an additional observation time. Interviewers typically visited participating households on a number of occasions, returning to the household for both halves of the primary respondent interview, and if applicable, both halves of the spouse or live-in partner interview. In addition, interviewers normally spent some unstructured, unrecorded time with family households, joining them for dinner or observing some other aspect of their daily routine. Every observation—interview, household, and neighborhood—was collected upon completion of the interview through an online form that included structured and semi-structured questions on the neighborhoods and unstructured spaces for open-ended observations. The compiled notes from these observations total to more than five hundred single-spaced, typed pages. Interviewers also collected photographic data during their interviews. They took pictures as they traveled around the respondent's neighborhood, documenting observations of other buildings in the area, relative level of disrepair, apparent economic status, racial and ethnic composition, and safety. Pictures were also taken of the exterior and interior of the respondent's home, documenting how the respondent's household compared to other residences in the area and on the appearance of economic situation evidenced in possessions internal to the residence. Racial and ethnic characteristics of the respondent and respondent's household and neighborhood were also observed. And if the respondent had moved within the past year, observations and photographs were also collected on the prior residence and neighborhood. The project collected more than one thousand photographs and accompanying descriptions. As background to all of this, the Science of Generosity Initiative also collected data through year-long ethnographies conducted in 2009 at four churches in the American Midwest—one evangelical, one mainline Protestant, one black Protestant, and one Catholic—focused on congregational finances and religious financial giving. As part of that phase of our study, we interviewed sixty-three adult members of three of those four churches about their financial giving and collected 724 pages of detailed, typed fieldnotes, based on our observations.

6. Data gathered from this phase of the study involved a collaborative, mixed-methods research project that, to explain it more fully, collected data in five phases, beginning in 2007 and concluding in 2009. The first phase consisted of telephone surveys conducted with all congregations located in three mid-sized contiguous cities of a Midwestern state. The survey was completed with a remarkable response rate of 98.9 percent (N = 269). Next, US Census (2000) data were linked to the congregational survey data by postal codes. Third, in-person interviews were conducted with a stratified quota sample of ministers from these congregations (n = 42). The first three phases of data collection

are detailed more thoroughly in Patricia Snell, Christian Smith, Carlos Tavares, and Kari Christoffersen, "Denominational Differences in Congregational Youth Ministry Programming and Empirical Evidence of Systematic Non-Response Biases in Surveys," *Review of Religious Research*, 51, no. 1 (2009): 21–38. The fourth phase entailed a continuation of the project via content analysis and participant observations with four religious congregations selected to represent each of four Christian denominational categories, defined by Steensland et al. (Brian Steensland, Jerry Park, Mark Regnerus, Lynn Robinson, Bradford Wilcox, and Robert Woodberry, "The Measure of American Religion: Toward Improving the State of the Art," *Social Forces* 79 (2000): 291–318) as mainline Protestant, evangelical Protestant, black Protestant, and Catholic. Religious worship services, committee meetings, youth groups, Bible studies, confirmation classes, Sunday schools, and other congregational meetings were observed throughout the course of a year, with a particular focus on processes around financial giving. A total of 229 discrete group events were observed with a total of 724 recorded pages in fieldnotes in each of the congregations. Content analysis included mission statements and other belief explications located on website and printed materials. The fifth phase of the study consisted of additional in-person interviews with congregation members, youth participants, and parents of youth participants (n = 233) with a response rate of 87.6 percent. Of these, sixty-three were conducted with adult members with a focus on financial generosity, volunteering, community involvement, and so on (the leaders of the black church opted out of the financial giving section of our interview questions). Congregation members were selected from a list provided by each congregation in which individuals were categorized by their giving and participation level—allowing us to use a stratified random sample to interview congregants with varying levels of church participation. The interviews, which lasted an average of one hour in length, were recorded and later transcribed for analysis.

7. Alfie Kohn, *The Brighter Side of Human Nature: Altruism and Empathy in Everyday Life* (New York: Basic Books, 1990).

8. Another general assumption we make in our analyses is that people's actions are determined by complex causes and processes operating at multiple levels of their lives. Some theoretical approaches in science tend to be "reductionistic"—that is, they reduce all explanation to one level or type of analysis. They want to explain lots of things by appealing to single genetic, biological, neurological, psychological, or sociological causes. Whether that is "selfish genes," the "pleasure principle," "cultural socialization," or something else, however, in fact no one level or force of causal explanation will suffice. Generous actions are the results of complex combinations of material, relational, cultural, psychological, chemical, and neurological processes. Of course no one analysis can account for all of those factors simultaneously. An additional assumption behind our work is that human motivations of a sometimes non-rational and often deeply social nature are responsible for producing generous actions. If humans acted in the way that the discipline of traditional economics describes them—that is, as rational egoists making choices to maximize their own "utility"—people would not be nearly as generous as they in fact are. In that case, people would only do things that served their own perceived interests. They might be generous with close family relatives. But otherwise we would expect them to devote their resources to their own well-being. But that is not how many people act. So the standard economists' model of human action is not what we assume. Instead, we take a sociological approach, which focuses not only on people's incentives and opportunities, but also on their cultural beliefs,

normative concerns, relational ties, and institutional contexts. Self-interest and incentives clearly affect people's levels of generosity, but so do many other factors. In this book we try to account for many of them. These assumptions are rooted in a particular philosophy of (social) science known as critical realism, about which I (Smith) and many others have written elsewhere. The first assumption here has to do with complexity, which critical realism emphasizes. The second assumption has to do with the "stratified" nature of reality and the fact that life, including that which science seeks to explain, usually operates in "open systems," which critical realism also affirms. For more on critical realism, see Christian Smith, *What is a Person?: Rethinking Humanity, Social Life, and the Moral Good from the Person Up* (Chicago: University of Chicago Press, 2010); Roy Bhaskar, *A Realist Concept of Science* (London: Verso, 1997); Roy Bhaskar, *Critical Realism* (New York: Routledge, 1998); Roy Bhaskar, *The Possibility of Naturalism: A Philosophical Critique of Contemporary Human Sciences* (London: Routledge, 1979); Andrew Collier, *Critical Realism: an Introduction to Roy Bhaskar's Philosophy* (London: Verso, 1994); Berth Danermark et al., *Explaining Society: Critical Realism in the Social Sciences* (New York: Routledge, 2002); Andrew Sayer, *Realism and Social Science* (New York: Sage, 2000); Andrew Sayer, *Method in Social Science: A Realist Approach* (New York: Routledge, 2002); Margaret Archer, *Realist Social Theory* (Cambridge: Cambridge University Press, 1995); Margaret Archer et al., eds. *Critical Realism: Essential Readings* (New York: Routledge, 1998); Justin Cruickshank, *Realism and Sociology: Anti-Foundationalism, Ontology, and Social Research* (New York: Routledge, 2002); Margaret Archer, *Being Human: The Problem of Agency* (Cambridge: Cambridge University Press, 2000); Douglas Porpora, *The Concept of Social Structure* (New York: Greenwood Press, 1987). For recommendations on how, as a novice, to learn critical realism, see http://www.nd.edu/~csmith22/criticalrealism.htm.

9. See Jonathan Haidt, *The Happiness Hypothesis* (New York: Basic Books, 2006); Douglas Lawson, *Give to Live: How Giving can Change Your Life* (La Jolla, CA: ALTI Publishing, 1991).

Chapter 1

1. Our survey only asked whether respondents had given blood in the previous year. That measure proves statistically insignificant in its relationship with our five measures of well-being. But there is a difference between having perhaps given blood in the last year versus being a regular blood donor. The latter might be significantly associated with well-being. Unfortunately, our survey measure did not make this distinction. Future research will have to investigate this possibility.

2. The answer choices were: very happy, somewhat happy, neither happy nor unhappy, somewhat unhappy, and very unhappy.

3. The control variables used were age, sex, education, household income, full-time work status, financial net worth, residence in the South, race/ethnicity, political party affiliation, how hard respondent was hit by the recession of 2008, number of close adult friends, frequency of religious service attendance, and religious affiliation. In addition, for all analyses concerning happiness, we included a control for the presence of teenagers in the household (increasing the number of controls to fourteen), because sometimes that factor is associated with adult happiness.

4. Those few not significant at the $p < .05$ level are noted in endnotes below.

5. The question wording was, "I regularly donate at least 10 percent of my income to religious, charitable, or other good causes." The sample over-reported tithing compared to exact dollar amounts reported giving relative to reported income, and compared to what we know from other surveys. Hence, some social-desirability bias is evident in this question, further discussed in Chapter 4.

6. $9.67 = 5.8/.6$.

7. See Christian Smith and Jonathan P. Hill, "Toward the Measurement of Interpersonal Generosity (IG): An IG Scale Conceptualized, Tested, and Validated," (2009): http://generosityresearch.nd.edu/assets/13798/ig_paper_smith_hill_rev.pdf.

8. Up to 45 percent of respondents on some questions did not agree that they practiced relational generosity as asked in the question.

9. Cronbach's alpha = .87. All scales reversed answers with negative question wordings to match all answer directions in the same direction.

10. Specifically: 1. more than once a week; 2. about once a week on average; 3. twice a month; 4. about once a month on average; 5. 5–9 times during the year; 6. 2–4 times during the year; 7. a few times during the year or less; and 8. never. Because of low frequencies on the high end, we combined "more than once a week" and "about once a week on average" into one category, "once a week or more often," reducing the spread from eight to seven categories.

11. Frequency distributions (weighted) are as follows: Extremely or Very Generous = 15.5 percent; Somewhat Generous = 36 percent; Neither Generous nor Ungenerous = 28.1 percent; Somewhat Ungenerous = 10 percent; and Very or Extremely Ungenerous = 10.2 percent.

12. Interpreting regression coefficients (not shown) allows us to note, for instance, that controlling for the possible related effects of thirteen other variables, the independent effect of giving away 10 percent of one's income itself increases the chance of being happier by one-third of one answer category on the five-point set of answer categories of the happiness survey question; that is, giving away 10 percent of income per se moves respondents one-third of the way from reporting that they are, say, somewhat happy toward being very happy. Volunteering in the previous year compared to not volunteering has the effect of increasing the chances of being more happy by .23 of one answer category; and a one-step increase in relational generosity (on a seven-point scale) has the same effect by .29 of an answer category.

13. http://www.redcrossblood.org/learn-about-blood/blood-facts-and-statistics. More broadly, see Kieran Healy, *Last Best Gifts: Altruism and the Market for Human Blood and Organs* (Chicago: University of Chicago Press, 2006).

14. See, however, the research by Jill Piliavin, including Piliavin, "Doing Well by Doing Good: Benefits for the Benefactor," in *Flourishing: Positive Psychology and the Life Well Lived*, ed. C. Keyes and J. Haidt (Washington, DC: American Psychological Association, 2003), 227–247.

15. That is, the differences are significant at the $p = .10$ level.

16. Although in this case the differences are significant at the $p = .058$ level, just above the standard $p = .05$ level.

17. Giving blood was significant at the very margin of $p = .049$.

18. Cronbach's alpha = .75.

19. After controlling for all control variables in an ordinal logistic regression model, the volunteering effect is significant at p = .074. This is the only life-purpose effect not significant at the p = .05 or greater level.

20. With the slight exception of the anomalously elevated strong life purpose percentages among the least generous on the point of self-evaluated relational generosity.

Chapter 2

1. Our argument here reflects a critical-realist philosophy of social science.

2. Peter Lipton, *Inference to the Best Explanation* (New York: Routledge, 2004); Gilbert Harman, "The Inference to the Best Explanation," *The Philosophical Review* 74, no. 1 (1965): 88–95.

3. Our account in no way claims absolute, positive knowledge about this or any other topic. All scientific knowledge is ultimately based on presupposed beliefs, not certainties (see Christian Smith, *Moral, Believing Animals: Human Personhood and Culture* (New York: Oxford University Press, 2003)), and so is fallible. Despite the fallibility of our knowledge, however, it is still possible and often actual for us knowledge-seeking humans to understand truth about reality. See Christian Smith, *What is a Person?: Rethinking Humanity, Social Life, and the Moral Good from the Person Up* (Chicago: University of Chicago Press, 2010).

4. For example, one poor woman, Osceola McCarty, who made a meager living washing other people's clothes, in 1995 donated her life savings of $150,000, earned from seventy years of work, to the University of Southern Mississippi, a school she had never visited, saying, "I wanted to give some children the opportunity I didn't have." Evelyn Coleman, *The Riches of Osceola McCarty* (Park Ridge, IL: Albert Whitman & Company, 1998).

5. United Healthcare/VolunteerMatch Do Good Live Well Study, March 2010, slides 38, 40, http://cdn.volunteermatch.org/www/about/UnitedHealthcare_VolunteerMatch_Do_Good_Live_Well_Study.pdf.

6. Sonja Lyubomirsky, Kennon Sheldon, and David Schkade, "Pursuing Happiness: The Architecture of Sustainable Change," *Review of General Psychology* 9, no. 2 (2005): 111–131; Z. Magen and R. Aharoni, "Adolescents' Contributing Toward Others: Relationship to Positive Experiences and Transpersonal Commitment," *Journal of Humanistic Psychology* 31 (1991): 126–143; K. Sheldon and L. Houser-Marko, "Self-Concordance, Goal-Attainment, and the Pursuit of Happiness: Can There Be an Upward Spiral?," *Journal of Personality and Social Psychology* 76 (2001): 482–497; M. Snyder and A. Omoto, "Basic Research and Practical Problems: Volunteerism and the Psychology of Individual and Collective Action," in *The Practice of Social Influence in Multiple Cultures*, ed. W. Wosinsak, R. Cialdini, D. Barrett, and J. Reykowski (Mahwah, NJ: Erlbaum, 2001), 287–307.

7. Other studies that have explicated causal mechanisms of generosity, on which we have partly drawn, include: Marc Musick and John Wilson, *Volunteers: A Social Profile* (Bloomington: Indiana University Press, 2008); Stephen Post, "Altruism, Happiness, and Health: It's Good to be Good," *International Journal of Behavioral Medicine* 12, no. 2 (2005): 66–77; Stephen Post and Jill Neimark, *Why Good Things Happen to Good People* (New York: Broadway, 2007), 10–11.

8. Musick and Wilson, *Volunteers,* 495–496.

9. Harold Koenig, "Altruistic Love and Physical Health," in *Altruism and Health: Perspectives From Empirical Research*, ed. Stephen Post (New York: Oxford University Press, 2007), 437; also see Barbara Fredrickson, *Love 2.0: How Our Supreme Emotion Affects Everything We Feel, Think, Do, and Become* (New York: Hudson Street Press, 2013).

10. C. Witvliet, T. Ludwig, and K. Vander Laan, "Granting Forgiveness or Harboring Grudges: Implications for Emotion, Physiology, and Health," *Psychological Science* 12, no. 2 (2001): 117–123.

11. Allan Luks with Peggy Payne, *The Healing Power of Doing Good* (New York: iUniverse, 2001), 180; also see J. Teasdale, "Negative Thinking in Depression: Cause, Effect, or Reciprocal Relationship?" *Advances in Behaviour Research and Therapy* 5 (1983): 3–25.

12. John Dovidio, Jane Piliavin, David Schroeder, and Louis Penner, *The Social Psychology of Prosocial Behavior* (Mahwah, NJ: Lawrence Erlbaum, 2006), 118–140; Barbara Fredrickson, "Gratitude, Like Other Positive Emotions, Broadens and Builds," in *The Psychology of Gratitude*, ed. Robert Emmons and Michael McCullough (New York: Oxford University Press, 2004), 145–166.

13. All the names of our interview respondents have been changed to protect the confidentiality of their identities.

14. Robert Weiss, William Buchanan, Lynne Altstatt, and John Lombardo, "Altruism is Rewarding," *Science* 171 (1971): 1262–1263.

15. Gail Williamson and Margaret Clark, "Providing Help and Desiring Relationship Type as Determinants of Changes in Moods and Self-Evaluations," *Journal of Personality and Social Psychology* 56, no. 5 (1989): 722–734; G. Manucia, D. Baumann, and R. Cialdinio, "Mood Influences on Helping: Direct Effects or Side Effects?" *Journal of Personality and Social Psychology* 46 (1984): 357–364.

16. Robert Cialdini, Mark Schaller, Donald Houlihan, Kevin Arps, Jim Fultz, and Arthur Beaman, "Empathy-Based Helping: Is It Selflessness or Selfishly Motivated?" *Journal of Personality and Social Psychology* 52, no. 4 (1987): 749–758.

17. Lara Aknin, Christopher Barrington-Leigh, Elizabeth Dunn, John Helliwell, Robert Biswas-Diener, Imelda Kemeza, Paul Nyende, Claire Ashton-James, and Michael I. Norton, "Prosocial Spending and Well-Being: Cross-Cultural Evidence for a Psychological Universal," Harvard Business School Working Paper #11–038, 2010; Elizabeth Dunn, Lara Aknin, and Michael Norton, "Spending Money on Others Promotes Happiness," *Science* 319 (2008): 1687–1688; "Money Can Buy Happiness—If You Give it Away," *Harvard Mental Health Letter* (September 2008): 7.

18. United Healthcare/VolunteerMatch Do Good Live Well Study, March 2010, slides 29, 43, 49–50. Also see Robert Wuthnow, *Acts of Compassion: Caring for Others and Helping Ourselves* (Princeton, NJ: Princeton University Press, 1991).

19. Stephen Post, "It's Good to be Good: Science Says It's So," *Health Progress*, July/August 2009, 18–25; Catherine Norris and John Cacioppo, "I Know How You Feel: Social and Emotional Information Processing in the Brain," in *Social Neuroscience: Integrating Biological and Psychological Explanations of Social Behavior*, ed. Eddie Harmon-Jones and Piotr Winkielman (New York: Guilford Press, 2007), 84–105.

20. Harold Koenig, "Altruistic Love and Physical Health," in *Altruism and Health: Perspectives From Empirical Research*, ed. Stephen Post (New York: Oxford University Press, 2007), 422–441.

21. Allan Luks, "Helper's High," *Psychology Today*, 22, no. 10 (1988): 39–40.

22. James Andreoni is the economist most associated with this idea; also see William Harbaugh, "What Do Donations Buy?: A Model of Philanthropy Based on Prestige and Warm Glow," *Journal of Public Economics* 67 (1997): 269–284.

23. Frank Riessman, "The 'Helper' Therapy Principle," *Social Work* 10, no. 2 (1965): 27–32.

24. Shankar Vedantam, "If It Feels Good to Be Good, It Might Be Only Natural," *Washington Post*, May 28, 2007, http://www.washingtonpost.com/wp-dyn/content/article/2007/05/27/AR2007052701056.html.

25. Andrea Marques and Esther Sternberg, "The Biology of Positive Emotions and Health," in *Altruism and Health: Perspectives From Empirical Research*, ed. Stephen Post (New York: Oxford University Press, 2007), 159–160.

26. Paul Zak, A. Stanton, and S. Ahmadi, "Oxytocin Increases Generosity in Humans," *Public Library of Science ONE* 2 (2007): e1128; Karen Ravn, "Give Till it Helps—We're Told it's Better to Give than to Receive. Now Scientists are Weighing In—and Say Generosity Indeed Has Benefits for Body and Mind," *Los Angeles Times*, December 24, 2007; R. Mitchum, "Donating to Charity is Good for the Brain, According to Study," *Chicago Tribune*, June 15, 2007; S. Bhanoo, "Doing Good Feels Good, Study Finds," *Baltimore Sun*, June 15, 2007; V. Contie, "Brain Imaging Reveals Joy of Giving," *National Institutes of Health*, June 25, 2007.

27. Jorge Barraza and Paul Zak, "Empathy toward Strangers Triggers Oxytocin Release and Subsequent Generosity," *Values, Empathy, and Fairness Across Social Barriers* 1167 (2009): 182–189; also see David McClelland and Carol Kirshnit, "The Effect of Motivational Arousal Through Films on Salivary Immunoglobulin A," *Psychology and Health* 2, no. 1 (1988): 31–52. Also see Paul Zak, *The Moral Molecule: The Source of Love and Prosperity* (New York: Dutton Press, 2011), in which the link here is modeled as indirect and reciprocating: people behave generously to others and the recipients' oxytocin levels increase, which then promotes further generosity and trust between giver and recipient—thus trust boosts oxytocin so the giver's initial level is also boosted.

28. Vera Morhenn, Jang Woo Park, Elisabeth Piper, and Paul Zak, "Monetary Sacrifice among Strangers is Mediated by Endogenous Oxytocin Release after Physical Contact," *Evolution and Human Behavior* 29, no. 6 (2008): 375–383; also see Jorge Moll, Frank Krueger, Roland Zahn, Matteo Pardini, Richard de Oliveira-Souza, and Jordan Grafman, "Human Fronto-Mesolimbic Networks Guide Decisions about Charitable Donation," *PNAS* 103, no. 42 (2006): 15623–15628.

29. Óscar Arias-Carrión and Ernst Pöppel, "Dopamine, Learning, and Reward-Seeking Behavior," *Acta Neurobiol Experimentalis* 67 (2007): 481–488.

30. Among a vast literature on this subject, see, for example R. Depue and J. Morrone-Strupinsky, "A Neurobehavioral Model of Affiliative Bonding: Implications for Conceptualizing a Human Trait of Affiliation," *Behavioral Brain Science* 28 (2005): 313–350; C. Sue Carter, "Neuroendocrine Perspectives on Social Attachment and Love," *Psychoneuroendocrinology* 23, no. 8 (1998): 779–818.

31. R. Bachner-Melman, I. Gritsenko, L. Nemanov, A.H. Zohar, C. Dina, and R.P. Ebstein, "Dopaminergic Polymorphisms Associated with Self-Report Measures of Human Altruism: A Fresh Phenotype for the Dopamine D4 Receptor," *Molecular Psychiatry* 10 (2005): 333–335. Also see R. Depue and J. Morrone-Strupinsky, "A Neurobehavioral

Model of Affiliative Bonding: Implications for Conceptualizing a Human Trait of Affiliation," *Behavioral Brain Science* 28 (2005): 313–350.

32. Luks and Payne, *The Healing Power of Doing Good*.

33. See A. R. Peirson and J. W. Heuchert, "Correlations for Serotonin Levels and Measures of Mood in a Nonclinical Sample," *Psychological Report* 2, no. 87 (2000): 707–716 and E. Williams, B. Stewart-Knox, A. Helander, et al., "Associations between Whole-Blood Serotonin and Subjective Mood in Healthy Male Volunteers," *Biol Psychol* 71 (2006): 171–174.

34. Heike Tost and Andreas Meyer-Lindenberg, "I Fear for You: A Role for Serotonin in Moral Behavior," *SNAS* 107 (2010): 17071–17072; M. Crockett, L. Clark, M. Hauser, and T. Robbins, "Serotonin Selectively Influences Moral Judgment and Behavior Through Effects on Harm Aversion," *Proceedings of the National Academy of Science USA* 107 (2010): 17433–17438.

35. B. McEwen, "Protecting and Damaging Effects of Stress Mediators," *New England Journal of Medicine* 338 (1998): 171–179; Shelly Taylor and Gian Gonzaga, "Affiliative Responses to Stress: A Social Neuroscience Model," in *Social Neuroscience: Integrating Biological and Psychological Explanations of Social Behavior*, ed. Eddie Harmon-Jones and Piotr Winkielman (New York: Guilford Press, 2007), 454–473.

36. See, for example, S. Dickerson and M. Kemeny, "Acute Stressors and Cortisol Responses: A Theoretical Integration and Synthesis of Laboratory Research," *Psychological Bulletin* 130 (2004): 355–391.

37. Elizabeth Dunn, Claire Ashton-James, Margaret Hanson, and Lara Aknin, "On the Costs of Self-Interested Economic Behavior," *Journal of Health Psychology* 15, no. 4 (2010): 627–633; also see G. Ironson, G. Solomon, E. Balbin, C. O'Cleirigh, A. George, M. Kumar, D. Larson, and T. Woods, "Spirituality and Religiousness are Associated with Long Survival, Health Behaviors, Less Distress, and Lower Cortisol in People Living with HIV/AIDS," *Annals of Behavioral Medicine* 24 (2002): 34–48.

38. Jorge Moll, Frank Krueger, Roland Zahn, Matteo Pardini, Richard de Oliveira-Souza, and Jordan Grafman, "Human Fronto-Mesolimbic Networks Guide Decisions about Charitable Donation," *PNAS* 103, no. 42 (2006): 15623–15628; also see C. Sue Carter, "Neuroendocrine Perspectives on Social Attachment and Love," in *Foundations in Social Neuroscience*, ed. John Cocioppo et al. (Cambridge, MA: The MIT Press, 2002), 853–890.

39. William Harbaugh, Ulrich Mayr, and Daniel Burghart, "Neural Repsonses to Taxation and Voluntary Giving Reveal Motives for Charitable Donations," *Science* 316 (2007): 1624.

40. William Harbaugh, Ulrich Mayr, and Daniel Burghart, "Neural Responses to Taxation and Voluntary Giving Reveal Motives for Charitable Donations," *Science* 316 (2007): 1622–1625; Holly Hall, "Sex, Drugs, and . . . Charity?: Brain Study Finds New Links," *Chronicle of Philanthropy* 19, no. 5 (2006): 6.

41. See David J. Linden, *The Compass of Pleasure: How Our Brains Make Fatty Foods, Orgasm, Exercise, Marijuana, Generosity, Vodka, Learning, and Gambling Feel so Good* (New York: Penguin, 2011).

42. See, for example, Jorge Moll, Roland Zahn, Ricardo de Oliveira-Souza, Frank Krueger, and Jordan Grafman, "The Neural Basis of Human Moral Cognition,"

Neuroscience 6 (2005): 799–809; Paul Zak, "The Physiology of Moral Sentiments," *Journal of Economic Behavior and Organization* 77 (2011): 53–65; Dharol Tankersley, C. Jill Stowe, and Scott Huettel, "Altruism is Associated with an Increased Neural Response to Agency," *Nature Neuroscience* 10, no. 2 (2007): 150–151; Roland Zahn, Jorge Moll, Mirella Paiva, Griselda Garrido, Frank Krueger, Edward Huey, and Jordan Grafman, "The Neural Basis of Human Social Values: Evidence from Functional MRI," *Cerebral Cortex* 19 (2009): 276–283.

43. Paul Zak, "The Physiology of Moral Sentiments," *Journal of Economic Behavior and Organization* 77 (2011): 62, 63.

44. R. Bodnar and G. Klein, "Endogenous Opiates and Behavior: 2003," *Peptides* 25, no. 12 (2004): 2205–2256; Marques and Sternberg, "The Biology of Positive Emotions and Health,"164.

45. Harold Koenig, "Altruistic Love and Physical Health," in *Altruism and Health: Perspectives From Empirical Research*, ed. Stephen Post (New York: Oxford University Press, 2007), 422–441; Luks and Payne, *The Healing Power of Doing Good*, 80, 88, 96.

46. United Healthcare/VolunteerMatch Do Good Live Well Study, March 2010, slides 33–34.

47. See Martin Seligman, *Flourish* (New York: Atria Books, 2012).

48. Research actually shows that volunteering time actually ends up creating more time for the volunteers—see, for example, Cassie Mogilner, Zoë Chance, and Michael Norton, "Giving Time Gives You Time," *Psychological Science*, 23, no. 10 (2012): 1233–1238.

49. S. Sprecher and B. Fehr, "Enhancement of Mood and Self-Esteem as a Result of Giving and Receiving Compassionate Love," *Current Research in Social Psychology* 11 (2006): 227–242; G. Caprara and P. Steca, "Self-Efficacy Beliefs as Determinants of Prosocial Behavior Conducive to Life Satisfaction across Ages," *Journal of Social and Clinical Psychology* 24 (2005): 191–217.

50. Marge Reitsma-Street, Mechthild Maczewski, and Sheila Neysmith, "Promoting Encouragement: An Organizational Study of Volunteers in Community Resource Centers for Children," *Children and Youth Service Review* 22 (2000): 651–678; Kristina Smock, *Democracy in America: Community Organizing and Urban Change* (New York: Columbia University Press, 2004), 37–38.

51. Musick and Wilson, *Volunteers*, 489. Also see Anne Stratham and Patricia Rhoton, *The Volunteer Work of Mature and Young Women: 1974–1981* (Columbia: Center for Human Resource Research, Ohio State University, 1985); John Wilson and Marc Musick, "Doing Well by Doing Good: Volunteering and Occupational Achievement among American Women," *Sociological Quarterly* 44 (2003): 433–450.

52. Rose Delvin, "Volunteers and the Paid Labor Market," *ISUMA* 2 (2001): 62–68.

53. Kurt Gray, "Moral Transformation: Good and Evil Turn the Weak into the Mighty," *Social Psychology and Personality Science* 1, no. 3 (2010): 253–254, 257. Note that, in the experiments, those who were cast in "evil" roles also increased in physical strength.

54. Musick and Wilson, *Volunteers*, 495–496.

55. United Healthcare/VolunteerMatch Do Good Live Well Study, March 2010, slides 25, 43, 44.

56. Smith, *Moral, Believing Animals*.

57. C. Park and S. Folkman, "Meaning in the Context of Stress and Coping," *Review of General Psychology* 1 (1997): 115–144.

58. Musick and Wilson, *Volunteers,* 510.

59. See Dovidio, Piliavin, Schroeder, and Penner, *The Social Psychology of Prosocial Behavior,* 210–213.

60. United Healthcare/VolunteerMatch Do Good Live Well Study, March 2010, slide 43.

61. Fidelity Volunteerism and Charitable Giving in 2009 Survey (N = 1,005 adult Americans), Executive Summary, Fidelity Charitable Gift Fund, 3, http://www.fidelitycharitable.org/docs/Volunteerism-Charitable-Giving-2009-Executive-Summary.pdf.

62. VolunteerMatch User Study, 2006, (N = 2,306), 12, http://cdn.volunteermatch.org/www/nonprofits/resources/hart_presentation.pdf.

63. Koenig, "Altruistic Love and Physical Health," in *Altruism and Health,* 422–441.

64. Mark Leary, *The Curse of the Self: Self-Awareness, Egotism, and the Quality of Human Life* (New York: Oxford University Press, 2004).

65. G. Matthews and A. Wells, "Attentional Process, Dysfunctional Coping, and Clinical Intervention," in *Handbook of Coping: Theory, Research, Applications,* ed. M. Zeidner and N. Endler (New York: Wiley, 1996), 573–601; George Valliant, *Adaptation to Life* (Cambridge, MA: Harvard University Press, 1989).

66. Robert Ornstein and David Sobel, *Healthy Pleasures* (Cambridge, MA: Perseus, 1989), 233–236.

67. Robert Roberts, "The Blessings of Gratitude: A Conceptual Analysis," in *The Psychology of Gratitude,* ed. Robert Emmons and Michael McCullough (New York: Oxford University Press, 2004), 58–78.

68. Robert Emmons, *Thanks!: How Practicing Gratitude Can Make You Happier* (Boston: Houghton Mifflin, 2007).

69. Nor, we think, does generosity have to entail the kind of "opiate of the people" quality that Karl Marx argued characterized religion, namely, making oneself feel artificially better about an unjust suffering by simply failing to face the facts about the real causes of the suffering. That too can happen in cases of apparent generous practices. But it need not be inevitable.

70. Graeme Wood, "The Secret Fears of the Super Rich," *The Atlantic,* April 2011.

71. Again, see Mogilner, Chance, and Norton, 2012.

72. Philip Watkins, "Gratitude and Subjective Well-Being," in *The Psychology of Gratitude,* ed. Robert Emmons and Michael McCullough (New York: Oxford University Press, 2004), 58–78; Rollin McCraty and Doc Childre, "The Grateful Heart: A Psychophysiology of Appreciation," in *The Psychology of Gratitude,* 230–255.

73. Paul Stiles, *Is the American Dream Killing You?: How "the Market" Rules our Lives* (New York: Harper Collins, 2005); Vicki Robin and Joe Dominguez, *Your Money or Your Life* (New York: Penguin, 2008).

74. M. Csikszentmihalyi, "If We Are So Rich, Why Aren't We Happy?," *American Psychologist* 54 (1999): 821–827.

75. Juliet Schor, *The Overspent American: Upscaling, Downshifting, and the New Consumer* (New York: Basic Books, 1998); Robert Frank, *Falling Behind: How Rising Inequality Harms the Middle Class* (Berkeley: University of California Press, 2007).

76. O. Lishtsey, "'Thinking Positive' as a Stress Buffer: The Role of Positive Automatic Cognitions in Depression and Happiness," *Journal of Counseling Psychology* 41 (1994): 325–334.

77. See, for example, Azim Jamal and Harvey McKinnon, *The Power of Giving: How Giving Back Enriches Us All—Creating Abundance at Home, at Work, and in Your Community* (New York: Tarcher, 2008); Lynne Twist, *The Soul of Money: Reclaiming the Wealth of Our Inner Resources* (New York: W.W. Norton, 2008); Jacob Needleman, *Money and the Meaning of Life* (New York: Currency Doubleday, 1991); Ken Blanchard and S. Truett Cathy, *The Generosity Factor: Discover the Joy of Giving Your Time, Talent, and Treasure* (Grand Rapids, MI: Zondervan, 2002); M. J. Ryan, *The Giving Heart: Unlocking the Transformative Power of Generosity in Our Lives* (Berkeley, CA: Conari, 2000); Dave Toycen, *The Power of Generosity: How to Transform Yourself and Your World* (Waynesboro, GA: Authentic Media, 2004). Also see Tim Kasser, *The High Price of Materialism* (Cambridge, MA: The MIT Press, 2002); Bill Clinton, *Giving: How Each of Us Can Change the World* (New York: Knopf, 2007); Jacob Neeleman et al., *Money, Money, Money: The Search for Wealth and the Pursuit of Happiness* (Carlsbad, CA: Hay House, 1998).

78. By "social networks" here we do not mean websites like Facebook and MySpace but rather the relatively stable strong and weak relationship ties that people have with other people that last over time.

79. Armida Salvati, *Altruism and Social Capital* (Boca Raton, FL: Universal, 2008); also see Aafke Komter, *Social Solidarity and the Gift* (Cambridge: Cambridge University Press, 2005); Helmuth Berking, *Sociology of Giving* (London: Sage, 1999).

80. See, for example, Debra Umberton, Chen Meichu, James House, Kristin Hopkins, and Ellen Slaten, "The Effect of Social Relationships on Physical Well-being," *American Sociological Review* 61 (1996): 837–857; James House, Debra Umberson, and Kenneth Landis, "Structures and Processes of Social Support," *Annual Review of Sociology* 14 (1988): 293–318; Morris Okun, William Stock, Marilyn Haring, and Robert Witter, "The Social Activity/Subjective Well-being Relation," *Research on Aging* 6 (1984): 45–65; Nan Lin, Xialan Ye, and William Ensel, "Social Support and Depressed Mood: A Structural Analysis," *Journal of Health and Social Behavior* 40 (1999): 344–359; John Rietschlin, "Voluntary Association Membership and Psychological Distress," *Journal of Health and Social Behavior* 39 (1998): 348–355; Elaine Weatherington, Phyllis Moen, Nina Glasgow, and Karl Pillemer, "Multiple Roles, Social Integration, and Health," in *Social Integration in the Second Half of Life*, ed. Karl Pillemer, Phyllis Moen, Elaine Weatherington, and Nina Glasgow (Baltimore: Johns Hopkins University Press, 2000), 48–74.

81. James Lynch, *The Broken Heart: The Medical Consequences of Loneliness* (New York: Basic Books, 1979).

82. Musick and Wilson, *Volunteers*, 470–471, 510.

83. United Healthcare/VolunteerMatch Do Good Live Well Study, March 2010, slides 31, 47.

84. Fidelity Volunteerism and Charitable Giving in 2009 Survey (N = 1,005 adult Americans), Executive Summary, Fidelity Charitable Gift Fund, p. 3. http://www.fidelitycharitable.org/docs/Volunteerism-Charitable-Giving-2009-Executive-Summary.pdf. This, however, was the least mentioned reason for volunteering.

85. United Healthcare/VolunteerMatch Do Good Live Well Study, March 2010, slide 47.

86. See Hans-Werner Bierhoff, *Prosocial Behavior* (New York: Taylor and Maddock, 2002), 315.

87. D. Shmotkin, T. Blumstein, and B. Modan, "Beyond Keeping Active: Concomitants of Being a Volunteer in Old-Age," *Psychology and Aging* 18 (2003): 602–607; A. Harris and C. Thoresen, "Volunteering is Associated with Delayed Mortality in Older People," *Journal of Health Psychology* 10 (2005): 739–752; Marc Musick, A. Herzog, and J. House, "Volunteering and Mortality among Older Adults: Findings from a National Sample," *Journal of Gerontology* 54B (1999): S173–S180.

88. United Healthcare/VolunteerMatch Do Good Live Well Study, March 2010, slide 34.

89. Fidelity Volunteerism and Charitable Giving in 2009 Survey (N=1,005 adult Americans), Executive Summary, Fidelity Charitable Gift Fund, 3, http://www.fidelitycharitable.org/docs/Volunteerism-Charitable-Giving-2009-Executive-Summary.pdf.

90. According to the most important theorist of ideal types, Max Weber, "An ideal type is formed by the one-sided accentuation of one or more points of view and by the synthesis of a great many diffuse, discrete, more or less present and occasionally absent concrete individual phenomena, which are arranged according to those one-sidedly-emphasized viewpoints into a unified analytical construct." Weber, *The Methodology of the Social Sciences*, trans and ed. Edward Shils and Henry Finch (New York: Free Press, 1997 [1903–1917]), 88.

91. A. M. Ziersch and F. E. Baum, "Involvement in Civil Society Groups: Is it Good for Your Health?" *Journal of Epidemiology and Community Health* 58 (2004): 493–500.

92. There may of course be other causal mechanisms at work. For instance, generosity may work to improve the quality of people's interpersonal relationships, which we know tends to increase happiness and health. In one study, for instance, generosity helped people overcome the confusions and misunderstandings that resulted in their interpersonal communications (P. Van Lange, J. Ouwerkerk, and M. Tazelaar, "How to Overcome the Detrimental Effects of Noise in Social Interactions: The Benefits of Generosity," *Journal of Personality and Social Psychology* 82, no. 5 (2002): 768–780.

93. United Healthcare/VolunteerMatch Do Good Live Well Study, March 2010, slide 44.

94. Doug Oman, Carl Thoresen, and Kay McMahon, "Volunteerism and Mortality among Community Dwelling Elderly," *Journal of Health Psychology* 4 (1999): 301–316; also see Peggy Thoits and Lynda Hewitt, "Volunteer Work and Well-Being," *Journal of Health and Social Behavior* 42 (2001): 115–131.

95. Terry Lum and Elizabeth Lightfoot, "The Effects of Volunteering on the Physical and Mental Health of Older People," *Research on Aging* 27 (2005): 31–55; also see Ming-Ching Luoh and A. Regula Herzog, "Individual Consequences of Volunteering and Paid Work in Old Age: Health and Mortality," *Journal of Health and Social Behavior* 43 (2002): 490–509.

96. Post and Neimark, *Why Good Things Happen to Good People*, 7. More generally, see E. Greenfield and N. Marks, "Formal Volunteering as a Protective Factor for Older Adults' Psychological Well-being," *Journal of Gerontology: Social Sciences* 59 (2004): 258–264; S. Brown, D. Smith, R. Schulz, M. Kabeto, P. Ubel, M. Poulin, and K.

Langa, "Caregiving Behavior is Associated with Decreased Mortality Risk," *Psychological Science* 20, no. 4 (2009): 488–494; Corey Lee Keyes and Carol Ryff, "Generativity in Adult Lives: Social Structural Contours and Quality of Life Consequences," in *Generativity and Adult Development: Psychosocial Perspectives on Caring for and Contributing to the Next Generation*, ed. D. McAdams & E. de St. Aubin (Washington, DC: American Psychological Association, 1997), 227–264; N. Krause, A. Herzog, and E. Baker, "Providing Support to Others and Well-being in Later Life," *Journal of Gerontology: Psychological Sciences* 47 (1992): 300–311; P. Moen, D. Dempster-McClain, and R. Williams, Jr., "Successful Aging: A Life Course Perspective on Women's Multiple Roles and Health," *American Journal of Sociology* 97 (1992): 1612–1638; N. Morrow Howell, J. Hinterlong, P. Rozario, and F. Tang, "Effects of Volunteering on the Well-being of Older Adults," *Journal of Gerontology: Social Sciences* 58 (2003): 137–145; Mark Musick, A. Herzog, and J. House, "Volunteering and Mortality among Older Adults: Findings from a National Sample," *Journal of Gerontology: Social Sciences* 54 (1999): 173–180; D. Oman, C. Thoresen, and K. McMahon, "Volunteerism and Mortality among the Community-Dwelling Elderly," *Journal of Health Psychology* 4 (1999): 301–316; C. Schwartz, J. Meinsenhelder, Y. Ma, and G. Reed, "Altruistic Social Interest Behaviors are Associated with Better Mental Health," *Psychosomatic Medicine* 65, no. 5 (2003): 778–785; Doug Oman, "Does Volunteering Foster Physical Health and Longevity?," in *Altruism and Health: Perspectives From Empirical Research*, 15–32; Robert Grimm, Kimberly Spring, and Nathan Dietz, "The Health Benefits of Volunteering: A Review of Recent Research," (Washington, D.C: Corporation for National and Community Service, 2007).

97. With the notable exception of Stephen Post and his colleagues. See, for example, Stephen Post, *Unlimited Love: Altruism, Compassion, and Service* (Philadelphia: Templeton Foundation Press, 2003); Stephen Post, Byron Johnson, Michael McCollough, and Jeffrey Schloss, eds., *Research on Altruism and Love* (Philadelphia: Templeton Foundation Press, 2003). The one classical sociological theorists who is an exception to this avoidance of theorizing love is Pitirim Sorokin, *The Ways and Power of Love: Types, Factors, and Techniques of Moral Transformation* (Philadelphia: Templeton Foundation Press, 2002 [1954]).

98. Yes, hats off to the Doobie Brothers.

99. For instance, research has shown that midlife adults and the elderly who give to their adult children, whether or not they receive anything back, enjoy greater psychological well-being than those who are mostly on the receiving end of their adult children's giving. A. Davey and D. J. Eggebeen, "Patterns of Intergenerational Exchange and Mental Health," *Journal of Gerontology Psychological Sciences* 53 (1998): 86–95; N. F. Marks, "Midlife Marital Status Differences in Social Support Relationships with Adult Children and Psychological Well-being," *Journal of Family Issues* 16 (1995): 5–28; E. Mutran and D. C. Reitzes, "Intergenerational Support Activities and Well-being among the Elderly: A Convergence of Exchange and Symbolic Interaction Perspectives," *American Sociological Review* 49 (1984): 117–130; E. Stoller, "Exchange Patterns in the Informal Support Networks of the Elderly: The Impact of Reciprocity on Morale," *Journal of Marriage and the Family* 47 (1985): 335–342. Similarly, see Stephanie Brown, Randolph Nesse, Amiram Vinokur, and Dylan Smith, "Providing Social Support May be More Beneficial Than Receiving It: Results from a Prospective Study of Mortality," *Psychological Science* 14, no. 4 (2003): 320–327.

1. Since salary was reported in categories, we did not have or use actual salary, but instead used the midpoints of each salary category to calculate this number, meaning that it therefore does involve a bit of measurement error in the calculation.

2. John and Sylvia Ronsvalle, *The State of Church Giving through 2007: What Are Our Christian Billionaires Thinking–Or Are They?* 19th ed. (Champaign, IL: empty tomb inc., 2009), http://www.barna.org/donorscause-articles/486-donors-proceed-with-caution-tithing-declines.

3. They are: Family & Neighbors, such as helping a family member or neighbor, working on issues to strengthen families or neighborhoods, crime prevention; Health, physical, mental, and emotional; Adult Education, such as tutoring, education, ESL, computer training, etc.; Children & Youth, such as tutoring, mentoring, education, after-school programs, ESL, recreational sports, camps, or 4-H, etc.; Homelessness; Poverty, such as low-income housing, welfare programs, job location, microcredit; Alcohol & Drug Abuse, such as counseling or education about substance abuse; Prisoners, such as visiting prisoners, writing letters to inmates, prison ministry; Abused Women or Children, such as domestic violence or child neglect; Elderly; Immigrant, Migrant, and Refugee Populations; Arts, Culture, and Humanities, such as performing arts, cultural or ethnic groups, museums, art exhibits, public television/radio; Animals, such as promoting animal welfare, ending animal cruelty, or protecting endangered species; Environment, such as recycling, reducing pollution, promoting "green" living; Food Issues, such as supporting local farmers, community-supported agriculture, sustainable agriculture, co-ops; Community Development, such as community revitalization, park cleaning, community gardens; Civil Rights, such as helping to promote racial, ethnic, or gender equality; Separation of Church and State; Supporting Military Troops; Anti-War; Supporting Gay and Lesbian Rights; Supporting Heterosexual Marriage; Prolife; Prochoice; Political Campaigns, such as supporting political candidates, nonpartisan political groups, and community groups; Disaster Relief, such as humanitarian aid, e.g. for the Haitian or Chilean earthquakes; Human Rights, such as domestic and international violations, including torture, political imprisonment, religious freedom, death penalty; Labor Issues; Umbrella Charities, such as United Way, community foundations, thrift stores; Religious, such as activities that are solely religious and not included in the above activities, such as teaching Sunday school, leading Bible studies, or serving as lay leaders for ministries, including as deacons, elders, etc.; Or is it some other kind of cause or issue? Other: (SPECIFY); Other: (SPECIFY); Other: (SPECIFY); Other: (SPECIFY); Other: (SPECIFY).

4. Brandon Vaidyanathan and Patricia Snell, "Motivations for and Obstacles to Religious Financial Giving," *Sociology of Religion* 72, no. 2 (2011): 189–214—a paper also based on Science of Generosity data.

5. We also placed a few generosity questions on the 2010 General Social Survey (GSS), for general comparison purposes. Generally, the GSS findings report somewhat higher levels of giving than the Science of Generosity Survey. For example, 77.1 percent of GSS respondents reported giving more than $25 the previous year (compared to 56.6 percent of Science of Generosity respondents); the average (mean) dollars reported given by GSS respondents who had given more than $25 the previous year was $2,110.18, compared to $1,767.57 reported of the same by Science of Generosity respondents; and

the proportion of income given by GSS respondents was reported at 3.7 percent, compared to 1.7 percent of income by Science of Generosity respondents (for the equivalent sample giving more than $25 and truncated at the 95th percentile). This shows that the relatively lower Science of Generosity numbers reported are not entirely due to the Great Recession, since the 2010 GSS was fielded at the same time. Differences in financial generosity reports are most likely due to the different methods of collecting the giving data, with GSS asking for total numbers and Science of Generosity using a more precise question about dollars given for up to thirty-six distinct categories of giving.

6. See for example, Christian Smith, Michael Emerson, and Patricia Snell, *Passing the Plate* (New York: Oxford University Press, 2008) and many references on this point cited therein.

7. Corporation for National and Community Service, "Volunteering in America 1010, Fact Sheet" (Washington, D.C.: CNCS, 2010).

8. Fidelity Volunteerism and Charitable Giving in 2009 Survey (N = 1,005 adult Americans), Executive Summary, Fidelity Charitable Gift Fund, 5, http://www.charitablegift.org/docs/Volunteerism-Charitable-Giving-2009-Executive-Summary.pdf.

9. *The 2007 Nationwide Blood Collection and Utilization Survey Report, Department of Health & Human Services* (Washington, D.C.: Department of Health and Human Services).

10. Tara Parker, "The Reluctant Organ Donor," *New York Times*, April 16, 2009. Others estimate the number somewhat higher, however, at about 52 percent of adult Americans (e.g., Testimony of James Burdick, Director, Division of Transplantation, Healthcare Systems Bureau, Health Resources and Services Administration, US Department of Health and Human Services, on "Organ Donation: Utilizing Public Policy and Technology to Strengthen Organ Donor Programs," before the Subcommittee on Information Policy, Census and National Archives, Committee on Oversight and Government Reform, US House of Representatives, September 25, 2007, http://www.hhs.gov/asl/testify/2007/09/t20070925a.html).

Chapter 4

1. Annette Lareau, *Unequal Childhoods: Class, Race, and Family Life* (Berkeley, CA: University of California Press, 2006).

2. Linda Waite and Erin York Cornwell, "Social Disconnectedness, Perceived Isolation, and Health Among Older Adults," *The Journal of Health and Social Behavior* 50, no. 1 (2009): 31–48; Nina Grant, Mark Hamer, and Andrew Steptoe, "Social Isolation and Stress-Related Cardiovascular, Lipid, and Cortisol Responses," *Annals of Behavioral Medicine* 37, no. 1 (2009): 29–37.

3. Heather N. Rasmussen, Michael F. Scheier, and Joel B. Greenhouse, "Optimism and Physical Health: A Meta-Analytic Review," *Annals of Behavioral Medicine* 37, no. 3 (2009): 239–256. Bert N. Uchino, "Understanding the Links between Social Support and Physical Health: A Life-Span Perspective with Emphasis on the Separability of Perceived and Received Support," *Perspectives on Psychological Science* 4, no. 3 (2009): 236–255. Peggy A. Thoits, "Mechanisms Linking Social Ties and Support to Physical and Mental Health," (2011): http://www.ncbi.nlm.nih.gov/pubmed/21673143.

4. "American Time Use Survey—2011 Results." US Bureau of Labor Statistics (2012): http://www.bls.gov/news.release/atus.nr0.htm/.

5. Alexis de Tocqueville, *Democracy in America*, trans. George Lawrence (New York: Perennial Classics, 2000 [1835, 1840]): 536.

6. Tocqueville, *Democracy in America*, 536.

7. "There are truths we do not see when we adopt the language of radical individualism. We find ourselves not independently of other people and institutions but through them. We never get to our selves on our own." Robert Bellah et al., *Habits of the Heart* (Berkeley, California: University of California Press, 1985).

8. Additional quotes: Shelly from Texas puts it this way: "Okay, other people with more money can help them out, what little I have, I'm going to help my family over there." Bill Kalon: "it's like me and my family first." Howard Philips: "I say family first."

Chapter 5

1. To what extent can patterns of bodily well-being be explained by generosity? Here we might consider married households in which one spouse is generous and the other not. Shannon's husband Bryan, for instance, who sees no good in being generous, claims that he is too busy to exercise, let alone take a break from work. During one of our interviews and a dinner out with Bryan, he drank five beers, perhaps betraying a problematic drinking habit. Similarly, Martin Cizec stays in shape enough to go scuba-diving regularly, but his wife Corrine, until recently, had avoided exercising. As another example, Rodrigo Martinez, who scores high on relational generosity, is a recovering alcoholic and regaining his health. His wife Shelly, who would rather protect her time and resources from encroaching family members in need, recently began a more extensive treatment to manage her Type 2 diabetes. In each case, and others not recounted here, even though these couples share the same access to resources and income, the generous spouse is healthier than the ungenerous spouse.

2. Michael Norton and Elizabeth Dunn, *Happy Money: The Science of Spending* (New York: Simon and Schuster, 2013). Cited in Norton and Dunn, "Don't Indulge. Be Happy," *New York Times*, July 7, 2012. Using a national sample of Americans, Norton and Dunn show that people earning $25,000 believe that if they were to earn $55,000 instead their life satisfaction would double. People who earn $55,000, however, are only 9 percent more satisfied than the people earning $25,000.

3. Barbara Oakley, Ariel Knafo, Guruprasad Madhavan, and David Sloan Wilson, eds., *Pathological Altruism* (New York: Oxford University Press, 2011).

4. Wendell Berry, *Jayber Crow* (Berkeley, CA: Counterpoint, 2001), 210.

INDEX